# BLACK EXPERIENCE, STRATEGIES, AND TACTICS IN THE BUSINESS WORLD
## A Corporate Perspective

## A HANDBOOK FOR PROFESSIONALS

By D

**Management Aspects Inc.**
Post Office Box 5729
Beaverton, Oregon 97006-5729

Published by:

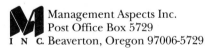 Management Aspects Inc.
Post Office Box 5729
Beaverton, Oregon 97006-5729

Library of Congress Catalog Card Number: 91-66614

ISBN 0-9630776-4-3: $19.95 Softcover

# About the Author

**B**orn in New Orleans, Louisiana, on May 31, 1953, Darrell Dean Simms completed high school in a school system with one of the nation's lowest literacy rates. With low grades he was unable to compete for college scholarship funds, so he joined the U. S. Navy in a quest to better his life. After a successful stint in the Navy, he married and, utilizing Equal Opportunity Programs and the G.I. Bill, entered the University of Washington. Upon receiving his degree in engineering with a physics minor, he entered corporate America.

For many years Darrell worked and spent time in many large corporations, most notably Westinghouse and IBM, where he noticed the lack of information available to help young Black and minority professionals to progress and excel in corporate America. He was inspired to write <u>Black Experience Strategies and Tactics in the Business World</u> (BEST) which allowed him to share the strategies and tactics that catapulted him into the tremendous success he has experienced.

Darrell started Management Aspects Incorporated, a consulting firm that specializes in working with corporations on how to manage "Diversity and Change" within their organizations. He was forced into starting a new division of his company when large publishing houses turned down the opportunity to publish Black Experience Strategies and Tactics in the Business World. He now publishes all of his own written material.

He spends a significant amount of time working with young at-risk Black youth in the Northwestern parts of the United States. He was very instrumental in co-founding a program aimed at encouraging young Black men to take responsibility for their lives: Project MISTER - Male Information and Services To Encourage Responsibility.

At time of authorship, Darrell resides in Beaverton, Oregon with his wife of 14 years, Nelda, and their children, Darsha and Thorin.

# Acknowledgements

This book was written to enhance the lives of people who should dare to read it, but it represents the people who I have had the opportunity to live, know, work and play with and, to you all, I say thank you.

I especially want to say thank you to my friends and cohorts:  R. Jack Morgan, Jerome Beard, Mary Lavern, Herb Stubblefield, L. Bonita Patterson, Paul Marshall, Jennifer Thomas, Linda Brown, Donna Harris, Serena Oka-Chow, Pete Melitz and Carolyn Vock; they were all very encouraging throughout the project.

I appreciate the time and effort put forth by Gretchen Meyer, my editor, and the finishing touches provided by Grey Jordan Nakayama, my grammar consultant.

I also appreciate the creativity granted to this project by Reyna-Moore Advertising, especially Dan Underhill.

A big thank you to Peggy Ross and her staff at Express Graphics Printing.

I would also like to acknowledge Delores Taninecz, a lady who has been a source of inspiration from the moment I met her at my first corporate interview.  The words she spoke to me still ring in my head, "Don't worry, you will get the job."

A big thanks to Kevin Kelly for teaching me how to write a complete sentence and introducing me to "Strunk and White."

Thank you to my mother, Ellenese Brooks Simms, a woman who has always found time to listen to my ideas and improve upon them.  Thanks to my father, Melvin Simms, who was responsible for giving me this opportunity to live such a fine life.

*To My Loving Wife, Nelda, for her patience*
*and to my children,*
*Thorin and Darsha, for their prayers*
*and encouragement,*
*and to God.*

# Table of Contents

**The Corporate Structure** *(cont.)*

**Managing In All Directions** *(cont.)*

# Purpose

From my own experience and investigation, I have found there are no classes, methodologies, thoughts, or philosophies that provide the information necessary to prepare young Blacks for the culture of the corporate and business world. At the time of writing, very few Blacks are rising to the tops of Fortune 500 corporations in America. There is not yet a Black Chief Executive Officer of America's Fortune 500.

The purpose of this book is to provide a handbook for Black professionals, college graduates or any other person preparing to enter or continue in the professional work-force of Corporate America, a Corporate America that is managed predominantly by the White male.

It will also offer a perspective on the challenges young Black professionals face when they leave the halls of America's educational institutions and how to deal with those challenges.

This book will discuss tactics and strategies for getting into the doors of Corporate America and staying in once you are there. It is aimed at helping the young professional plan and achieve his or her goals and, once the plan is formed, to provide strategy to assist in the execution of that plan, which will ultimately lead to a successful career.

This perspective is offered to the corporate executive who is mainly White, extremely educated and highly intolerant of perceived inadequacies of the Black professional—perceived inadequacies due to the historical evolution of Blacks out of slavery into educated Blacks deprived of White cultural experiences.

I caution the Black professional not to go into this book thinking I have worked some supernatural power on its pages that will lead to instant success. There are indeed answers provided to many questions, questions you may have at this time or questions you will have as you migrate from green university campus lawns to lush corporate carpets. I would like to offer early on: it is a fact that every person who has ever become successful in America accomplished it either through birthright or by excellent planning and thorough execution of that plan, complemented by hard work. This book is aimed at the latter.

# Who Should Read This Book

This book should be read by the young Black pre-professional who is about to graduate from one of America's educational institutions and about to enter Corporate America. Whether you are studying business, engineering, law, laboratory technology, medicine, pharmacy or any other professional discipline, you will want to read this book. You who are preparing to embark on a career in Corporate America should read this book. You who are capable of success if given the proper encouragement and information should read this book. You who are armed with confidence, enthusiasm and a drive to be the BEST should read this book.

Black professionals in corporations who are stymied by a lack of understanding of corporate politics should read this book. You who wish you had a little more insight into your boss and the corporate ladder in business environments should read this book.

Anyone who is truly interested in moving his or her career ahead in the business world should find this book helpful. You might simply need a little more insight into what gives an individual the edge when you try to propel yourself forward in a progressive fashion.

White corporate executives who really care about moving their corporations forward into this decade should read this book. This decade is going to require the business world to embrace the Black college graduate as well as other minorities, a graduate who brings a new challenge to White corporate executives and their management staff.

Finally, this book should be read by anyone truly interested in the success of Black people and the strategies and tactics that can be used to enhance their success.

# Chapter

# 1

# The First Generation

---

*T*he "Decade of the Nineties" has sneaked into existence reminding us "time will imminently continue" for all of its subscribers. I would like to step back in time for at least one chapter and set the stage for why the information in this book is of grave importance and great significance to the readers of its pages.

There is "a people" who hold the position of being the oldest minority group in America, after the Indians who are native to this land. They arrived upon this land called America in approximately 1619. They were taken from their motherland called Africa. These people were brought here against their will and stripped of their pride and dignity. Blacks have been upon the continent of America for approximately 370 years. Freedom arrived for us in America a mere 125 years ago, in the year of our Lord and Saviour 1865, when the Constitution was amended to provide Blacks with civil rights. Civil Rights for Blacks, we all know, did not fully come into existence until the late Sixties when segregation was legally ended in public places.

The Sixties were a progressive yet turbulent time for Black Americans, a time when the American Black decided it was time to stop turning the other cheek. Martin Luther King, Jr. and his supporters grabbed America by its political necktie and forced it to pay attention to a people who had contributed so much to a land that did not care about them. The Kennedy/Johnson Era marshalled a tremendous amount of White philanthropy and social programs aimed at trying to help Blacks become part of the American Society. A land of opportunity and acceptance for every other ethnic

---

representation still rejected Black Americans.

During the Sixties, Blacks demanded the opportunity to attend institutions of higher learning. Universities found themselves with numerous sit-ins and demonstrations by Blacks and Whites alike. They were forced to respond to an influx of a different breed of student who was full of fire and enthusiasm yet unprepared to receive the knowledge in the manner it was being presented. Many universities responded with programs which supposedly bridged the gap between poorly-administered-ghetto-high-school lesson plans and highly-sophisticated college curricula.

I attended high school in one of the most illiterate states in the Union. When I found myself faced with the opportunity to attend a very prominent state university (an opportunity afforded by a successful stint in the U.S. Navy and the accompanying G.I. Bill) and a desire to be a medical doctor, I was met with a letter of rejection. The letter was appropriate since I could not meet the standard entrance requirements. Fortunately, I was pointed to the last of the remaining Equal Opportunity Programs(EOP), which were a direct result of those Sixties sit-ins and demonstrations. Over the last 20 years, programs of this type have resulted in "The First Generation" of Black professionals arriving on the corporate scene.

The Seventies were exciting times for Black Americans. The doors of the White colleges cracked open by the Civil Rights Movement provided a few Blacks a good education. Affirmative Action Programs helped us to squeeze through corporate doors and take a peek at the corporate bullpens. Equal Opportunity quotas gave us a shot at sitting next to our White counterparts in those thriving yet restricted office environments. We learned to network and found the experience to be a test of how to keep management from thinking we were planning to overthrow them or thwart their system in some manner. We actually tried to buck the system and found it to be fully intact and "not to be bucked by no one." Set Aside Programs allowed us to take chances on hanging out our own shingles, and we fared OK! A few of us were "quick studies"; and, before anybody could figure it out, we slipped into a few executive chairs.

The Eighties allowed us to actually make a few dollars and to begin having some fun. For the past ten years, this country has experienced a positive turnaround in the economy and setbacks in affirmative action programs. The "Reagan Era" grabbed us around our neck and reminded us not to fall asleep while the "Republican Machinery" was trying to set its course. We allowed drugs and crimes to take their toll on our numbers which we could not afford. We began to empower ourselves by learning the rules of economics. This type of knowledge allowed us to start shaping our own destiny. Opportunity placed a new glow into our "eyes of understanding."

The Eighties also found Blacks stepping into the main tent of the political arena. Jesse Jackson and company (the Rainbow Coalition) took one giant step forward. (A plethora of Blacks entered mayoral jobs in key municipalities, and a few others were elected governors.) I think the Eighties allowed us to look back and see for the first time how far we had come and how far we still had to go in order to achieve some sense of parity in the business world. It was a time to be sharp and alert, yet we were tempted to be lulled to sleep by a sense of accomplishment!

We made great progress in the Eighties, and we must be very careful not to lose any ground as we step through the Nineties. The opportunity to get a piece of the action is quite near. The Vietnam baby boom is starting to manage corporate America; and, although they are a conservative brood, they are sensible and sensitive if for no other reason than to make money. The representatives of various European cultures who helped shape America's successful industrial age are no longer struggling for their share of American wealth. They are the owners of the large corporations. This country is going to have to turn back to the ones who helped those Europeans build America, those who sweated and bled to make America the beautiful. When corporate America starts to plan for the workforce of the future, "Workforce for the year 2000", Blacks, Asians and women are going to figure heavily into the equation. Economics are not quite in our favor. Affluent is a word most Blacks recently learned to spell. We have smelled the aroma of success, and we like the fragrance. Hence, we have decided we are going to participate. We now have educated Blacks in every part of this country's economic structure, including corporate America. Yet we have not had the opportunity to control a major commercial enterprise.

The Nineties will finally offer Blacks the opportunity to realize, at least in part, The Dream that was so vividly presented to America by Dr. Martin Luther King, Jr. I must point out, however, the number of Black college graduates available to enter corporate America continues to decline even as I write this paragraph.

# Obstacles

African-Americans have endured every test and hardship America has presented to them. The lingering effects are many large obstacles that must be overcome before we as a people can mass produce success. All who are truly intent on getting the most out of this book must take time to understand the progress we have made as well as the obstacles we continue to face.

The first obstacle we Blacks face in the business world is the color of our skin. The darker the color of our skin, the more of an obstacle it becomes. It is amazing how our society reacts to the dark-skinned American Black. Foreign Blacks, especially those with a noted foreign accent, are better received. A foreign accent seems to negate some of the stigma of a dark skin color which has long been an obstacle for the American-born Black.

The color of your skin truly becomes an obstacle when you try to move into a management position in a corporation. Appearance is weighed very heavily when you move into a visible managerial position in a corporation, especially, when you become a manager of managers. I will deal with this topic more in a later chapter.

For the most part, our skin color is an obstacle we must face, but it can be overcome if you possess very good skills and utilize all available resources.

The Black woman faces the unique obstacle of being feminine. Being a woman as well as having black skin can create challenges not experienced by the Black man. The progress achieved by the feminist equality movement helps to mitigate some of the challenge. Nevertheless Black women face obstacles not faced by Black men.

Women are making great strides in the workplace. Black women must continue to position themselves to take advantage of the opportunities being afforded to women who are seen as the solution to a shrinking male population.

A third obstacle Blacks will face in the business world is the use of the English language. As I mentioned earlier, Blacks from foreign lands usually are received by corporate America with more credibility than American-born Blacks. The Black cultural language, which I find useful and colorful, is often a major stumbling block in the business world. In fairness to my White colleagues, initially they will tolerate what has been deemed as incorrect use of the English language by Blacks.

In my college career, I received high marks in all of my English and technical writing courses, but my language skills came under harsh scrutiny when speaking in the corporate environment. My enthusiastic approach to getting things done helps me to live with this obstacle, but it does not solve the problem. I have taken an audio course to increase my word power and improve the enunciation of words I never realized I was mispronouncing.

Now that we have discussed the "quality" of the language, I would like to deal with the "quantity and volume." We must continue to pursue the art of correctly using the English language. It is the most highly regarded skill in the business world. We Blacks have a tendency to speak loudly and become boisterous when we become excited. I often find myself speaking very loudly when I am trying to get my point across, for example, debating issues in a meeting. I have found myself, on occasion, speaking very loudly when confronted on an issue about which I have strong opinions.

Whites often react to this obstacle by shutting you out. (I have been told by my White colleagues that we are often avoided due to this tendency to speak louder than what is perceived necessary by our White colleagues.) I once managed a White employee who often misread my compliments as insults because of the tone and volume of my voice.

Whites sometimes become afraid and feel intimidated by our loud speaking. There are times when this obstacle can be an asset if used properly and at the appropriate times. But most of the time it is misread by your corporate colleagues as a display of anger and is seen as a negative attribute.

The fourth obstacle presents itself as a stigma in

corporate America: "Blacks are generally lazy." Unfortunately, a few of us perpetuate the stigma by not working up to our full potential. Be aware, the average White manager views the average Black employee as lazy. I have engaged some of my co-managers in conversation on this topic, and they have told me their Black employees did not work as hard as their other employees. They were convinced this was the case, and they were trying not to be unfair. This type of thinking is not left to the White manager alone; my Asian counterparts also think this way. I also believe there are many Black managers who experience this sort of thinking in spite of their own struggle. They become obstacles to the progress of advancement for their own people.

We must be careful not to perpetuate this stigma that society has placed on us. We too often learn the job we are asked to do, and then we put ourselves in a mode of doing just enough to meet minimal expectations. Once you have learned a job, you must immediately try to improve upon it or start looking for that next level of responsibility.

As a professional, I am often viewed as being impatient. Once I learn and thoroughly understand a job, I am ready to move up to the next rung in the ladder. This impatience has often worked in my favor and has been read as enthusiasm. Impatience can sometime be viewed negatively, however, if a corporation has a policy that employees spend a certain amount of time in a particular job whether they need to or not. Putting forth the extra effort will allow you to overcome this obstacle. Personal pride should also spur you on in this endeavor to overcome this obstacle.

This next obstacle stems from Corporate America being made up of many different kinds of mind sets; some people call them cliques and circles. The business world is often representative of the real world, and you will find there is a lot of back-scratching in order to get things accomplished. Black Americans are often outside of this major form of networking.

The cliques and inner circles which form in the business world are often bound by color as well as other identities, including social status. For example, golfing and snow skiing are two key sports which will allow you to break into inner circles or cliques in the business world providing the parties with whom you are interested in co-mingling are golfers or skiers. Golfing and skiing are not the usual sports a young Black kid has had an opportunity to experience or become skilled at. I have learned to golf and ski, and I must add they are fun sports. When preparing to participate in these sports, I found them to be a bit spendy to get involved in, and they have a fairly expensive continuing cost.

A lot of business professionals form their associations around sports such as these, and this can be a major hurdle to overcome. This obstacle can be overcome by persistence, patience, time and money. Studying and understanding the process that shapes these circles and cliques, as I will later in the book, can be of great importance if back-scratching is to work for you. Most important, corporate information flows through these systems like mini-grapevines. The smaller vines intertwine themselves throughout the larger corporate networks. They are powerful mechanisms in the corporate political structure.

You can also gain entrance to the White inner circles if you bring something to the table. Being very good at what you do will help you gain entrance and acceptance to some circles. Being the best at what you do will almost assure you a seat at somebody's table.

Beware. Circles and cliques which are exclusively Black can also be stumbling blocks. We are often afraid to find ourselves in a meeting room with two or more Blacks for fear of the "What. Are They Up To?" syndrome. There is a definite perception by Whites in management that, when several Blacks talk amongst themselves, they must be unhappy about something.

Normally, when we congregate, we are seeking social interaction, and we often do not take the opportunity to exchange business-related information. We are often afraid to share information for fear we are going to let out the last secret which might lead to our own success. We often share concerns when we come together, but it is often out of fear and uncertainty rather than out of confidence and assurance. The cliques/inner circles can be very useful in our quest to gain and share information. We must continue to reach out and enter into these business networks.

The very fact we are a minority people sets up a

major obstacle. You will notice right away the absence of our race when you first arrive on the corporate scene. It can make you paranoid. You will find yourself worrying whether you can meet the challenge or whether you will be able to deliver when you are called upon to do so. I will let you in on a little secret: your White counterparts experience the same feelings, maybe not to the same degree, but they have similar fears. It is a strange feeling to go to a seminar and be the only Black in attendance. I often try to attend meetings, classes and seminars with a buddy, and I usually do not care what their origins are. If they are friendly, I will be friendly. After you become comfortable with your own capabilities, you will continue to notice this phenomenon, but the uneasiness will become less and less.

When you join the ranks of corporate management, you often wish there were more Black managers available in the corporation. I have found that, when there were other Blacks available to consult, we were all better off. Being few in number hinders us in setting up good support structures. You will find in most corporations the success of the individual lies with the resources s/he can bring to bear on a given set of requirements. A lack of the necessary support structure is resulting in fewer and fewer Blacks arriving at the top of large corporations. The Blacks who are at ground level in a "fend for yourself" mode struggle a great deal to accomplish their goals. The Blacks who are successful usually find Whites and other minorities to use in their support structure. But, as I mentioned earlier, you never get something for nothing.

Our own prejudice against one another is often a major obstacle in our endeavor to move things forward. I personally have had thoughts about my fellow Black professional that I am not proud to share. I have found myself thinking, "I hope they do not mess it up for the rest of us." Blacks who understand how to use their strengths and who have honed their skills will often strike out on their own. The more confident we get, the more we feel we do not need one another. I have found the time to truly band together is when success is inevitable. We should continue to foster helping one another.

An obstacle that stems from our own thinking is we Blacks often feel a lot more is expected of us than of our counterparts. (Chapter 4 is devoted to this topic.) This can be true in many instances but not to the degree we impose on ourselves. We often perpetuate this thinking within the ranks. We become very impatient and think, "I am doing twice as much as I need to, and I am not being rewarded for the efforts." This can be a self-made trap created out of our own desire to succeed. Corporate America expects a lot from all parties, and you will find that the more money there is involved, the more there will be expected of you. A rule of thumb to follow: Do your Best!

Our love for the "Black Culture" can often be our biggest obstacle. We do not want to give up our style of dress for fear it somehow makes us less Black. I am guilty! When our White co-professionals make a comment on our use of the English language, we are often offended. Being from the southern part of the country and now residing in the northwestern part of the country, I have truly come to observe and understand this obstacle. We must remember, we do not have to give up our cultural ties because we change the way we speak and dress. The Asians have been very successful at preserving their culture and, at the same time, fooling the business world into thinking they are willing to give up their cultural ties for acceptance. (We will discuss this more in a later chapter.)

The Black cultural use of English is often one that does not serve us well in the business world. I must admit, I am developing a professional language at work and a cultural language when I am amongst my Black friends and colleagues. You might say I am becoming bilingual!

Be aware, all Black professional do not subscribe to the use of the Black cultural language, and I have had it work against me in various situations. I have met Black co-professionals who would not put away their corporate etiquette when I attempted to include them in my network or enter theirs. They did not shun me or anything like that, but they appeared to protect what they had built for themselves. So, I conclude this section with this thought: Do not hastily assume things will be the way you think they ought to be with your Black cohorts.

"Institutional Racism" is an obstacle that lurks in the halls of corporate America and stifles the ability of young Blacks to move into and up through corporations. It is probably one of the most accepted forms of racism today. This type of racism is non-confrontational, which most Blacks have learned to deal with by this time. Here's an example: You are now ready to take on more responsibility. Your boss is convinced you need to spend more time developing because you have not spent the prescribed amount of time that s/he has decided should be spent in a given position. Climbing the corporate ladder is always met with some form of institutional racism, and you must develop skills to overcome this monster from the executive offices.

The "White woman" is definitely an obstacle for young Blacks attempting to enter the workforce of the Nineties. White women have won the battle to be a part of corporate America and rightfully so. (Statistics show the workforce will be fifty percent women by the year 2000.) The workforce will have plenty of room for them and for us as well. At this time, White women are entering the workforce faster than any other minority. Yes, I said, they are a minority! They understand how this game is played, and we had better understand they are a direct competitor. Here is an example of how prevalent they are in the workforce today. I was participating in a management staff meeting called to discuss awards to be given at an upcoming meeting. Each manager was responsible for nominating their employees as candidates to receive awards for contribution to the business. After listing all the candidates' names on the board, we were asked to consider several things: how many senior people have we considered to receive awards; how many employees who were associated with different products or job classifications have we considered to receive awards; and how many WOMEN have we considered to receive awards. We were never asked how many Blacks or minorities have we considered to receive awards.

Another example: There were only two Black managers on the entire management staff of twenty-four. There were eight women on that staff and one of them was Black.

Black women appear to be progressing better than the Black man due to the number of them entering the workforce and gaining access to jobs at this date and time. Women are starting to arrive! And we should take our lead from their accomplishments. As a Black man I am spurred on by the progress!

An obstacle a lot of Blacks face is their inability to assimilate into the corporate environment. Make it clear to yourself, the business world is predominantly White. The sooner you understand this, the sooner you will be able to deal with it properly. The more you fight it, the more it will fight you. I have observed many of my Black colleagues who have become very frustrated with what they have termed "The System." (We will discuss dealing with The System in a later chapter in more detail.) Before understanding how it works, they were off trying to change it to suit themselves. The System is bigger than all of us, White or Black, and it is capable of working for or against all of us.

Now let me make one thing perfectly clear—oppression, segregation, prejudice, overt and covert racism—all these things are still prevalent in our society today. They are all still problems to be faced and obstacles to be overcome, but we must keep those problems in proper perspective. If we are truly going to finally participate in America's socioeconomic success, we cannot spend our time and resources focusing on the negatives. If allowed, the obstacles outlined above and the problems we have faced for the last three and a half centuries can be insurmountable, especially when trying to become successful in America. But we are overcoming them all, surely! The rest of this book is focused on that effort.

# The Black Chip

I wanted to put this discussion into a separate section because it is worthy of its own book, and maybe, at a later date, I will take up the challenge. My first inclination was to present it as just another obstacle, but that would have been a sad mistake. You will find yourself returning to this section many times to reread and understand how you can possibly benefit from this discussion. Truly it fits the category of being an obstacle and has presented itself in many ways as just that. I will describe it and then present it as a secret weapon which can help us achieve the levels of success we desire.

The "Black Chip" is our ability to turn time back to an era of pure hell and oppression, a time when we were treated like animals and lower life forms. It is our ability to cry

"Foul" and "Time-out" when we perceive we are being treated unfairly. It is founded in the deepest and most protected thoughts of our minds and souls. It is indeed a part of our cultural make-up and heritage, though not necessarily by choice.

We Blacks know our ancestors were brought into this country against their will. We were not allowed to assimilate into America, and we did not want to even if we would have had the opportunity. Had we chosen to assimilate at that time, I am not sure we would have known how. I do not want to dwell on the historical significance as much as I would like to deal with the current thinking process. The Black Chip is a result of inborn anger, misgivings, lack of opportunity and many other negative factors that are brought about from a people being oppressed at different points in their lives.

Now in today's light, the Black Chip is perpetuated by lack of positive experiences. It is very often reinforced by the actions of various anti-Black groups of today. A lack of opportunity continues to promote the Black Chip. By exploring the Black Chip, we can continue to understand the forces that are behind it and hopefully come to an appreciation of how to utilize these forces. I have observed the Chip in others as well as in myself.

We often acquire an attitude of constantly protecting ourselves even when it is not necessary. Because the Chip is seated in our deepest emotions, it is easy to stimulate and unleash as a protection mechanism.

The Chip will diminish risk-taking which is essential in the business world, even if it is only calculated risk. The Chip can lead us to a point of only doing what we are asked to do for fear if we do more, we may do the wrong thing. The lazy syndrome, which is so often unfairly placed upon us Blacks, can be a manifestation of the Chip. "I am not going to do any more than has been asked. If I do more and it is not done properly, I will be penalized for it."

The Black Chip can stifle sincere desire and healthy ambition. It can get in the way of genuine enthusiasm and your own personal drive. It can interfere with all things essential for one to be successful. It most often presents itself in a negative fashion. It often shows up as an inferiority complex. It can create a lot of unnecessary problems for all who witness it. If unleashed in an uncontrollable fashion, it will cause violence. It can lead us to be over-sensitive, impatient and unwilling to pay the dues required to be successful in today's world.

But, the Black Chip is also a secret weapon. If we take time and understand it, we can harness the energies of the Chip and use them to our advantage. I have learned it can work for us now just as much as it has worked against us in the past. Those same energies can enhance our motivational drive. If recognized and understood, they can be extremely useful to the young Black professional. A positive use of the Chip is the thinking process that encourages us to go after a "piece of the action." I am motivated by the Chip to help as many of my African American brothers and sisters as I can. I often feel I want to do my best because I have something to prove. This is the way we want the Chip to operate—positively. We must be on guard not to let it sway us back to the negative side where we simply want to get back at society for the bad hand it dealt our forefathers. The powerful forces of the Chip can be used to push us forward.

It is interesting to observe that our White business counterparts neither recognize nor understand the Black Chip. When it presents itself to them, it usually causes fear due to their lack of understanding. They often have seen it as a negative attitude and an impatient nature. They often see us going against the flow. I have had the experience of meeting individuals in the business world who I immediately sense dislike me. I started to think, "He does not like me because I am Black," and I started to build up my own prejudices based on my own conclusions stimulated by the Chip. I had to learn to suppress all the emotion brought on by the Chip and start to channel the energy into a healthy competitive nature. I started to work harder and aggressively approach my assignments with vigor. I found I could gain respect through creativity and hard work. The Chip can increase your drive when you try to be more aggressive if you will take the time to understand it and channel it into positive energy.

Everyone needs something that will act as a driving force; an energy from within. The Black Chip can fulfill this need better than any other energy source I have been able to acquire. The hunger and thirst for success is born out of the Chip. This can truly give you an edge. The average corporate player is driven by his or her own "guts." We have the guts to succeed when enhanced by the positive side of the Chip, and it will allow us to truly become over-achievers.

The Black Chip must continue to be monitored for proper motivational use. There is a thin line that separates whether the Chip is working for you or against you. Aggressiveness can stem from the Chip, but it must be tempered so that we can use it as a positive motivational force.

The Black Chip is a common force we all have, and it can be a force used to rally Black co-professionals. I truly believe it appeared in this form during the Sixties Civil Rights Movement which we all benefitted from and are still benefitting from even now. We must take caution to keep it positively motivated and well controlled.

It is very important that we, as Black people and as Black professionals, take time to acknowledge, understand and control what I have defined as "The Black Chip."

# The Glass Ceiling

Say the words "The Glass Ceiling"; they sound so elegant, so fragile, so beautiful. This is the obstacle of all obstacles for those who would dare to scale the ladder of success in the business world. It exists for most of us who are non-White and often for those who are not male. It is a mystery to most of us because when you gaze up to look for it, it is not there except for the occasional smudges that are left by those who have the pleasure of being supported by it. Yet it has a solid structure that has been erected by years of uninterrupted construction. It is fortified by those who say they are helping those of us beneath it. There is no door. Every time we try to get near it, it disappears and re-materializes above us, again and again. Even as I attempt to expose it, it looms over my head like an invisible yet solid barrier.

The proverbial Glass Ceiling is made up of all the obstacles discussed earlier and a whole lot more. It is very difficult to comprehend and even harder to remove. Everyone understands how it works, yet no one seems to have a solution to remove it. It is not easy to see even for those who have broken through it. The ones who created it are at a loss to remove it even when they have the incentive to do so.

What we are really describing is the inability of Blacks, minorities and women to enter into the hallowed halls of Business America, into senior management positions of large corporation— the positions where decisions are made and direction for corporations is determined and handed down; the place where goals are created and strategies are often put in place.

For Blacks, the glass ceiling is a very real obstacle, and it looms large over even the lowest level of management positions. Blacks are often promoted into supervisory positions where they stagnate when they try to go any higher. Most of the time they become frustrated trying to prove they can do the things they are more than qualified to do.

The Women's Movement was the first to attack the Glass Ceiling, and it has since haunted them. Many women today are trying to break through it, but every time they get close, it moves away, protected by those who continue to re-create it. I acknowledge all of those women who give up their lives attempting to break through it—women who have decided not to get married or not have a family in order to keep themselves mobile, women who work 12 to 14 hour days as well as weekends hoping to show they are worthy of joining what has been an all White Men's Club for years. I am of the belief that it will be those women who will finally punch a hole through it and who will allow the rest of us finally to squeeze through. Once we are presented the opportunity to walk on the upper side of the Glass Ceiling, we had better be properly prepared to perform at that level.

If one percent of all who read this book could break through the Glass Ceiling, that would be something to behold. I would simply like to see some of us at least have the opportunity to break through it or at least force it to move out of the way.

# Chapter

# 2

# The Essence of Success

---

**W**hat is "success"?  It is easily defined for most people because most people base their definition on what someone else has accomplished.  Before reading on, take a minute and look the word up in your dictionary:  success. I would like to share my own definition of success with you: Success for me is to "attain the goals and objectives I have set for myself and to accomplish those goals and objectives in some predetermined time frame I have chosen."  Your definition for success should be determined by you and only by you.  Your definition of success should be modifiable as you go through life.  Your goals and ambitions should change based on your accomplishments.

Success is defined by different people in many different ways.  People often confuse the definition of success with the way success is measured.  Every corporation has its own definition of success, and you will see it posted in clear view for everyone to see.  A well-run corporation has learned to communicate what success means to its constituents, employees and owners (shareholders).  If success is not clearly defined, it is usually very hard to achieve.  There are many people who put large amounts of pressure on themselves because they have not clearly defined what success really means to their lives.

Most Americans define success in material accomplishments, and most of the time this translates to mean MONEY.  Money, however, is a vague measurement for success. Many people find success to be a major disappointment when they use money as their sole basis for measuring success.

There are many ways to measure success.  But it can be confusing to a person who appears successful to be told s/he is successful when s/he does not yet feel successful. Measuring your sense of success by someone else's standards is the most misused standard of success.

Some people measure success by how they feel. Others measure success by what others think about them. I strongly believe the standard of success is very individual and should be measured only by the individual who seeks it.

I am intrigued with the individual who is successful one day and loses it the next. One should be flexible in trying to define or measure success, but not to an extreme. Success can only be measured by accomplishments and achievements. Financial wealth and material goods are misused as measures of success and can make real success difficult to attain.

Success should be experienced throughout your life and career, and this can only be accomplished if your "levels of expectation" are set properly. When you are defining your factors for success, clearly define your measurement system. You will thereby reduce your frustration and the need to redefine success every time it appears but is not yet attainable.

Success can be measured by how well you accomplish the goals you have set for yourself. Success can be measured by how well you bring your dreams into reality. Dream realization is one of my own major measurements of success. Success can be measured by how well you please yourself or your loved ones. Happiness should definitely factor into your measurements of success. Success can be measured in many other ways. Explore for yourself which ways best measure your own success.

Take time to define success clearly and the ways you will measure it. Do this in light of what your skills are, what you want to do, and what you will have the opportunity to do. Defining something you may never be able to obtain is a sure way to induce failure. For example, smaller corporations are often guilty of not having a realistic measurement system for their standards of success. They often try to use the same measurement systems being used by larger corporations.

# Planning, Preparation & Performance

In order to be successful, planning is essential and will always allow you to be ahead of the crowd. Planning is simply sitting down and deciding what you need or want to do in order to accomplish the tasks which stem from your well-thought-out strategies, strategies that will only come about from crisp, thorough planning. Planning will use your personally developed goals and will be based upon your dreams and ideas. Your goals should be measurable as I discussed earlier. I call these measurements "objectives." A good planner is one who not only creates a good plan but also one who precisely executes that plan.

If you show me a successful person, I will show you a planner. Good planning is a key to success and will almost always bring about desired results. Most people think planning takes a long time. In fact, whatever you are trying to accomplish will take longer if you do not take time to plan it. People who refuse to plan are usually procrastinators and have a tough time completing tasks. In the business world those people tend to be your "run of the mill" folks. They rarely accomplish anything!

Planning allows you to organize your thoughts and think through strategies which will support a good idea. Planning is a process that will make ideas become reality.

This book was only an idea for over two years. I made several false starts and finally realized I needed a plan. After a lot of procrastination, I finally put together an outline which led to some significant planning, hence, this book.

In the following paragraphs, I offer you my simple methodology for planning that has led me to achieve numerous goals and my own success. My methodology is not the only way, and it can always be improved. The following is my basic methodology of good planning:

**Goal Setting** — This should be quick and simple. Please do not make it complex. Take one idea at a time and turn it into a clearly stated goal. Do this for each idea.

Example:

"I will arrive at work on time!"

This is a simply stated goal. This goal may or may not lead to a set of very complex strategies. But before I discuss strategies, I want to discuss ways to measure the goal. I call these ways the "objective."

Objectives allow us to measure when we have successfully completed a goal. They tell us the when, how much, or how long of reaching a goal. Objectives are usually defined for a particular goal.

**Define Objectives** — This is the way to measure the success of accomplishing a goal.

Example:

"I will have accomplished this goal when I arrive at work on time for 60 consecutive days. I would like to complete this goal in six months."

Corporations live and die by how well they define and accomplish their objectives. You should be no less concerned in your quest to define your objectives. As I stated earlier, it is hard to accomplish something you do not know how to measure.

Once we have decided how we will measure the accomplishment of a goal, we can then put strategies in place that will lead to tasks for completing the objectives and achieving the goal. Hence, we must create strategies.

**Create Strategies** — Strategies are simply ways to accomplish a goal. There can be more than one strategy to accomplish one goal.

Example:

"I will get up at 5:30 a.m. in order to arrive at work by 7:45 a.m. I am due at work by 8:00 a.m."

It is not hard to set a goal, but creating strategies to accomplish that goal can often take time. Take the time to fully think through your strategies. The time you take to put well-thought-out strategies in place will save you a lot of time later during the execution of the tasks and activities they generate.

This methodology can be as elaborate as you want to make it. I suggest you start out with simple planning. I can now do most of my personal planning without always having to put it down on paper. You should write it down until you have mastered the skill. You will find planning is the first step in being prepared.

"Preparation" is probably the hardest skill to master. This is where you identify resources needed to execute your plan, and this can take time. In the example we used above, the preparation may be as simple as purchasing a good working clock or making sure your car is in good working condition. I have found a lack of preparation can be the show stopper for executing a good plan. For instance, if you try to write a book using a word processing package and you do not understand its functions or features, you have just missed your opportunity to be prepared to write a book.

In the business world, you will continuously be preparing to accomplish various tasks. Preparation, along with organizational skills, is essential if you are going to successfully accomplish your assignments. Surprising your co-workers by bringing donuts to a meeting will make you well-liked by your peers, but do not forget to bring the napkins so they can tidy up after eating the donuts. With good preparation you are finally ready to execute your plan.

The execution of a plan is called "Performance." Whether the plan is your personal plan or the company's plan, you must perform the plan the same way an actor performs a script on stage. Performance can be readily measured both objectively and subjectively. Performance is something young Black professionals are going to have to understand better. Doing what you are told is just the start of performance. Understanding how you will measure the performance of a plan is key to helping you measure the success of the execution of a plan. If you do not perform, the plan will fail and you will fail.

You are going to find as you move through your career, there are many factors that will contribute to good performance. You should learn them and make them a part of you. They will ultimately lead to your success.

# Elements That Lead to Success

In reading the opening paragraphs of this chapter, you have discovered how important it is to define what success means to you. In this section, I will discuss some of the factors that have led to the success I have already achieved in the business world. I do not wish to sound as if I have already obtained all of what I have defined to be success for me, but I have already experienced some measure of success. You probably have already started to observe some of these elements becoming a part of you as you worked your way through school. Hopefully, you have started to add many of them to your tool kit for success.

The order in which these elements have been presented is not of significance. You will understand which should come before the other as you acquire them and they become a part of your tool kit. I will try not to use any formal definitions for these "elements of success." I wish to draw from my own experience and observations of other successful professionals I have had the opportunity to work with or observe in the business world.

**Initiative** — This element is essential to getting things started and "off and running." I believe you can never have enough initiative in your tool kit.

It is hard to learn "initiative", but it can be developed if there is the slightest hint of it in a person.

Initiative is the ability to point out, direct and get things started when trying to accomplish a task. It is often mistaken for enthusiasm which we will discuss later. It can be viewed as threatening by your colleagues. I encourage you to be aware of how it is being viewed when you are using or displaying it.

It is an element that can put you in the spotlight and can attract a lot of attention, whether you want it or not. Management usually tries to control initiative in the ranks, yet they sanction it almost all the time. If you have many talented people showing initiative all at once, it can be chaotic for the whole.

I have learned to treasure initiative, and it has carried me through many situations where I was trying to establish my credibility. Taking the initiative has allowed me to move through the corporate structure swiftly, and I feel neither I nor the corporation has suffered for it. If initiative is complemented with any amount of expertise, it should lead to a measure of success. You will find most professionals encourage initiative. In the business world, you will find it to be one of the top characteristics sought when hiring professionals.

Initiative should not be looked upon to be self-serving. It should be used to help others in your department or corporation to move ahead and become progressive.

As Black professionals, we do not walk into the business arena with a lot of historical success. I have observed many of my Black colleagues who are knowledgeable and talented but who have no initiative.

Case in point — When I arrived in my first management position, there was a Black male marketing professional who had been in his assignment for seven years. I had only been in the company for five and half years. This individual had been very successful in his current position. I asked him, "Why are you still in this position?" He looked at me as if I had no right to question him in that manner. After some preliminary jockeying for position and helping him feel I was in a position to help, I immediately started to educate him about what I knew of the corporate structure we were both a part of. We immediately put a plan in place to initiate his being promoted within this office. He had a lot of the elements for success; he just did not know how to take the initiative. The plan worked so well he was promoted by the end of that year and is still on an upward swing in the business world.

**Self-Confidence** — This is where many Blacks fall short! Self-confidence is a characteristic which can be developed in an individual. A good family structure and support system can foster the environment for self-confidence to develop naturally. If you did not have the luck to grow up in such an environment, self-confidence can be obtained by gaining knowledge and experience. If you gain knowledge in a particular subject or profession, self-confidence should be a by-product of the process.

I have observed individuals who had nothing more going for them than their self-confidence and it carried them a long way in the business world. It allowed them to appear confident, and it made them insurmountable. Individuals who understand this element of success and how to use it are well on their way to a successful career in the business world.

Be aware, however, self-confidence can be mistaken for "cockiness" and conceit. It can be interpreted as arrogance if not tempered with common sense and a little humility. Self-confidence will almost always intimidate at least one of your peers. It is very powerful; it is capable of convincing yourself that you are invincible, and this could lead to self-destruction.

Self-confidence is interwoven through the other elements of success. There is no better feeling than knowing you can accomplish what you have set out to do. Self-confidence is my foundation for learning what I need to know and for not letting anyone stop my progress.

You must be careful not to let anyone pull this "security blanket" away from you. I have had my confidence tested in many ways, and I have lost it several times. It is not hard to regain if you keep your wits about you. I once had a staff assignment with a gentleman who had been in the company longer than I and who was better skilled than I for this particular job assignment. He was comfortable at tinkering in the back room rather than being out in front of people. I was just the opposite.

When he discovered I was very comfortable in front of people, he felt threatened. He began to point out my areas of weakness to our peers. He also challenged everything I brought to the table in meetings. Needless to say, I became somewhat insecure when he was around and I felt threatened. I created and planned a program and made it obvious I did not need his help to implement the program. The plan was well received by management, and I was given the resources necessary to execute the plan. My confidence was restored, and he hesitantly worked beside me until I completed the assignment.

If there is any element I would like to perpetuate in Black professionals, it is self-confidence. It can be the foundation for building a wonderful career and can bring you through a lot of the obstacles that have been placed in the way of young Black professionals in the business world.

**Self-Control** — You will never make it in the business world if self-control is not a part of your tool kit. In fact, you will fail miserably without this element. If you do not have it already, it can be learned or obtained through experience. I have found it to come and go based on the situation I am facing. The Black professional needs this element just as much as he or she needs self-confidence.

Due to our historical background in America, the self-control element gets tested often. I am never sure if someone is addressing me or thinking about me in a certain way because I am Black or because of the circumstances.

Self-control is the element needed in order to take advantage of the "Black Chip" which I discussed in the chapter entitled the "The First Generation." Self-control allows us to keep the Chip in its harness. I have found myself struggling to maintain my composure when I think someone is looking down at me due to my color and/or my cultural heritage.

Once, I was driving several customers to lunch, all of whom were White. We were talking and discussing various business subjects when all of a sudden another car pulled along side us. The car was full of White teenagers. Then the unthinkable happened: one of the children called me a "nigger." Yes, right in front of several managers of a fairly large insurance company. My first thought was to retaliate in some way, but the self-control element kicked in and I simply smiled. The people who were with me, of course, all made comments to console me; but I must admit I was steaming the rest of the day. An incident like this can blow your whole day if you do not exercise self-control.

Self-Control can be enhanced many times over; and the more you practice it, the more it will be available to you when you really need it. If you ever have the opportunity to manage other people, you will cherish your ability to maintain self-control. When there are ten different personalities to deal with and you may have to deal with five of them within one hour on a subject matter that is not pleasant, self-control may be all you have to keep you from bursting into "diplomatic flames."

You will be presented with numerous opportunities to sharpen or lose your self-control depending on what you are having to deal with in a given day. Your manager can also be a tester of this wonderful element. If you are in a job where you have to deal with customer situations, and you have to live by the adage "the customer is always right", self- control will often come into play, especially when you know the customer is wrong!

**Order/Clarity** — This element is really divided into two parts which are the basic building blocks of professionalism. If you want your work to be noticed, whatever the discipline, you must have clarity and order in whatever you do. I, as a Black professional, struggle with this when I am trying to communicate. When I am placed in a situation of having to write or speak the English language in its purest form, it is difficult. As I stated earlier, I was educated in a very illiterate setting by the standards of most state education boards. I am now educated and in a very technical business. I spend most of my time talking with White America, and it is not easy. I worry about my diction and my pronunciation. Being from the southern part of the U.S. only tends to complicate what I need from Order and Clarity.

While going through sales training and conducting a practice sales call with a manager, he evaluated the call and raised several issues he felt a need to discuss with me. At one point he looked across his desk and looked me square in the eyes and said, "You must learn to pronounce the word ASK!" It was the first time I was told I had a problem with my diction. Because I am from the south, I pronounce ask as "axe." He went on to explain that if I was trying to sell somebody on my ideas and they were paying more attention to the way I pronounced 'ask' than to my ideas, I might lose the sale. I was devastated, and I had lost the very part of me I thought was a great strength, my confidence in speaking. I recomposed myself and started to practice the pronunciation of 'ask.' I now over dramatize the "k" when I pronounce 'ask.' It seemed like such a small word to make such a big difference. The session helped me realize how important it is to speak clearly and concisely.

I have given many presentations in corporate America, and I am still self-conscious of the way I speak. I will always continue to enhance this skill and to perfect it as much as possible. I am aware of this weakness, but I do not let it hinder my progress.

The other major way you communicate in corporate America is through writing. I struggle with this a little less than with speaking. I can always ask someone to look over my writing to see if I am being clear and orderly with what I am trying to say. There are a lot of computer software tools that will assist you with clarity in writing. The editor of this book was essential.

The "order" part of this element should also be taken into consideration when you are looking at your organization skills. I will not spend a lot of time discussing organization here, but organization definitely comes into play if you want clarity and order in the way you go about getting things done.

**Objectivity** — This element is simple. I like to think of it as "the pay attention to what is going on" element. Objectivity allows you to observe more than speculate. In the business world, there are plenty of people willing to read more into a matter than is there; there are people who will jump to conclusions quicker than you can bat an eyelash.

I believe that, if you can master being objective, you will gain great respect from your peers. You will appear to have wisdom in your business dealings. You will listen more than you speak when considering a matter.

Objectivity works for me when I am considering others. I have been successful at understanding when an individual is giving 100% or only 95%. I miss the mark with this element when it comes to the skill of listening. I am struggling to develop the most elegant and artful skill called "Listening." I will discuss listening in the chapter entitled "We Need to Communicate—A Valuable Skill."

Being objective will help you sharpen your corporate "dagger" when you are ready to "go for the juggler." If people find you to be objective, they are more apt to consider your opinion and ideas. If you add a measure of sensitivity to your objectivity, you will be a force to reckon with. When your ideas are questioned objectively, do not let the dark side of the Black Chip make you defensive. Allow your co-professionals to question your work and help you clarify your ideas. I have learned to enjoy sharing my work with others and soliciting their opinions about my work. Constructive, objective criticism can help you immensely. When you are called upon to provide input, go into the situation with an open mind and try to help the individual or team as much as you can. Learn to set your emotions aside and use your skills. Strategizing with your co-workers is very important; there is a lot of jousting involved within the process that will lead to quality creativity, and it can be a lot of fun.

I strongly recommend that you take the time to understand how objectivity can become a part of your arsenal. It is not an innate skill. It definitely has to be learned and continuously honed if you are going to make good use of it.

You must also try to understand when someone else is using it, especially if it is being applied to you. It will present itself during evaluations of your performance and accomplishments. You will always hope for a manager who is more objective than subjective when evaluating subordinates.

**Self-Image** — If you are reading this book, this is evidence that you are already trying to improve your self-image. It goes hand-in-hand with self-confidence. The most important thing to know about this element is it will always be with you. You are either projecting a positive image or a negative one. This is where your talents and attributes are first presented and continue to be presented throughout your life and career.

Self-image can be observed more than any other attribute; it is how people see you and formulate opinions about you. It is made up of the way you dress, talk, walk, and even think. All other elements you possess will help make up your image. The way you go about getting things done projects your image. We will discuss image more in the chapter called, "The Corporate Dress Code."

**Risk-Taking** — Risk is the ability to think you can accomplish what you set out to do, unsure if you will win or lose. A true leader is a risk-taker and usually has an understanding of what is at stake. Most people who are self-made are risk-takers. There is a difference between taking risks and being foolish. Some people do not understand the difference and continue to call their foolishness risk-taking. Investing in the stock market when interest rates are low is good risk-taking because stocks usually go up. Playing the local lottery is foolish, especially when the pot is big because the odds of winning are lower!

To understand this element is to use it. There are levels of risk-taking, and you should understand how much you are willing to risk to get what you want from a given situation. There are rules to risk-taking, and I have come to believe you define for yourself what they are for you. Risk can be calculated once you fully understand what is involved and what is at stake.

Risk-taking is probably the most elusive element of success for the Black professional. It is not as though we do not take risks or do not want to take risks. It is more that we do not understand how and when to take risks. If there is any one thing that can make you or break you, it is your ability to calculate risk. We have learned in America to by-pass or minimize risk if at all possible! Those who have become great in America have set plans in place that allowed them to take risks.

We as Blacks have truly learned to avoid risks in general at all cost. We do not understand risk or how to manage it. Sure, we will take a gamble if we feel we are in control. The reason we have obtained the treasures of freedom we enjoy today is because Blacks were willing to risk in the late Fifties, Sixties and Seventies, and there were many risk takers from Rosa Parks to the likes of Malcolm X and H. Rap Brown; Barbara Jordan, Jesse Jackson and Shirley Chisholm. Of course, I cannot forget Martin. Blacks have taken most of their risk as a threat to life and limb. Slaves used to try to outrun their masters, and now-a-days Black youth try to outrun the local authorities. The journey we face today will definitely require risk-taking.

In the business world, in order to move ahead of the pack, you must be a risk-taker. You must be willing to sacrifice your time, talents and efforts in order to obtain what you want. I find myself taking risks almost every day. I was responsible for bringing a demonstration center to readiness in my office location. Once the center was in place, we started to invite customers from different parts of the city. I was told not to invite a certain customer because of the politics between my upper management and the branch management that served the other customer. I realized how much it could help our branch and the company if I could get this particular institution to join ranks with our office and adopt our strategy over that of the competition. My boss chewed me out because of the politics involved; but, after the dust settled, everybody thought it was a good idea. The institution was willing to implement the center on their campus and everybody won.

In the world of investing, risk-taking is paramount to your success. The most important thing to remember is how much is enough. You can lose your shirt if you risk too much. If you plan your investments carefully, you can minimize the risk. If we Blacks are going to ever gain personal wealth, we are going to have to take more risks. The one risk we are going to have to learn to take is the risk of investing in and trusting in one another. We will discuss risk and how it pertains to the business world in a later chapter.

**Proficiency** — This is an element that stems from wanting to be the BEST! This is an attribute most professionals strive to have as a part of their tool kit. Proficiency is not easy. If you reach a level of professionalism that includes proficiency, you have probably obtained a lot of the other elements that have been discussed in this chapter. Another way to describe a proficient person is one who seeks out the best way to accomplish a given task.

I have not found many of my colleagues whom I thought were really proficient. You will find there are a lot of good people in the business world, but there are more who are average. Average is often good enough. There are some who strive to be the best, and I like to think of myself as one who is reaching for the best in my professional career. However, I lack patience, and, to truly become proficient, you must be patient, especially with yourself. Time is also important. It takes time and great effort be proficient.

The Asian corporations put the "P" in proficient, and America has paid a great price because of it. The Asian corporations have sold out to their workers, and that has allowed them to gain a competitive edge.

Blacks already understand proficiency in their mastery of the sports where proficiency in training is required to become a great athlete. Now we must "step up to the plate" and learn to hit home runs in the business world. This will be a challenge because it requires great skill and proficient thinking on our part, and the ability to educate yourself is paramount.

**Analyzer** — Being an analyzer is a great skill to have. We spend most of our business years performing analysis on many different things. I believe analysis is a basic part of planning. Sometimes the analysis can be as simple as taking time to think through an idea before you move to the application.

I have also found many of my colleagues who like to analyze things to death. This is one of those elements that can hold you back if you are not careful. You can get in a mode of being such a careful analyzer you forget to take risks. There are many times when you must simply do something and not waste a lot of time studying whether it is the right thing to do. In this case, I would suggest you are on the side of too much analysis rather than too little. The ability to analyze must be balanced with the ability to take risk.

**Presentation Skills** — This is a skill you must have in your tool kit in this day and age. You are going to find that, no matter what business you are in today, you are going to spend time in front of a group of people. Whether you are spending time to inform or educate them or trying to sell to them, you will need presentation skills.

Presentation skills require you to listen, to think on your feet, to handle objections, and to field questions properly. You must take time to prepare yourself and the media that is most appropriate for your audience.

Presentation skills will help you when you try to convince people of your own credentials and self worth. I have observed that people who present well also seem to interview well.

Presentation skills are made up of more than just getting up in front of the group and speaking. It is a strong method of communication. It is a way to gain instant credibility, especially if you truly know and understand your subject. You must spend time listening to your audience and responding. I have not found one job or discipline where this skill cannot help you or is not required.

Presentation ability definitely can be acquired, even purchased, fairly easy. There are many courses being taught on effective presentation. You can achieve some level of proficiency in being a presenter if you practice in front of a mirror.

Using this skill is a lot of fun; and, if you have a decent command of the language, it can be a great way to communicate ideas.

**Writing Skills** — Writing is essential in the business world, and it is the most important form of communication. You will find yourself writing all the time. Most professional positions will demand this skill.

Most college graduates take the minimal writing requirements. It is easy to overlook the development of this skill when you are trying to learn a discipline. Most schools are now requiring students to take more writing courses in order to finish their programs.

Do not be fooled into thinking some secretary will do

all of your writing. Secretaries are really conduits for getting your work done. Most corporations have word processing pools, and they are trained to type what they see. I have had the experience of having a secretary proofread a document and have still found numerous errors in what was thought to be the final product. You must be able to put your words in text before they will ever get to a word processing station. The days of the personal secretary are gone for everybody except the CEO of the company. It is just not cost effective to have secretaries be ghost writers for corporate executives. Many executives have personal workstations on their desks that they use to communicate with their colleagues without a secretary ever seeing their work.

Writing is a skill you want to have; and, if you are already in the business world, you should take additional writing courses when they are available. The better you write, the better you will be able to communicate.

**Integrity** — It is the keeper of excellence and fights compromise. I have known many individuals of high integrity, and I am glad to have met them. One of the biggest downfalls of a business person is a lack or loss of integrity. Integrity is a value most people do not have to develop; it is usually passed down by parents. It can be acquired through common sense. The business world used to demand integrity, but now a company is fortunate if 50% of its people are of high integrity. Integrity is usually accompanied by high moral standards. The "me generation" weakened the integrity of this blessed nation. In the Eighties, Ronald Reagan can be credited with trying to bring back the desire for integrity.

One characteristic which makes an employee proud is when the company's executive officer has a high regard for company standards, if the executive officer stands behind the slogan or motto of a corporation and tries to deliver a quality product to the customer. An employee can hold her head high when she knows the product she is representing is of the highest quality available.

It is easy to represent an organization that it is built upon a foundation of integrity. The employee wants to contribute to meeting the goals and objectives of the corporation. You as an employee will take pride in your work if integrity is a part of your organization. Some people call integrity "scruples." American business needs to focus on bringing integrity back to the corporate meeting rooms and bullpens. The fear of God used to be enough to keep businesses moving on an honest path. God has been pushed out of the organizational structure, and now it is simply up to the customer of a corporation to decide whether he or she is being dealt with fairly.

**Results-Oriented** — Employees who are results-oriented are usually very effective in their jobs. They tend to strive for perfection. They are sought after in the corporation because they can be counted on to get things done, and they usually perform very well against a set of objectives. Co-workers desire to have results-oriented employees on their team because they are the higher contributors. This element allows you to compete effectively, working towards bringing about desired results. This can be an acquired skill but is usually acquired with experience. This does not mean you just want to see things get done, but it also means you like to meet objectives. People who are results-oriented are often driven and strive for completion and perfection.

The business world has become less bureaucratic and more aimed at completing its mission. The business world is becoming much more task-oriented and seeks accomplishment of its stated set of objectives.

Results-oriented professionals thrive on accomplishing what is asked of them. Results-oriented managers are easy to please if you also are results-oriented. I was a part of an office that had such a manager. He was not a friendly guy, at least not at all times. He went by the numbers or, as he would so often put it, the companies stated objectives. He was moody, and you could usually tell if the office was making its numbers or not. His mood swings were very good indicators of how well we were meeting the objectives. If the branch was meeting its objectives, this guy was in a good mood. If the branch was behind in its objectives, you did not say "Good morning" to this executive.

If you can get others to produce the desired results like our manager above, you are probably a good candidate for management, if you are not already there.

**Optimizes Resources** — Optimize is one of those corporate buzzwords that really is valid and provides something to shoot for in the business world. One who can learn to optimize is going to be looked upon very favorably by his colleagues. One who optimizes resources is truly going to contribute to the productivity of a corporation and to the profit margin. The business world today is constantly trying to cut expenses and expenditures. Optimization becomes necessary. I might go so far as to say that it is a requirement to optimize the resources you use.

The days of "do what it takes to get the job done" are gone. This is the era of "minimize your resources and still have a good return on investments." Managing resources is one of the foremost things to do in a corporation. Hero status can be obtained easily if you know how to optimize the resources and meet your business objectives.

Planning the use of resources required to get a job done is a part of the optimization process. Good planning, as we stated earlier, is necessary for proper utilization of resources. I was once responsible for meeting a quota objective and was asked to downsize my requirements. It is not easy to reduce resource requirements and still accomplish objectives in the same amount of time. To be successful, you must be very resourceful with what is available to you.

**Utilize the Network** — This is just another name for understanding what information is being passed via the political grapevine. We as Black professionals have learned how important this capability is to our professional growth. There are many types of networking, but I would like to focus on networking inside of a corporation. Understand who and what is important to know and who can help advance your career once you have the necessary skills.

The network is a required communications vehicle that can transmit anything from what resources are required to accomplish certain company objectives to who is having a baby on the 10th floor of your building. Understand what contribution this can make toward your goals and how you can become a contributor to accomplishing other subscribers' objectives.

We must take care and learn to utilize the network element and allow it to work for us and the corporation. The network can be abused and can work against you if it simply becomes a rumor mill or carrier of negativity. A company can really become a place of doom if the employees use the network to spread discontent. If the network performs in this fashion in your company, you should cancel your subscription to the network. We will discuss "networking" in more detail in a later chapter.

**Motivator** — This is my favorite element of success. I enjoy moving people forward, and this is the element necessary to move people forward. If you allow this element to consume you, you will indeed become a leader of people. If the business world needs anything, it needs more people who are motivators. Motivation in a lot of corporations today is very low. Companies are spending a lot of time trying to keep their heads above water, and this leads to low morale in a company.

The motivator is usually an upbeat individual. S/he is usually a true optimist and a pleasure to be around. Corporations thrive off the motivator. You can walk in the office on a Monday morning feeling down and out. You run into a motivator, and s/he will make your day by saying just the right thing to give you a boost.

A self-motivator is an individual who can really get things done. If you are a self-motivator, you have one of the best attributes you can have. You have the ability to move forward and encourage yourself. These people are in no way average people. The self-motivator is highly sought after for team projects and becomes very valuable the first time he uses his skill to bring the level of enthusiasm a team may need to get its project back on schedule.

**Respect for Others** — This is necessary if you are going to need others to help you accomplish your goals and objectives. Respect is your ability to understand what is important to another person. It comes out of understanding what other people care about. It also comes out of caring about what a person can contribute to an organization.

I had the opportunity to work for a company who took respect for the individual very seriously, and I learned a lot about respecting one's work and capabilities. I learned a lot about what respect can do for a company. I firmly believe that if a corporation works at respecting an individual, an individual becomes very loyal to that corporation. I would not work for a corporation that did not show respect for its employees.

Remember, your peers do not have to like you, but

they must respect you.

**Ability to Empower** — There are many good leaders who understand how to use their power to help make others effective. That is what I call empowerment. Having the ability to help others take responsibility for what needs to be done will achieve grand success for the organization. A corporation will be very successful if it is capable of granting power effectively to the people who make up the corporation.

Many of us suffer from "personal power ambiguity." This simply means we want to be powerful without understanding how to use that power. If you look around a corporation, you will find the people who are a part of what I call "the power tower." These are the people who are very good at using and sharing the power.

Empowerment is one of the most overused and misunderstood words of the Nineties. But, I like it if it is being used in the same sentence with my name. I hope we African-American professionals will build this skill as it is slowly being entrusted to us by the corporate business world. Then, I hope we learn how to use it on one another.

I have presented you with a set of attributes, characteristics and skills that have been the essence of success for most of the successful people we know. People who are successful do not get that way by a miraculous bestowal. They work hard, and they press towards excellence and perfection. They may never obtain what they have set out to do, but they are successful, simply, in the trying.

If you truly want to be successful in the business world, add all of the above elements to your tool kit for success. If you read through this chapter hurriedly, go back and read it slowly. If necessary, study it for a week. Toy with these different elements to see if you can make them a part of what you are all about. I am successful because I have learned to think and do what other successful people have done and are still doing. Get on with it!

# Chapter

# 3

# Perpetuating the Work Ethic

*P*lease do not be confused by the use of the word "ethic." I simply mean be serious about doing your best in front of the work-clock. A profound professor once told his class of industrial engineering students, "Work smarter, not harder." "Learn to use your mind, not your back." I say, "Provide a good day's work for the salary you are paid. Then you can say you earned it." I once heard a good business instructor say, "Work for the money and not to make money." I believe he was saying that you should not come to work just to get a paycheck but that you should come to work to earn a paycheck and to provide worth to yourself.

Doing a good job will become the norm in the Nineties! The workforce is calling for the highly educated and highly trained individual. Corporations are being managed by some very high-achieving individuals who strive for perfection and set their sights on excellence. The work ethic is part of our culture again. In fact, we are overshooting the target on the amount of time people are spending at work. In the last office I worked, most of my colleagues worked every weekend. I do not believe it takes working every weekend to be a highly productive employee of a corporation. But, I do believe the quality of the time worked must be very high if you are to remain competitive. Many people have decided the quantity of time worked is a substitute for the quality of finished work. Doing quality work is equally as important as completing the work.

In the "Industrial Age," workers could show their worth by how many parts were produced or by how much material they could process. As we move deeper into the

"Information Age" and/or the "Service Age" (The product many industries are providing to their customers today is service.), quality has to be the number one measurement. Our work measurement system is evolving to accommodate this change from quantity of work completed to quality of work completed. When you are in the business of providing service, the way you measure quality will become more important than measuring quantity. We as Black professionals are going to have to understand these measurement systems in order to be sought after for our work.

If we focus on the quality of our work, a good work ethic will emerge. This should be a given—the ability to do your very best and to exceed what is asked of you. The employer should be able to have confidence in you and to take pride in what you do.

We should not take for granted the opportunities afforded to us just because we have trained and prepared ourselves for them. The employer may owe us an opportunity based on historical significance, but they do not owe us a job. I have been guilty of saying, "They owe me this job, and they had better take whatever I am willing to give." American business is in an interesting era, and we need to understand what has happened to the equal in "Equal Rights." Quotas are becoming business objectives, which means they now become prioritized with all other business objectives of corporations. If that objective is not top priority, it will not receive attention. The Jesse Jacksons of the world should still continue to focus on the issues, but we must do our part by continuing to understand the business climates and the objectives placed in front of us.

# Overcoming the Stigmas

As you read through this chapter, you will ask the question, "Is he talking about stereotypes and calling them stigmas?" The answer is yes! The reason I use "stigma" instead of stereotype is because I want to over-emphasize the importance of the negative thinking you will face in the business world. Webster says that stigmas are scars. The thinking process used by management is a diseased type of thinking when it comes to African-Americans and other minorities. What we consider stereotypes, they believe to be real and stigmatic, hence the use of stigma.

African-Americans have lived with numerous stigmas for a long time in America, and some of these stigmas are not just figments of White imaginations. Some have merit, while others are unfortunate misunderstandings due to ignorance on the part of all involved. For instance, we Americans have always managed to get our message across by slowing down production or stopping work when we deemed it necessary to gain management's attention. The most powerful method of getting the attention of those in control is by rebellion, slow-downs and decreased production. When Blacks try to employ these methods, especially as a concerted effort, stigmas arise. I offer this section of the book, as an explanation of the results and maybe as justification for some of the methods that brought about such results.

Blacks have tried to employ rebellion, slowdowns and decreased production but often have not been successful in getting the message across. When we were mistreated by the workforce (pre-Seventies) or were passed over for promotions or job opportunities, we often retaliated by slowing down our work efforts. Whites and others did the same thing but did not have their intentions misinterpreted or were not perceived as a negative influence on society. When you try to convince the majority to give you what you think is rightfully yours and they think you already have enough, long-lasting stigmas are established. Stigmas are easy to create but very hard to dissipate.

An example of this is Blacks are perceived as being "lazy." In the eyes of White corporate management, Blacks are still seen as "lazy" and often perceived as being less productive than their White counterparts. The Asians have complicated this perception by coming to America and working harder and longer than all Americans - White, Black, etc. The "laziness stigma" comes from long ago from the protests of the 1800's when slavery was the norm. Pavlov's theory was valid then and is still valid today. If you condition any species that has the ability to learn to a certain behavioral pattern, it will continue to perform to that behavioral pattern for as long as the stimulus is there. This is what happened to us as African-Americans. When the master of yesterday wanted more work from his slaves, he whipped them and told them how lazy they were. The slaves became infuriated and worked harder just to show this master how proud a people they were. But they then learned there was no end to this perpetual production/stimuli phenomenon. They realized they were working themselves to death. They learned to slow down their pace and to work at a much more consistent pace. The masters continued to call them lazy and another type of phenomenon developed. They started to work just hard enough to stay the whip. Today we Blacks are still living with those perceptions of the past, hence we have a stigma.

The "laziness stigma" is an easy one to overcome by outstanding performance. You will find the business world will quickly move away from this stigma if you do your job well. Remember, a business does not have time to hire you just to have you fail. Management wants you to be successful and will usually work to that end. That is why I have chosen to call these particular obstacles stigmas rather than calling them prejudices. The stigma stems from past beliefs and can be overcome by bringing about the desired behavior. In the business world, the desired behavior is excellent performance. I have never had to deal with the laziness stigma personally, but I have observed other Blacks who were considered lazy.

We must also be careful we do not fall into the trap of living up to the laziness stigma by letting the Black Chip provide a negative influence. I observed a young Black woman who allowed herself to get so frustrated with trying to overcome the laziness stigma, she gave in and allowed her performance to become inadequate. The result was decreased self-esteem, lower performance, ridicule, and hence, perpetuation of the stigma.

Another stigma Blacks face in the business world is, "Blacks are inferior mentally." This one will hurt when you encounter it for the first time. You might be sitting in a meeting and be very eager to demonstrate your capabilities as a contributor. You will somehow get edged out of the discussion and get virtually shut down. You will go away wondering what happened to you. I have had this happen to me numerous times. You will want to retaliate in some way, but I suggest you go away and plan your next move for perfect execution. Sweet revenge will only come from showing professionalism. The next meeting you attend will be a fun one. I have found that, once I knew what had happened to me, I enjoyed engaging and mastering the game. I become twice as conscious of what is going on around me, and I become twice as creative. Your White co-professionals will be startled when you first present the best idea on the table. It will be as if an old country hound dog started to speak perfect English. If they have had minimal dealings with African-Americans, you will have the opportunity to teach them the proper behavior and consideration. There are times when they will not be willing to listen, and you will become frustrated. This is the time to sit back and stay focused; and when you have your wits about you, get back into the game.

A third stigma we Blacks face is, "Blacks are not neat." This is one stigma that is very easy to remove. Dress and look your very best. I strive to be the best dressed individual in the office. This is not to be flamboyant, but rather to be the professional that I am.

Keep your desk neat, your work area secure. Having a nice working environment is very important to you and to others who work with you. A clean work area is something that is very easy to control. You will be labeled a slob by your peers if you keep your work area or office messy. The old adage that says, "A cluttered desk is the sign of a creative mind" is outdated. People who are known to be neat are perceived to be very organized, and that is one perception you want people to have of you.

Take care to be neat. Every time you go into the rest room, look at your hair and the rest of your grooming. We Blacks often have very dry skin. Whenever we wash our hands and face, our skin becomes very ashy. Be sure to keep lotion handy for those occasions. I am very proud when I see other Black professionals looking their best and I can see the time and care they took to present a well groomed appearance. The more time you spend thinking about this, the more you will care about these things. Remember, we must overcome the stigmas that are placed on us. God forbid we perpetuate them any further.

I hope you are starting to formulate a plan that will allow you to be better prepared to take on the corporate environment with a slightly better edge than those who were not fortunate enough to have the information presented in this book.

# Prove Excellence

"Prove to yourself what makes excellence for you, and you will never have to strive for it."

I decided to "Prove Excellence" in the things I do. If you have proof of something, you are usually very confident about it, and it is easier to accomplish. When you are put to the test, you can fall back on what you know, on what you have proven. Scientists do this all the time by first establishing what they want to prove. They call this their hypothesis. They then set up experiments to prove what they believe to be true. If you prove excellence, it gets embedded in the way you go about accomplishing the various tasks and strategies you have developed. If a plan is well thought out and executed using proof of excellence, success is inevitable.

Attitude is very important when you are trying to prove excellence. A winning attitude is the only true way to bring about excellence in everything you do, that is, winning from the standpoint of having the confidence in yourself, to believe anything you propose in your heart you can achieve. My mother once ran for city government. Her campaign slogan was, " Believe It! Achieve It." What a winning attitude she projected throughout all of her campaign! The attitude she projected during that time was very infectious to everyone who was associated with her.

A professional must have a great attitude. It will take you through most tough situations. A great attitude can "stand the test of time," and it will always come through for you, especially when things are not going well for you. Remember the times you found yourself enjoying someone you had just met? Not a sensual or erotic attraction, but a good-to-know-you type of an attraction. This person made you feel good about being around him or her. If you investigated a little further, you probably found this was a person who cared about others as well as himself. He  did his best at all costs. This is a person you learn to trust in a very short period of time. She appeared to work hard at accomplishing what she set out to do, and she did not compromise her values. At the time you were observing this person, you were witnessing the projection of excellence.

Now there are many levels of excellence, and I believe we all subscribe to one. There is bottom level of excellence, and it usually borders on failure. A taste of failure, if properly analyzed and put into proper perspective can help bring about excellence and can be a deterrent to mediocrity. Mediocrity is the exact opposite of excellence in my opinion.

Many of the people I have known to achieve excellence in the things they have accomplished were once failures and will probably be failures again. You see, excellence does not stop you from failing, but it does make it hard for failure to continue.

Excellence breeds success in all of its truest forms. The highest level of excellence is when others know you have executed flawlessly and have accomplished the things you have set out to do. You prove excellence not only to yourself; you also prove it to others. No matter how well you do things, excellence will always say, "You can do better." I found some of the most exciting times of my life were when I knew I was executing and performing better than the world around me.

Excellence takes a lot of planning, execution and hard work.

I have had the opportunity to work for a corporation who had for its motto, "A Commitment To Excellence." The company tried very hard to live up to the motto and has probably come closer than any other corporation to accomplishing and proving excellence within its hallowed halls. For a corporation to prove excellence throughout its entire organization, it must be made up of people who are willing to take this on as their personal goal.

The time is now for African-American professionals to make excellence the core of everything we set out to accomplish. There is one thing I have come to know about excellence since I started my quest to prove it to myself: You are no longer just getting by or struggling to make it. You know what you are doing. You are now a leader. One of the best things a White man has ever said to me was, "I know you want to encourage excellence in this department, but you are pushing too hard." I will treasure that comment for the rest of my life.

Another way to prove excellence is by accepting criticism from your cohorts and yourself. People who are critical of themselves can move rapidly toward excellence. They are way ahead of what others are expecting from them and have learned to push themselves for maximum output.

However, there are people who take criticism of themselves too far. Those who criticize themselves too harshly will allow it to become something that does not motivate and that will not lead to proven excellence. I have played golf with people who spend more time being frustrated with themselves than enjoying the game. You must never lose sight of the purpose of what you are trying to do. Allowing criticism to become the focus will slowly consume you. Allowing others to criticize you and your work constructively will bring improvement in whatever you are trying to accomplish. Finding colleagues who evaluate your work will not be hard. Be careful not to let them simply put you down as opposed to providing constructive criticism.

We as Black professionals must stop settling for second best or being the best amongst other Blacks. We have got to set our sights on being totally competitive with everyone. As will be pointed out in a later chapter, the Asians have mastered perpetuating the work ethic. They are now starting to earn the dollars which allow them to take over segments of the markets where they choose to participate. We should learn to push ourselves for excellence and allow the natural causes of success to motivate us.

Having the right support structure in place is essential in our pursuit to prove excellence. A positive environment is an absolute must not only at work but also at home. The friends you associate with can influence how effective you are going to be at accomplishing your goals. Your friends should help create a healthy environment for you. They should be good people, clear and creative thinkers. They should help stimulate you, encourage you and promote your ideals and standards. The interaction between you and your friends should be two-way; and you should be able to contribute something to their lives, as they contribute to yours. A motto I live by says, "If I cannot help you in some way, I cannot be your friend." Friendship should be a mutual interaction for all parties concerned and is indeed necessary if you are going to overcome the obstacles and challenges that you will face in the business world.

I believe you should be very selective when choosing your friends. They should be honored to be your friend, and you should feel the same way. Mutual friendships are the only kind to have. You need to be able to trust someone with your thoughts, secrets and ideas. You have control over this part of your environment, and you should exercise it. Your friends are very important in helping you live a good and productive life. Many people take for granted the ability of people to affect one anothers' lives. Remember when your mother used to tell you not to hang around with certain individuals because they were troublemakers or they were not going to amount to anything. That applies as much in your adult life as it did when you were a kid. When the pressures of this life come to rest on your doorstep, you are going to need all the support you can get. Getting support and giving support work together for the good of the whole. We Blacks really need to pay attention to this structure more than others.

Family structure has deteriorated over the years, and we really need to concentrate on building it back to what it was when slavery existed. We were displeased with anyone splitting our families apart, and we fought it with all the resources we had at the time.

Yes, it takes all this to bring and maintain excellence in your life. Strive for it and it will come; and it will stay.

# Be Organized

Organization is the key to keeping a business healthy and thriving. Business will bog down quickly if the company is not carefully organized to accomplish its objectives. The people who make up a company are essential to helping maintain the structure of a corporation. Organization can be perpetual if a corporation has ingrained in its management and staff the need for tight organizational practices.

If you have not yet spent time assessing whether or not you have a certain level of organization in the things you set out to accomplish, you should spend some time making this assessment. Organizational assessment should be the first step in learning to work at maximum potential. For instance, look at your desk and see if you know what is on your desk. If you have more than four stacks of files or papers on the top of your desk at any one time, you are either extremely organized or your desk is out of your control. Look in your file cabinets. If you do not have a clearly defined system for putting your files or datasheets into your files, you lack organization. Do you enjoy going into your desk or files or even your clothing drawers at home? If you do not enjoy opening a drawer, you probably lack organization.

It is possible to be organized in a particular area and not in others. If someone comments on how neat you keep your files, you can probably assume this is an area where you are skilled. Be sure you are not skilled in one area and lacking skills in numerous other areas. This is where knowing your strengths and weakness comes into play. Learning organization skills is not easy if you have not been taught this skill as a child. I feel very strongly about teaching children how to be organized as early as possible. If the skills of organization are bred into you when you are a young child, they will be a part of you forever. And if you have not been taught organizational skills, you can learn to be organized.

Most of the African-American professionals I have worked with lack organization skills initially. I was not taught to be organized until I was an adult. I must admit, the U.S. Navy taught me how to be disciplined and how to get things done. I am still a bit regimental, but I enjoy working in this manner. We should not view a lack of organization skills as a put down but more as a skill deficiency which we need to develop and or improve. We too often allow the Black Chip to trick us into believing a skill deficiency is another way the White man is trying to oppress us; and it may be true in some cases. But that is not the issue to focus on at this time. We must overcome the temptation for self pity and admit when we have a skill deficiency. Once an alcoholic admits he or she is an alcoholic, then and only then can s/he be helped. We must become the assessors of ourselves and deal with our problems and overcome our deficiencies.

As I stated earlier, if you are not organized, you can learn to become organized. It is amazing what a simple time management course can do for enhancing organization skills. Keeping a calender adds tremendous improvement to tracking day-to-day activities. A calender can be a basic system for tracking obligations. A simple "to-do" list will enhance your ability to follow up on uncompleted tasks. Once you start to develop organization skills, you will continue to seek ways to improve yourself in this skill area.

Becoming organized is one way of adding a business nature to your life. We need this more than ever, especially if we are ever going to run a piece of corporate America.

One final note on organization. When you attend a meeting, sit up straight in your chair. Always bring a note pad and pen. Be prepared for the discussion, and always position yourself to contribute.

# Time

If you live a normal life of 75 years, which is 27,375 days and nights or 657,000 hours, you can consume 67 days of your life sitting at a stop light! You can find yourself standing in a shower for one and a half years of your life. You will need to spend 37 years of your life in a bed in order to get the required amount of sleep! You could possibly spend 62,400 hours of your life working in a given profession! The above statements describe the various activities requiring TIME from our lives.

Yes, time! We have all heard that time is money or the time is now. Time is an important measurement and is a key element for helping to perpetuate the work ethic. Time is the only asset that has immediate value when you first acquire it. We do not always know or understand its value until someone wants to purchase, take, or demand a portion of it. You started learning the value of time from the time you were born; even as a child you valued the time you were allowed to watch television or play with your friends. Time can become very valuable overnight or get devalued in a matter of seconds. Think of college athletes: one day they are on a university campus as a mere student on a varsity squad; the next day, due to some draft, they are millionaires. But if an athlete injures a vital limb, he can become a "has been" worth nothing but sympathy.

The most precious asset in the business world is time. Time is the factor that allows a corporation to know if it is making or losing money. Time is used by the corporation to measure the value of a dollar. You will find the business world can and will consume as much time as it is allowed, and often comes back for more. Understand the value of your time and know what it is worth to your employer and the current job market. Understand what value your employer puts on the time it uses to accomplish the tasks necessary to achieve its measure of success. The time spent in a corporation must be utilized properly by all concerned if a company is going to meet its objectives. Many people often take for granted and misuse the time that is allotted to them for accomplishing the work of a corporation. Time is one thing that can be so easily wasted. Its major enemy is procrastination.

The work ethic thrives on the use and management of time. The management of time is the biggest chore you will have in the business world. Today there are hundreds of tools and methods for allowing you to track and manage time. The way you manage your time can be the difference between whether you are giving a good performance in a job or thought of as a slouch.

Many professionals are guilty of mismanaging their time. I have observed people who are very good at what they do but were perceived as not doing a good job because of the time it took to accomplish the tasks of the job.

Many people infringe on the time of others. Be very respectful of others' time. You will find people treasure their time and hold it as a most valued commodity. If you are respectful of others' time, you will be viewed as a professional who has sensitivity for others. If you say you are going to be at a given place at a given time, then do your best to be there. Others will quickly become aware of your professionalism if you are a punctual individual.

In a provider/customer relationship, time is an important element. If you are a salesperson and you commit to making a presentation at a certain time, starting the presentation on time is a key part of the presentation. Starting tasks of the job on time is highly professional and will be viewed as part of your work ethic.

Punching a time clock is long gone in most corporations at the professional level. Expectations of the time an employee is required to give to the company are not clearly spelled out. Professionals are entrusted with the time of the corporation. You will quickly be thought of as a slouch or slothful if you often arrive at work late. Arriving at work on time is the first step toward showing a good and healthy work ethic.

If you are a professional, you will be expected to work as long as necessary to complete tasks that help meet objectives. If you arrive at work on time and leave on time, you will be thought of as a "nine-to-fiver." Try to arrive at work ten to fifteen minutes before the published start time of your company. If you are not up against a deadline, try to stay a half hour after the published quitting time. I often spend time after work visiting with my peers and discussing work related issues. This helps me to seek out the knowledge of other professionals, and it allows me to be seen as part of what many corporations call the "A Team." If you spend a lot of time visiting with your peers during normal work hours, you may be viewed as someone who keeps others from getting their work done.

Remember, the challenge is to perpetuate the work ethic in your work environment. Try to be a positive influence on your peers and co-workers. You are going to find plenty of negative factors in the work place that were there long before you arrived. Do not become part of the problems your work environment may have. Be known as upbeat and an optimist. This will enhance your contribution to the organization where you are now a vital part. If at all possible, avoid those who are the low contributors to the corporation. You will know who they are if you are striving to become an added value to the corporation.

You can help the corporation a great deal if you are giving 110 percent! As Black professionals, we have to continue to show we work very hard, and we are now ready to take a bigger role in the business world. The corporate world needs as many highly-trained and hard-working individuals as it can get, and you must tell yourself you are going to rise to this occasion and not be left out. The work ethic is another essential part of keeping African-Americans vital in this country. We want and need to succeed!

# Chapter

# 4

# Twice as Good – Can Be Good Enough

We as Black Americans, along with women and other minorities, are often led to believe we have to be two to three times as good as our White male counterparts if we are to gain the recognition and success we seek. In my experience, this remains a part of the thinking of the business world. There is often resentment on our part because of what is expected of Blacks in the work place. These unreasonable expectations, along with the other obstacles, are often deterrents to achieving success. The workforce is now being forced to accept us at an even par with our White co-professionals but only for entry into the work place. Do not be satisfied only with acceptance! We do not want to be just average in the work place; we must strive to far exceed all of the expectations. We should settle only for being "twice as good as what is expected."

It is expected that we are not overachievers, and we do not advance to the seats of power and decision. These are expectations we do not want to meet. We want to be considered and placed in the seats of power and decision. Being twice as good is now good enough to achieve the success we have wanted for so very long. We must teach ourselves and our children to settle for nothing less than being the BEST!

## Perception

"Perception is reality" is not just an old adage; it is true for all who strive to attain excellence, which I defined in an earlier chapter.

I was once on the staff of an area vice president who

was responsible for about $1.1 billion in sales and for approximately 1,100 people. I had the opportunity to work for a very meticulous, yet fair, manager. She was a very good communicator, and she was also very good at appraising the work performed under her guidance. I sent her an electronic note which is a normal method of interoffice communication in most companies today. She called me to her office and told me I needed to be more careful when sending out electronic notes. She pointed out spelling and formatting errors in my notes. I had not given much thought to the quality of these notes which were being sent throughout the division. It was a matter of laziness on my part because the system we were using was quite capable of pointing out the errors electronically had I taken the time to use it. She said the work you do for the field organization is going to be judged based on the notes you send out. The people on the receiving end of the notes do not all know you, and they only see your notes. If the notes are of poor quality, your clients will perceive you to be a poor communicator and discount the work you do. Remember, "perception is reality." Needless to say, I became a very good user of the electronic mail system, and I learned to take advantage of the tools that could help me to do a better job.

How people perceive you is going to influence how they think about you, and their perception will quickly become reality when your co-workers and superiors start to discuss your contribution. I was working with a senior level individual who had been in the corporation for quite a while. This individual had moved up through the corporation and become a manager and then decided to go back to the office where he was first hired. He was a fair performer and was a contributing member of the team. For some reason the word got around the office that this individual was an "eight-to-fiver." He was also perceived as under-skilled. We put a plan in place to fix the skills issue and then tried to move the person into more of a leadership role in the office. This, indeed, was a tougher job than he or I ever thought it would be. We were met with a lot of peer resistance. Nobody wanted to work with this individual nor did they want him on their team. It was mainly a perception problem on the part of the people in the office. We were not able to fix the problem for this individual and he remained very frustrated in the assignment of lesser responsibility.

You must constantly be aware of how you are perceived in the work place by your peers and your manager. Do not take for granted people who appear to like you. They could possibly like you for your personality and be critical of your work habits. You will find people may start off liking the way you go about accomplishing your work; and then, due to some factor you may or may not know about, they become your critic rather than your advocate. Be sure you understand the perception your manager has of you. Managers are often asked their opinion of their subordinates and, for the most part, are fair with their assessments. Be sure you understand how your manager feels about you as an employee and as a person. A manager may like your work, but may not like your approach to getting things done. Do not assume your manager is fully aware of everything you have accomplished over some period of time. Misguided perception on the part of a manager can be the downfall of an employee. Your co-workers are usually well informed of what you are capable of doing, but they too can be swayed by what they hear and think they have observed about you. I have learned to solicit criticism from my peers, managers and co-workers. Their comments have not always met what I thought they were thinking. Learn to listen for what is actually being said about you. Do not think, if you are doing a good job, all is well. The business world is full of political hoops; perception is one of those hoops!

# Reality

Reality can be whatever you make it to be and is very often driven by perception. If you do not shape reality, it will shape itself (perception), and you may or may not be happy with the outcome. You are the author of reality in the work place. People will think you are a good performer if you are constantly putting on a good performance, and this must not manifest itself as effort alone. There must be results!

Overcoming perceptions some people may have of you is a reality of the work place. Overcoming unwanted perception can make it a little harder to bring about the reality you desire. Nevertheless, reality will prevail. You should often check the reality of whether things are going well or poorly. If you find yourself becoming very comfortable in a job, make sure you are not entering the tunnel of complacency.

If you are a hard worker and an exceptional performer, the word will spread quickly. High-achieving African Americans always take the business world by surprise because of our small yet progressive numbers. It will be a long time before we are totally and unequivocally accepted by the business world, and our numbers are such that we become the status quo. Good performance allows us to take advantage of what used to be an obstacle — the lack of our ability to excel in the professional community due to lack of opportunity. Fortunately, the business world has stopped accepting the notion that there are just a few highly trained Blacks entering the job market. You now have the opportunity to control reality; and, when the spotlight is turned your way, you must be prepared to take center stage. This does not necessarily mean we must all become the CEO or President, although I hope many of you will try. We simply need to become one of the best — the one sought after for what s/he knows and can accomplish. We should be tired of just being a corporate statistic helping to meet some corporate business objective (i.e., minority quota).

Reality is now in our own hands, and we must learn to shape it and form it into what will help us continue to progress, an image that will allow us to continue to own a piece of the American business.

I often take advantage of being selected to represent the Black professional community. When I am asked to sit at the vice president's table, I am fully aware I have been asked to sit there as the token African American. I am delighted, and I keep in mind there was a time when we were not considered for the opportunity to sit at the head table. I prepare myself for the event. I keep reminding myself I am representing the other Blacks in the corporation and those who may have a chance to join the corporation in the future. I make sure I have something to contribute to the conversations at the table and work hard at continuing to positively shape reality for me and other Black professionals. This is evidence we are starting to have the opportunity to shape reality for ourselves.

One of the most important things I have learned since I arrived in the business world is there is plenty of room for those who dare to shape reality. I enjoy every time I find myself in control of my own destiny. This is something I want to get used to: understanding the when, where, how and why I am capable of accomplishing whatever I choose to do.

Not spending my time trying to catch up, but continuously moving forward. We can make and shape reality.

Do not spend all your time worrying about whether the amount and quality of your work is good enough to meet the requirements of the job. You will find that your counterparts are no better than you are, although they do have their heritage and background to fall back on. You can experience most of the things you need in order to develop the skills being required to do the job. Yes! It will take you a little longer to accomplish what you want, but it's the end results that count. It will not be an easy task to equal the accomplishments of our White counterparts, but we must persevere; and we can enjoy the here and now. We can start to make the new day and create the reality we desire.

"Are we disadvantaged?" or "Do they have the advantage?" are the questions I am still trying to answer. If reality is what we are after, we must be honest with ourselves. Being disadvantaged is only a bad thing if we do nothing to rectify the situation. I know I am disadvantaged every time one of my White colleagues corrects my English or says not to worry about it.

I asked to be promoted to a job I had already demonstrated I could do. I was told that it was understood I wanted the job and they (upper management) would do the best they could to make it happen. Yet, I was made aware the current open position which I was already filling and wanting would not continue to be filled by me. They were bringing in a person (a young White women who was once a part of the office) from another part of the company to fill the position. And they did just that. You bet they have the advantage. They are already totally networked into a game we are still learning how to play.

Reality tells me to dig deeper — tapping the powers of the Black Chip—and learn how to overcome the obstacles reality will continue to throw my way. I have already come to understand frustration as a motivator; and this is where we can turn the Black Chip into a powerful weapon. I must admit there are many experiences like the one in the paragraph above that are not easy to push aside. I can tell you becoming angry does not help me overcome such experiences. Understanding what is happening to you during these experiences can strengthen you to go the next mile and allow you to become smarter as you plan your next move.

Now is a good time to discuss skills analysis again. I promise to discuss this topic in several different sections of this book and from several viewpoints.

We must not fool ourselves into thinking we have all the skills necessary to conquer the world of business. Upon completing the college education curriculum and a summer internship, we are merely ready to start learning what the business world will require of us. The good news is that they are willing to teach us but not with a lot of handholding. We must constantly inventory our skills and evaluate how we need to enhance those skills. Reading, writing, and arithmetic are now assumed, and most corporate aptitude tests will screen these fairly well before they let you in the door. You will be surprised to find college has only given you the basic foundation for a corporation to build on before you become a productive contributor. I was very surprised to find I had to attend in-house education for a year upon entering a large corporation. Corporate education is a continuous process, and they will do all they can to keep you current in the business of the corporation. Talk about reality! It can be overwhelming to see how unproductive you are for at least the first three months after you arrive on the corporate scene.

Reality is the one thing you want to keep close tabs on in the business world because it can change very rapidly. One day you may think the company is doing well and making a lot of money. The next day you find they are going to shut down a whole division because of cash flow problems or because they decided this is not the business they want to be in. Do not allow reality to manipulate you into something you do not want to be. Keep your skills honed and stay well informed. Take advantage of every opportunity to become smarter and more powerful. Create and build upon your own reality. Create and formulate your own perceptions about you and your work. Make you the best breeder of perceptions about you. If at all possible, do not allow others to formulate perceptions about you. Let your reality be so powerful it will negate others' perceptions.

# Managing Expectations

Your expectations are going to be the hardest thing to manage in the business world. The reason why most executives in large corporations keep a bottle of antacid in their credenzas is because what they expect to happen does not happen or what they did not plan to have happen did. In order to manage your own expectations, you must first assess what kind of a person you are. Are you a risk-taker? If you are, how much risk are you willing to take? Are you conservative? If you are, what are you willing to risk? Your expectations are something you ought to spend a lot of time assessing, and I recommend you try to capture a description of what you expect out of a corporation and write it down for later referencing. You will be surprised at how much you will expect from yourself, from others and from the corporation you have become a part of. Understand what to expect and have some idea about your reactions to certain events you will experience in a corporation. Managing expectations is very important to your longevity in a given corporate environment. I have observed individuals who change companies every year because the company does not meet their expectations. I have met individuals who continue to go back to school because they cannot deal with the business world, and school becomes their profession.

What kind of a company will meet your expectations? I believe all professionals do not spend enough time thinking about the characteristics of the place they would be most productive in a corporation and what they expect of a company. We spend a lot of time thinking of the career we would like to pursue. (At least I hope we spend a lot of time researching and choosing a career.) But the first offer that has the right amount of dollars associated with it is what we accept. We should think long and hard about the type of company where we hope to spend at least five years of our lives.

Before completing my degree, I was offered a job by a very good company. The job sounded very exciting when described to me by the company's recruiter. I accepted the position after doing very minimal research. I had a lot of responsibility, my own office, a wonderful title and a handsome salary. After six months in the position, I found myself bored to death. I was offered a job for the second time by a corporation that had offered me a position earlier. After a lot of research, I accepted the position at a lower salary. It was a very good move, and I thoroughly enjoyed the job and the opportunities it afforded.

A large corporation can be a good place to start if you are easily bored. It will provide you with greater opportunities to change job assignments if that becomes necessary. I find after two years in an assignment, I am ready to move to a new assignment. I love to be very busy; and if I am not, I start to get anxious. In a large corporation, you have the flexibility to move around and change job assignments. Large corporations are easier to assimilate into because you will usually find a ready population of Blacks. You will also find less focus on your particular job.

Small corporations can give you more freedom if you do not like a lot of structure. A small corporation may have very few Blacks, and this can be detrimental if you need a support structure around you. If you have a lot of initiative, a small corporation can allow you to be more creative, but it does not allow a lot of time for you to learn and develop skills. A small corporation often wants immediate results.

In the business world, it is very easy to think something is going to go in one direction, and then it goes in another direction. I wanted to be a manager because I truly like people. I set my expectations toward being a champion of the underling, and I thought it would be fun to manage people and reward them for a job well done. It was a lot of fun promoting a highly enthusiastic, gung-ho performer. I never thought about what do you do when you are managing a poor performer and have to force someone out of the company. It is a terrible headache to try to convince an employee to change job assignments when they truly like what they are doing but are not very effective. I must tell you, never go into management if you like people. You will have a much better chance of meeting your expectations if you are working along side rather than over others.

Learning to manage others' expectations is part science and part art. It will take a lot of your time and energy;

but if you master this skill, you are well on your way to a great career. If I were to size up all the things you need to learn successfully, managing others' expectations is close to the top of the list.

If you are in sales, you will have to manage the customers' expectations. You must also manage your manager's expectations (which we will discuss in some detail in a later chapter). If you are on a team, you must make sure everybody understands what they can expect from you.

It is okay to take time to figure out what is going to be expected of you, but then you will get in the driver's seat and guide these expectations into something you can manage. It is fun to observe the new kid on the block who is raring to go and ready to get up under the yoke of success. S/He quickly learns what is expected and starts to manage the expectations of those who are a part of the team. If you are not a high-initiative person, you will soon be relegated to being a "doer", not a leader.

Managing the expectations of those who are in a position to impact your state of being in a company is key to making sure you are perceived in a manner which is most beneficial to you. I enjoy reading the people I work with and setting their expectations toward my concerns.

Cognitive Dissonance - This is the ability to bring one's thoughts and emotions in line with reality. My first encounter with this term was in my Psychology class, freshman year, fall quarter. You know the one where you get credit for showing up for some simplistic study that takes about an hour of your time. I never in my wildest dreams thought it would be such an important concept to understand. It is really a simple concept once you understand how often you experience it.

Remember the last time you wanted something that was red, shiny and neat. You went to a store keeper and you asked for what you want, explaining in excruciating detail what your heart desired. The store keeper went behind the counter or into a cabinet, came back and said, "Sorry, we don't have a red one, but we do have an orange one." You pondered the thought of having a red one, and you went through the full range of emotions from storming out of the store to throwing yourself at the mercy of the salesperson and saying, "Whatever it takes, please get me a red one." Finally, you came back to reality and you realized the orange one was not only just as good as a red one would have been, but was probably better. You have just experienced cognitive dissonance. Well, how does this help us to manage others expectations?

If you understand someone is expecting something from you, and you are the person empowered to deliver it, you should always be in a position either to meet their expectations or to manage their expectations until you can deliver. The ability to understand how to manipulate one's thoughts and emotions is a very important skill to have. In the sales environment, it is fundamental and will work in your behalf. This understanding of how you can manage a person's expectations works in almost every aspect of the business world. I am sure by now you are remembering some instance where a salesperson manipulated your emotions and sold you something you were not quite ready to buy. Cognitive dissonance can also be brought about in an individual who was not planning to have a certain experience take place in their life. It often comes into play when you are in a meeting. You are trying to convince the committee that your ideas are great and should be implemented as soon as possible. You will find yourself, many times, in a position of having to convince someone to accept your way of thinking. Changing people's minds, especially when they have already arrived at certain conclusion, is indeed a valuable skill. And you thought that Psych class was just for a few easy credits!

Understanding how cognitive dissonance works in a person can be one of the best methods in assisting you to manage expectations in the business world. You may have already discovered how well it works on a spouse or on other family members.

Projecting Your Potential - The business world thrives on the potential of its parts, especially when it comes to planning and measuring productivity of the individual worker. Projecting your potential can lend itself well to managing expectations. You must be able to clearly explain and project what you are capable of accomplishing. Remember, perception is very often reality; and they both must be managed by you. We as African American professionals must learn to attract attention to our work and demonstrate that we are more than capable of performing the job of the profession we choose. We must learn to ask to be put on the more challenging assignments that can lead to upward mobility and greater responsibility.

The only way we will truly gain the opportunity to make decisions that will enhance the quality of positions held by Blacks in large major corporations is to be prepared and ascribe to decision-making positions. We must fight the fear which so easily impedes our efforts as we battle our way to the top of America's corporations. This fear is really a fear of failure which is so devastating to the risk-taking which leads to success.

This fear is also a fear of succeeding. Why? Because to succeed means to take a chance of reaching all the potential that is within ourselves, and this could lead to areas beyond one's current capabilities. I have observed African Americans who did not want to accept management positions or other positions of responsibility. Their explanation was simple. "I don't want the hassle that goes with that level of responsibility." The very thing we need to have control of for cultivating Blacks in the business world is the very thing we do not want to be a part of. We must be able to shift into the next phase of the American dream. Equal opportunity does not mean equal authority, wealth or power.

# Workforce Issues

In the opening paragraphs of this book, I introduced a new discussion on a very old topic. Where do Blacks fit in the workforce of today and what does the future hold?

Quotas are now almost nonexistent; and we need to know that, understand it, and accept it. I used to tell myself as a young engineer of the Eighties that I know I will always have a job because I will be one of the token Blacks in one of America's large corporations. For the most part, this has proven to be true and has worked to my benefit. In counseling other young Black professionals who sought me out for advice, I often provided them with what I have come to think of as warped logic: the minority quota is just another characteristic that is used in the decision process of selecting individuals to hire. Quota can be compared to a person being attractive. Considering all things equal, an attractive person has a better chance of getting hired than someone who is not as attractive. Another example I have used is that quota systems can be compared to knowing someone in a particular company and asking that person to get you an interview. Quota systems in corporations often allow us to get our foot in the door.

Minority quota was America's answer to Blacks' anger at their inability to get a job based on the color of their skin. Quota was a good attempt at addressing the issue and has been in front of this country for the last 20 years.

Blacks have made great strides in becoming a part of the workforce, and quotas have helped greatly. It is time for American corporations to move past the quota system because corporations have learned to manipulate this process easily. No, it is not an issue about which Black professionals should be angry. It is something we must continue to understand, especially since times have changed.

I have observed the quota system in action. In fact, I have actually helped to administer it in a very large corporation. First, understand quotas are not called quotas in most large corporations, although they are administered similarly to the way they were first implemented back in the early Seventies. Quotas are now called "business objectives." At first glance, you might think this a good transition. I assure you that this is an attempt by corporate America to get rid of ugly and distasteful terminology. Quotas have evolved to become part of the business strategy, and they now receive a lot less attention. They are monitored on a quarterly basis; and if they are missed (most of the time they are missed to the low side of the objective), they spawn an action plan in the same way a business would address an expense overrun.

Quotas should be the last thing Blacks rely on to get a good job; although, as I stated earlier, they can help get you through the doors of the corporate world. I believe quotas may soon be dropped from the board room discussions.

At the time of writing, the President of the United States is trying to get rid of quota systems. He wants it to be solely on the backs of American corporations to continue to bring about equal opportunity in the work place. I admit I am very afraid to leave something which is so vital to Black American growth and prosperity in the hands of those who are mainly concerned with making their next dollar.

You can quickly see the quota equation does not add up in the favor of African Americans. Ah! But I would not dare paint such a bleak picture without following it with hope and desire.

We Blacks must continue to desire management positions and strive to be the best—not only the best, but Twice as Good! Corporations continue to look at the future availability of a trained workforce. And guess what! Black professionals figure into the right side of this equation. White women minus fewer White males equal more minorities necessary to get the work done in business America.

## Workforce 2000

The year 2000 will mark the end of a God Given Century, a century which has allowed the United States to become wealthy and powerful. And we as Black professionals have just begun to participate in that wealth and power. We are currently entering the single digit percentages of the Upper Class. We are significantly a part of the middle working class and still a very significant part of the non-working poor.

We are now on the brink of something big! What is it? OPPORTUNITY! From now until the year 2000, the U.S. work- force is going to turn to the Black professional as well as to other minorities and White women to bolster the work-force. The American economy is going to continue to grow at a relatively healthy pace. Only a small percentage of the new entrants into the workforce are going to be White males as compared to their numbers today. This unique opportunity is going to present itself to Black professionals. There are going to be jobs without people to fill them.The jobs are going to be mainly in the service industries such as consultants and people strong in computer knowledge, and management of the service-related industries. These jobs, as you know, will demand high skill levels. A sad note is that there will continue to be very few jobs for those who cannot read or follow directions and use mathematics. Those of us who are prepared are going to be able to take advantage of the opportunity. We should be able to soar through organizations and make salaries comparable to those our White counterparts have enjoyed for the past century. This book focuses on some of the things we need to do to prepare to take advantage of this opportunity. First, we are going to have to control the "Black Chip" and use it to our advantage. We must become skilled in every way shape and form. Second, we must become proficient in every way to continue to make inroads into the corporate board rooms. We must become great analyzers of information and know when and where to use it. And we must truly learn how to market our skills in every arena that will allow us.

This opportunity is already starting to present itself in many industries. For those of us who possess an aptitude for scientific and technical information, there are many opportunities here today. The bulk of the opportunities will become available over the next five years and will continue to present themselves for years to come.

Workforce 2000 is what, I believe, may help us realize another part of the dream Dr. King presented to the world. Do you think he knew?

# Chapter

# 5

# Ego and Where It Fits

---

*T*he "ego" is something we all seem to shy away from, yet we know it is a part of us that must be revealed and utilized. In America, if one is said to have an ego, they are looked upon with negative connotation, and they are often shunned by those of us who supposedly do not have an ego. The truth of the matter is, we all have egos. Ego was given to us by the creator right along with our fingers and toes. It is the most important part of us when it comes to protecting our self-esteem and our ability to believe we are somebody. It does often present itself in strange ways, especially if sensitivity for others is not involved in its presentation. Another truth is that the ego is that part of us that mediates for us between what is perception and what is reality and the adaptation thereof.

The ego is often misused and often mistaken for other cognitive mechanisms that manifest themselves in our persons. I was often told during my earlier years in the business world, "You have a big ego." I did not deny having an ego and I tried to use it the way, in my humble opinion, it was meant to be used. I was often misunderstood to be self-serving because I talked about what I wanted to accomplish to everyone who would listen. I later realized that I was continuously trying to convince myself I could, indeed, accomplish what I had set out to do.

It is so easy to think about what you want out of life, but it is hard to make it come true if you are not convinced you can do it. The ego is the best part of our being that urges us to get on with the task of becoming successful. As Black professionals, we face so many obstacles that can possibly set us back. Each segment of our journey is filled with numerous opportunities for discouragement and, so very often, failure. We have not quite learned how to get behind each other and to motivate one another although great strides are being made in this area of our quest. I am convinced that the better we become at motivating each other, the less ego will be necessary. Remember, the ego, through self-motivation, assists us in actualizing what we dream. You might say, the ego is a reality-maker.

I have yet to meet a successful person who does not have an ego. I am not talking about people whose family afforded them wealth, or lottery winners. And even those people who have obtained wealth through some other means rather than earning it themselves, if you dig deep into their roots, you will find someone with an ego had a role to play in their success. I have only met a few people who have learned to hide it and carefully utilize it at the appropriate times. (I am striving for this position within myself.) Most of your successful business executives have large egos, and they are not ashamed to display them when necessary and appropriate. Keep in mind, it is lonely at the top, especially if you had to claw your way there. There are many ways the ego will be observed. The ego is displayed on walls of offices, in the way people carry themselves, and even in the kind of car they drive.

I have often watched professionals who have learned to control their normally unruly ego. They are fun to observe, and you can learn a lot by observing them. First of all, they know how to give strokes as well as receive them. They are often on the giving end rather than the receiving end because they usually know how to get what they want.

I once had a co-manager who was very good at working with her people. She was thought of by her people as one who worked well with others. I found her to be less effective than most of the other managers when attempting to develop her people and very good at getting them to work for her cause. She knew how to champion people, even those who were poor performers. She was very good at making her people look good to others. When she was rewarded herself, she gave the appearance of not wanting the limelight shining on her. But you knew she was one of those people who knew she deserved all the recognition that was bestowed upon her.

Yet, she still was worried about how others viewed her being selected to receive the recognition. She was once given the challenge of convincing an employee of twenty plus years to leave the company. She talked with her, spent time working with her and soon convinced the employee this was not the company for her. She gave the impression she was very sorry for the individual, and I think there was some compassion in her actions. I later watched her walk around the office with a slight bit of pride on the way she had handled the situation. Her ego served her well, and she was thought to be a good manager.

The ego, clearly, can work against you, and I am sure you have seen many cases of this. I have worked with many egotistical people, and they can often irritate the work environment. I once was teamed with an individual who, because of our job titles, was given the overall responsibility for an account. He was the sales representative and I was his technical support. Because I had been first on the account, I was already fairly established in the account. After finding out I was calling on a key decisionmaker in the account, he appeared disturbed. He instructed me not to call on the decisionmakers in the account. He informed me he wanted to be the one to call on this decisionmaker. After several weeks on the account, he discovered the account was not going to do much business with us. He decided, to give me the freedom to call on whomever I wanted, and he did not call on the account very much thereafter. I must admit, I was amused at his approach and his discoveries, and I did not go out of my way to tell him how wonderful this account had been in the past. I would say our egos clashed in this instance. He went on to be very successful in the business, after bringing his ego under control and allowing others to participate in his success.

To position yourself, it is very important to assess your ego and what it is capable of doing for you. I find it essential in the business world to partner myself with a person who has an ego that complements my own. Finding yourself working with egos that are not compatible with yours can be career threatening. Here again, you will find, you are at a disadvantage if you are paired with a White counterpart and your egos clash. We Blacks usually are forced to retreat and regroup. If you are a student of the ego, you can learn to manage and win. If you learn to demonstrate to management you have more to offer or more to contribute than your counterpart, you can win.

Learning when to allow your ego to operate will be invaluable when dealing with the various personalities you will encounter. My ego is the best motivator I have ever had. Many times I found myself feeling inadequate in the business world, and then my ego came to the rescue.

It is truly amazing how the mind can store away different events and then recall them at the proper moment of importance. You will learn behind every event of success, the ego has more than likely invalidated the opportunities for failure. The ego can be the best protection mechanism for dealing with various negative events and not allowing them to overcome you. I once functioned as an expert in one of the companies where I was employed. It was a very rewarding experience, and I enjoyed performing the job. I was often asked by my peers to accompany them on various visits to their customers. I usually had very little time to prepare for these visits, and I believe that was what really gave me credibility with my co-professionals. I do not want to give you the impression I did not spend time preparing. I was constantly refreshing my knowledge of the products and concepts I was responsible for knowing. What was so very gratifying was I could dazzle most of the customer executives by simply asking more questions than I answered. My cohorts would often come away from these meetings with a list of things the customers were interested in knowing. I cannot explain the feeling of accomplishment I got when an executive made a multi-thousand dollar decision based on the information I provided them. I often had to reel in my ego when I felt myself becoming over-confident.

There are many times when the ego can push you past the tidal mark of accomplishment and into more work than you are capable of handling. The ego can often make you say yes when you really should say no. The only reason you say yes is because you do not want to give up the position of being in the limelight. Saying yes when you should say no is one way you can allow your ego to take advantage of you. When you find yourself overworked, go back and see if your ego was the culprit. I often tried to accomplish more than was expected of me because my ego got in my way. How many times have you tried to take on more than you knew you could handle for the sake of recognition? I will answer the question. Too many times!

The ego can allow you to feel very confident about yourself. This can enhance the way you perform in your profession. It can allow you to take on missions that will help you grow. We African Americans must learn to broaden our skill base and our accomplishments. Anything that will stimulate us to grow is great. The "Black Chip" has an element of ego associated with it, and this is the part of the Chip we should take advantage of and continue to embellish. If the ego can allow us to push toward that measure of success we seek, allowing us to demonstrate excellence, it is indeed a good thing. If the ego steers us into idiotic blunders that we cannot recover from, it is detrimental. If we allow the Chip to evolve into a fully-functioning, positive ego-type motivation, we will truly have an awesome secret weapon in our professional arsenal.

I like the ego when it becomes the motivation for risk-taking, as long as it is not accompanied by stupidity. If we find the ego urging us on to prosperity-laden risk-taking, we will definitely find ourselves further ahead in this game of "go for it." Too often we are not motivated to put more on the line than we care to lose, and the ego can help us to maneuver into position to be successful at calculated risk-taking. Yes, it does mean losing a little for the possibility of gaining more than we have.

As we allow this ego to become an operational mechanism governing reality, we must not lose our human side. Let people know you care about helping them get what they need or want as you attempt to get what you want. You want people to feel good about working with you or beside you. You also want them to feel helping you is not a one way opportunity. Do not allow your ego to fence you away from helping others, especially your Black co-professionals. If you learn to manage this ego and keep it under control, many may be benefitted by you. The ego will be stroked royally if you help others.

# Self Esteem

As was stated earlier, the ego is a mental mechanism

which can protect our self-esteem. The most important point to be made in this chapter is "you must believe in yourself." This may be a startling realization to a lot of people who read these pages. You may think I am trying to insult your intelligence, but there are many of us who have become weakened in our struggle to have self-worth. Nevertheless, it is something Black professionals must continue to build: believing in yourself equals confidence, and confidence leads to self-worth. Confidence comes from deep within, and we must learn to cultivate it and allow it to work on our behalf. One of the elements of success is self-confidence, and it will function as our shield as we attempt to grow our self-esteem. This will give us self-worth.

I am a firm believer that whatever a person thinks about her or himself is what s/he will eventually become. If we can think about ourselves as a vital part of the American business world, we become capable of learning what it takes to participate wholly in its transactions. We then can prepare ourselves to start looking back, making sure we are paving a way for others to follow. To pull those who are behind us onto the highway of success allows the ego to fully transform itself into the self-actualizer it always seeks to become in us. Self-esteem will become the recipient of nourishing strength, which will eventually lead to a quest for total accomplishment. This can only strengthen us as a people who are capable of helping themselves. What does all this mean?

We then have a desire to attain higher positions in American business, and we are now capable of empowering ourselves and one another. Learning to support one another and perpetually building up one another can only lead to greater self-esteem which in turn leads to self-actualization. Simply put, this is feeling very good about what we are capable of accomplishing. But, if we stop when we just start to feel good about it, we have not won. And, too often this is where we stop.

If we can come to a point of being a professional who is actualized with high self-esteem, we should be unstoppable in reaching our goals and objectives. This is when we will stop being angry about the lack of opportunity. We will then seek opportunities and capitalize on them and thereby provide more opportunities for ourselves. I know some of this may sound easier to say than to do, but this is where our egos can really help us. It is all about turning things that have been viewed so negatively in the past into things that are viewed very positively today. These things will start to work for us instead of against us and start to move us closer to some sort of parity and autonomy.

You are going to find that there are many things you will want to control in the business world; and, if you are not prepared mentally, they will often grow to control you. Your ability to thwart this frustration will add quality to the time you spend going after the things you want to accomplish. If we can learn to control the ego and allow it to be the foundation for our self-esteem, we then fortify our ability to maintain our drive and motivation. That means nothing will be able to stop us.

The business world requires a resilient attitude, one that is not easily moved to the negative. It appears to me that, when a corporation is having morale problems, the African American professionals seem to experience it in some greater degree than our White counterparts. I believe this is due to a lack of a strong self-esteem to rely on when the chips are down. Again, this is where we need to build to a state of mind that will allow us to endure these various aspects of the work environment.

One final subject to discuss under this topic: Instill self-esteem into our young Black children. We must understand and learn how to imbue our children with confidence and self-worth. The opportunities for success are now on the horizon, but are our children going to be able to take advantage of these opportunities? We must become a people willing to lay life and limb on the line to see our children get the opportunities they deserve. I am not talking about violent protest or any of the turbulent, yet progressive, stuff we went through in the Sixties. These are the Nineties, and if we have not yet learned to use cognitive power to get what we want, we are still behind the times. Our children must be viewed as our most valuable asset. We must work two and three jobs if that is what it takes to put our children through quality schools. We must learn to provide appropriate experiences and environments in order to nurture our children to success. You may feel I am preaching to the choir, but if you the educated Black cannot understand this, than it is a hopeless cause I have taken on. All other cultures have a preservation of the species program strongly in place, and we had better follow suit. This book is mainly focused on making it in the large corporations of America, but there must come a time when we can strike out on our own and be successful. Then, and only then, will we own a piece of America.

I would like to conclude this section by going back to the same tenor with which we started this section—the ego is a very valuable part of our psyche. It works hard on our behalf and allows us to move towards the center of our stability, especially when it comes to self-confidence which can lead to a strong self-esteem. Ego must not be misused. If it is cultivated to be properly used, it will serve us well.

# Chapter

# 6

# We Need To Communicate
# – A Valuable Skill

*B*eing able to communicate is both necessary and essential to your success in the business world. No matter what profession you are in, you will always need to communicate effectively. I reduce most communications to buying and selling. Whether it is convincing (selling) management you are the best person for the job or explaining the benefits of an engineering change, it boils down to buying and selling. You may have to sell your boss on why your project will save the company money. You may have to be convinced (buy in) that your colleague's proposal is the best way to go. If you are the seller, you must convince your buyer you have the best product in town. Selling starts with being able to describe, in great detail and with great clarity, the product you are selling. If you are the buyer, you must be able to describe what you want in a product or at least be able to ask if the qualities exist in the products that are made available to you.

Black professionals often neglect building this skill because we communicate very well within the Black culture. But what works very well within the Black culture works against us in the business world. We really must focus on building these essential communication skills which are such a vital part of professionalism. The business world will utilize all the skills you have, but it will only reward what is excellent and proficient. If you truly want to be respected by your peers and colleagues, be a good communicator. We need to communicate.

# Listening Skills

One of the most valuable skills which I am continuously learning to use is the skill of "listening." Some might say this is not a skill. It is an art, and I have observed it used to that level of perfection. Listening is a skill I have taken for granted most of my life probably because I have not used it. It is a skill that can be used to overcome a multitude of challenges. I have missed many opportunities acting upon what I thought I heard. Listening is often a challenge for most people. I myself have to work very hard at listening. I like being a source of information, and this is often a downfall when I should be listening. One thing I have learned in recent years is you can be a better provider of information if you are a good receiver of information. And that only comes by listening.

If you enjoy talking as much as I do, you may have trouble listening. I can tell you talking is the biggest obstacle to listening, and talking does not have to always be in the form of physical conversation. I define talking as the ability to source and send out information. Using my definition, there are many examples of talking that we do not often consider. We can talk verbally, which is the most familiar method. We can talk through writing. We can talk through others which has so often been dramatized by politicians. Politicians work very hard at communicating verbally, and they fail miserably when listening. Talking is necessary in the business arena as long as it does not get in the way of listening.

Your first methods of listening were probably taught to you by your parents, but for all the wrong reasons. We Blacks may be guilty of making listening a negatively viewed skill because of the methods we employ when teaching our children how to listen. My father used to say, "Shut up, boy, and listen." We often use loud speaking and yelling as a method of discipline, and our kids learn early in life to tune us out. If you tell someone to shut up every time they attempt to speak, they will stop talking; but they will also stop listening. This method of disciplining can definitely work against us when it comes to teaching our kids how to develop the skill of listening. Most of the things we learn in our developmental stages carry over into our adult life. Kids learn to keep quiet. They consider themselves listening when they are not speaking. This leads to a very warped sense of listening when they reach adulthood.

I have learned that the skill of listening is much more encompassing than what I thought it was before I joined the business community. It is much more than being quiet while someone else is speaking. It is an essential skill for conducting good business. I have learned that hearing what someone has to say does not always equal listening. And, just as verbal talking should not be the main focus for communicating, physical hearing is not the main form of listening, especially in the business world. Hearing is our ability to receive the information that is being communicated to us. Listening is our ability not only to receive the information, but to understand and internalize the information as we hear it. To be able to quickly disseminate information we receive is of the utmost importance; we must decide what is fluff and what is substance. When you have these capabilities, you are probably listening effectively.

Understanding the pertinence and relevance of information is of the greatest importance. Case in point: We spent a whole year selling a new product to a customer. We were so caught up in trying to convince the customer our product was the one they should buy, we forgot to listen to the customer as they presented us with their business objectives and requirements. We convinced the customer to install our product. We also convinced the customer to be a beta test site. This allowed the customer to receive the product before general availability to all our other customers. They would basically have the opportunity to kick the tires on the product. We installed the product at the customer site with great difficulty. The marketing manager on the account kept prompting me to bring in the big guns and fix the problems. We did just that but to no avail. The customer persistently told us this product was not going to meet their business objectives. We insisted it would and kept convincing them to stick with the product. The customer missed every deadline and spent a large sum of money trying to make the product work. Finally they threw the product out, sued our company and won. This was a clear case of our not listening. We lost the customer and a lot of money in concessions.

Since I have become a part of the business world, I have found listening is the essential part of being a good communicator. I guarantee if you do not listen, you will never be a good communicator and you will be unsuccessful.

# Verbal Communication

In the business world, you can speak what you want into existence if you know how to put into words what it is you want!

Proper use of the English language is a must and cannot be substituted. The business world prefers proper speech and can be very unforgiving of poorly spoken English. As I mentioned earlier, I am from the South; and we Black Southerners put the "c" in colloquialism. If you are in the Northwestern part of the United States, the business world finds the southern accent irritating, especially when it is mixed with certain Black dialects. We must understand the requirements for communicating in different business environments and situations. We must do whatever we have to in order to acquire good verbal communication. This is another area we need to assess in order to see if we are measuring up to the standards required.

When I first arrived on the corporate scene, I thought I could speak quite well. I did not know I was not eloquent. I had the opportunity to make a practice sales call on an executive. After the completion of the call, he critiqued me. The first thing he said was, "You must give a firm handshake. Shake my hand like you mean it." He then presented me with something I was not quite prepared to accept. He said, "You should learn to pronounce 'ASK'." You say 'AXE'! I was startled and hurt. I felt demeaned and all the other feelings you can have in a situation such as this one. I went away feeling quite inadequate; I lost confidence in my ability to speak, which I thought was one of my strengths. I think what amplified the hurt I was feeling was when I tried to pronounce "ASK" and I could not. I immediately started to practice the proper pronunciation of this word. I can now pronounce "ASK" with confidence, although there are times when I sound as if I am over stressing the "k".

Once, I was over the initial shock of having someone criticize the way I spoke, I then progressed to becoming a very good speaker and presenter. I am not the greatest orator that ever lived, but I can be heard in the business world. I am forever grateful to that executive who took time to improve my speech, and I am still working on improving my grammar and the pronunciation of certain words in my vocabulary.

From that incident, I learned I cannot waste precious time becoming angry when I am criticized for a deficiency I have, whether it is perceived or real. Criticism can be used as a motivational tool for improving yourself. I must caution you, do not try to change every time someone is critical of you. Do not try to change everything about you all at once because someone pointed out a problem area. Work on the problem area and then make an assessment of how well you have corrected the problem.

It is not always easy to make the changes necessary to improve our speaking ability, but it can be done. I have been away from the South for a very long time. It is becoming harder and harder for people to tell if I am from the South. I have made it a game, and I often enjoy when people are trying to figure out where I originated. They have no problem knowing that I am Black, although I have been told, I have a business dialect and a home dialect. I am proud of both. I still use words like "man" quite often. What is most fun to observe is when our White counterparts start to use some of our sacred colloquial terms.

Having a good speaking vocabulary is very valuable. You are perceived to be very bright if you have a decent vocabulary. People often think you are smarter than you actually are if you use proper English. This does not mean you have to learn a thousand words nobody understands except you and your last English professor. A good vocabulary consists of words that have more than one syllable and which are easily recognized when spoken. They should be words you can conjugate and edit without having a secretary help you.

Knowing when to speak and, most importantly, when not to speak is a part of verbal skill. Two wrong words can kill a promotion. Three right words can get you the assignment. We African Americans often get in trouble because we allow ourselves to be put on the defensive. Learning to hold back your comments will afford you a lot more information in the end. Speaking allows you to put out the information others may want and need. But remember, what you say may be something you have to live with for a long time.

Case in point: I was promoted into management. Soon after I arrived in my new management assignment, I addressed all eight of the people who were reporting to me. I was very excited about being a manager, and I wanted my enthusiasm to show. I stood up in front of my new unit and begin sharing some of the things I wanted to accomplish with them. Then I said something that would haunt me for the next two years of my career. I said to the unit, in true openness, "I am a fast tracker." (A fast tracker is a person who spends enough time in an assignment to learn the job and then get promoted. They usually are highly motivated, very enthusiastic people.) This was said among many other positive statements but was heard as a negative statement. Little did I realize how much was decided about me by the people who heard me make that statement. Eighteen months later, I was conducting a opinion survey, feedback session, with the unit, and we were discussing the section of the survey that had to do with trust and confidence. One of my best employees said, "When you first arrived here, you told us you were a fast tracker, and that meant to me I couldn't put a lot of trust and confidence in you." He also stated, "I thought your statement two years ago was very arrogant." I was staggered by his comments. I asked if that judgment bore out in the way I approached the job. He answered, "No, but you established a perception you've had to live with for the last two years."

We must learn the art of verbal communication. I do believe we must take the skill to its art form. Learning when to say something or when not to say something could be the difference between whether you win a situation or lose it. I have spent many mornings wishing I had the opportunity to take back words I had said the day before. People are very unforgiving once a statement is made that they do not like. You will suffer long and hard in the business world if you make a practice of saying the wrong thing. Even genuine openness, or as we often say it, "I am going to give them a piece of my mind," may come back to haunt you. I do not want to make it seem as if everything you say will be held against you, but I do want you to know that, if you make a statement, expect to be held accountable for it.

The tone of your voice is also very important,

especially for us Black men. Because we speak with such heavy voices, we are often misread by our White colleagues. There are many times when I was thought to be angry when I was simply trying to make a point. It is my experience that White women are very sensitive to the heavy Black male voice. I once had a White woman working for me. I was told she thought I treated women very different from the way I treated the men who worked for me. She said I often raised my voice at her and she thought I was angry with her. She was correct in that I raised my voice from time to time, but it was not because I was angry.

Many of us Blacks have a tendency to increase the volume of our voices when we are excited and when we are trying to make a point. And some of us are just plain loud. I was. You do not have to agree with all of this, but please be aware that these conditions exist for us in the business world.

Good verbal communication is a must in the business environment. The quality and the skill with which it is used can be of great value to you. An African American professional who has mastered this very valuable and necessary skill can be a real winner. You must be comfortable at using this skill. This is also one of those skills that will improve as you continue to use it.

Speak with authority and understanding and be heard by all who will listen!

# Written Communication

The skill of writing is very important to your success in the business world. It is assumed that you can write if you are a professional.

Writing is one of the most difficult skills to acquire. It is very complicated and can be a very complex form of communication. You will be presented with many opportunities to communicate through the written word, such as interoffice memos, documentation, letters to clients, presentation materials, etc.

The latest and greatest form of written communication is electronic notes and messages. I spent at least an hour a day reading and writing electronic mail when I was a part of a corporation. With the advent of the computer, you can be sitting in Boring, Oregon and send a note to

Madrid, Spain in a matter of minutes. You must be able to write effectively.

I have learned you do not have to be a fancy writer. The business world is perfectly comfortable with simple sentence structure. A subject - verb - object is a good way to write. You can build from there. You should have a dictionary, thesaurus, and a handbook or guide to English at your fingertips. (Keep them with this handbook.) These books will be invaluable to you in your work space. You will find numerous opportunities to use them until they are thoroughly worn. You can often buy them in sets that will include other useful reference books.

If you find you are afraid to write, you are not alone. I have found some of the most intelligent professionals often struggle when they are forced to write. If you write only when you are forced to, you will struggle and probably be a very poor writer. Writing is a procrastinator's nightmare. If you are expected to respond in writing, do it as soon as possible. The fear of writing will often cease once you start to write.

It is an absolute must that you have a computer with a very good word processor at home. Having the capability to prepare documents at home is essential. It will afford you the opportunity to write when not under pressure. I often help friends with document preparation. I use the computer for newsletters, home accounting and other projects. The computer will prove to be invaluable once you get past the initial outlay of money. There are numerous tools on the market to aid and assist you in your written communication.

There is a new computer software writing tool on the market that will help the poorest writer. It is called a "grammar and style checker." Basically it is like having a proof-reader on your desk. They are fairly inexpensive and prove to be invaluable. You produce your document on your favorite word processing software, and then you run the document through the grammar and style checker. (Be sure to check compatibility of your word processor and related software.) This tool will help you with grammatical considerations such as verb tense, parallel construction, punctuation, as well as reading levels.

Understand what writing is capable of doing for you. The most important thing writing will allow you to do is to leave an audit trail. I cannot tell you how many times you will be asked how you handled a certain problem or issue. It is a tremendous feeling when you can say, "Wait a minute, let me check my files." If you are in a job assignment that has high visibility, this kind of documenting will be essential. I was once working a problem that involved my having to work with my local company organization, a support group in New York, another one in Los Angeles, and one in Paris. We had a Paris organization which acted as a liaison for us and a Paris-based business which transacted a lot of business with us. We had problems with their products. It was necessary to be in weekly contact with all the support groups and the Paris company we were doing business with. A lot of information traveled to and through each of the organizations before arriving in my office. Once the information arrived in my office, we scrubbed and summarized the data before sending the information in a formal letter to our customer. It was a documentation nightmare. We kept this flow of written information going for three months before the problem was resolved. My "hot issues file" grew to huge proportions. Here was a clear case of having to communicate through writing, and there was no better way.

There will be many times when your written communication will save you a lot of trouble and frustration. It will often be used to "cover your backside" when nothing else can. You will find times when you use written communication to "pat someone on the back." This is a very good way to build your network. You will be surprised at how much your colleagues will appreciate a note of thanks, especially if you copy their manager on it.

The computer has made writing easier, but it will never substitute for the skill of writing well. There may come a time when you will write by simply speaking into a microphone or some other device, and the computer will transform your verbal communique into written communication. But there will always be some form of documentation in the business environment.

Practice writing as often as you can, and you will become very proficient at it. If you do not have this skill now, then you should immediately enroll in your local community college and take a course in writing. I guarantee this will not be a waste of your time. I have often heard people say, "I don't need to know how to write. I'll just have a secretary do it." You will never have a secretary if you do not know how to prepare business documents. Secretaries today are conduits to word processing, and they usually will not change grammar. Besides, you want to be sure you are the effective communicator, not a secretary.

# Body Language

Your smile is an important form of communication in the business world and should not be overlooked in the role it plays when communicating. As Blacks, we tend to be more up front with our opinions and expressions. We speak loudly and with conviction and are often mistaken for being angry when we are excited and unsmiling. We have a tendency to frown when we are deep in thought, and this can be misread as dissatisfaction. We know the smile as a sign of deception and weakness. This may be one reason why we do not take advantage of it as often as we should. We must learn to use the smile to soften our presentation. A little smile tells people you are not angry.

The smile can be used as a gesture of agreement or it can be used to say just the opposite: "I don't believe what you are saying." The smile can be used as a reward in some cases. I often feel grateful if someone gives me a smile of approval for work that I am doing or have completed. On the other hand, a smile from higher authority could mean "Back off!" or "Don't bring up that subject at this time!"

Be consistent in your use of the smile, and try not to confuse people in the messages you send. Remember the opposite of a smile is a frown. Please use it carefully. People who frown too often will be shunned.

We African Americans also communicate by the way we walk. Do not be surprised if your business colleagues do not understand and may even be offended by your walk. Make sure your walk is very professional and is sending the signal you want it to send. The "dip and swing" does not work very well in the business world. I have seen Black professionals snubbed by their counterparts because they walked with arrogance in their stride. I try to have a walk that says I am not arrogant but I am proud of myself.

Using your hands when you talk is a sign of animation

and is usually regarded as positive and friendly. I use my hands when I am trying to make a point or accent something I am trying to get across. I have often put my hands in my pockets when I am deep in thought or I am waiting for a response from someone.

Be careful not to use extensive touching of individuals to communicate. Touching can often be misread and can really be used against you in some instances. I tend to put my hand on someone's shoulder when I am being friendly. I am very careful, however, how I use touching with the opposite sex. (My Black sisters, you are not exempt from this warning.) The business world is full of pitfalls, and this can be a big one. I will deal with this topic more specifically in a later chapter.

The business world is very uncomfortable with people who swing their arms wildly when they try to make a point. John Madden, who was once the coach for the Raider's football team, is very animated in this way. He is now making a lot of money with his wild arm flurries. In the football world, he was known as a highly emotional person. However, Blacks are often thought of as being too emotional, and we do not need to add to that type of thinking.

Tapping on a table can be very distracting. Be careful how you use this one. If you are trying to send a signal using this method, make sure the receiver is in tune with you. This is not a discreet method of communication. It can be effective if used at the right time and in the right place.

I only use pounding of my fist to get the attention of someone that I am not pleased with or when I really want to make a point. This can be a very effective method of showing strength. This is an extreme use of body language, but no one is likely to misread what you are trying to say. I have been known to use this in a theatrical manner during a business meeting. I appear displeased, but I really am not. Use this method as rarely as possible or you could find yourself categorized in a manner you may not like — authoritative, directive, stubborn or hard to deal with.

Folding your arms can send different messages. It usually is read as, "I'm not sure if I agree with what you are saying" or "I don't follow that line of thinking." It can also be read as a sign of boredom especially if you also lean back in a chair.

Your eyes can send all kinds of signals. Shifting your eyes, or what we Blacks would call "rolling your eyes," can be signals of displeasure or disagreement. Lifting your eyebrows can say you are pleasantly surprised. Women can use their eyes easier than men because they tend to have better eye contact.

Nodding your head is very handy if you want to attract the attention of the person speaking in a meeting. The speaker will tend to direct the presentation towards the person who appears to be paying attention. If you nod your head in agreement, you will often attract the attention of the person who has the floor.

Body language is an important form of communication, but it can very easily be misread. Black professionals are easily misread by their business counterparts, and we should take a little extra care when using body language to communicate.

All of the forms of communication should become a part of your skill base and used when necessary. Communication should be clear and concise. If you are to be successful in the business world, you will communicate often and you must do it well. There is no other option. "Say what you mean and mean what you say." You must be an effective communicator or you will always be relegated to receiving instructions rather than giving them.

# Chapter

# 7

# Interviewing Tactics

Y our first encounter with the business world as a professional is usually in the interview process. It is the first time a corporation has the opportunity to see what you are all about. It is also the first time you have an opportunity to see what a particular corporation is all about.

When you interview for a job in a corporation, you must think of the interview as the first step towards a partnership between you and the corporation. You must want to become a part of the corporation. Too often we prepare to be interviewed by the corporation, and we forget to prepare to interview the corporation. You must feel good about the services and products they sell or provide. You must agree with the way they conduct their business. If they asked you to join them, all the more reason why you must understand what you are being asked to become a part of. Many people get so caught up in the process of preparing themselves to impress their prospective employer, they forget they also need to be impressed by the corporation.

When you are brought into a corporation, they are really going to make every effort to get to know as much about you as possible in the time allotted. Do not forget your objective is to be hired, but it is also to make a selection of where you want to spend a major portion of your daily life.

## The Corporate Interviewer

In order to get and keep good talent, corporations have professional recruiters in-house or they contract with professional talent search firms. More than likely the first member of a corporation you will meet will be an employment recruiter, especially if you interview on a college campus.

Recruiters are often from the human resources or personnel side of the corporation. They are usually trained to look for the hot-shot student or candidate. They usually spend a lot of time in the placement offices of college campuses. They often participate in career fairs and hospitality suites for different college organizations such as fraternities, campus associations, and other student organizations.

If the recruiter is experienced, s/he may have connections with some of the officers of student organizations and school placement workers. If they are truly experienced, they will tap into the college infrastructure such as professors and other faculty members. When I was being recruited, two very large corporations were interested in me. One of the recruiters was acquainted with one of the professors in the department of my major study. This particular professor took time to send me out of class to meet the recruiter. I had my first interview for this particular company while wearing blue jeans and a T-shirt. I was later offered a summer job but turned it down in order to take a course that was being offered that particular summer.

College recruiters are usually looking for candidates they can initially interview on campus and later invite to their company. They will usually research prospective candidates through available school records. They will often ask the placement center staff for information on students. This is a good reason why college students should register with the placement center. There is usually part of the placement center staff dedicated to minority placement. In the university I attended, this staff was invaluable.

While in the winter quarter of my junior year, the second corporation approached me for an interview. They were in dire need of engineers and held their own hospitality suite in a local hotel. I was invited by the college recruiter to attend their interviewing session. I was interviewed in a hotel room by two people, the college recruiter and an engineer from the company. I was then invited to fly to their site for further interviews. I was offered a job that summer. I started my senior year with a job offer and was the first to be put on the salary board in the student lounge of my department. It was a very exciting time of my life.

If you are already in the job market, keep in touch with a good talent and/or executive search firm. Another name for these individuals is "headhunters." Many smaller companies will use these firms to supplement their own efforts to recruit good talent for their organization. But beware. There are often fees associated with these firms, and they may or may not be paid for by the company needing the resource. The fees are usually some percentage of the starting annual salary of the placed individual. Search firms have been known to negotiate their fees. If you enter into an agreement with one of these firms, be sure you take time to understand their terms and conditions up front.

Getting past the initial interviews of a college recruiter or a search firm is not very hard. They are usually trying to meet and interview a certain number of candidates to attain a quota of some sort. On the other hand, getting invited for an on-site interview is most important and can be a very rigorous and intriguing experience.

Profile of the corporate interviewer — The corporate interviewer is usually one of the management staff. Many corporations now have peer interviews. The peer interview is conducted by one of the potential peers of the prospective employee.

The corporate interviewer usually has the power to hire you or at least recommend you for hire. They are usually very happy to interview a candidate. There is very little training provided to them on how to interview a candidate. Most corporate interviewers are professionals and usually have some tenure of years with the corporation. They usually have worked their way up through a corporation and often think of themselves as an integral part of the corporation. They are usually proud of their accomplishments, and their ego may come out during various parts of the interview. If you have the opportunity and the know how, stroke your interviewer's ego. The corporate interviewer is often in need of the resource they are looking for and are usually excited and anxious to find a candidate that they can hire and put to work.

The corporate interviewer will spend a lot of time assessing your sense of style, personality and all those other attributes and characteristics that make up a person. They do pay attention to the way you are dressed and will down- grade you for such things as not having your shoes shined, even though their shoes may need shining. If they care a lot about their own attire, they are often more critical of others. I give very high marks in my interviews if a candidate is well dressed. I become a very tough interviewer for a candidate who has not taken the time to dress for the interview. I have interviewed Black candidates who looked great, but they were not in the proper attire. Most interviewers appreciate the candidate who takes the time to prepare themselves for the interview and being appropriately dressed is the first step.

Interviewers can be very clever in their line of questioning. If they are experienced, they will definitely structure the interview with certain questions to help them decide what type of a person you are. I was once a corporate interviewer, and I always asked the question, "What would your mother say your strengths are, and what would your father say your weakness are?" These questions always caught the interviewees by surprise. If they took their time to think about their answers before presenting them to me, I viewed that as positive on the mental score card I kept. I almost always received very interesting answers. Most interviewers like to explore the individual's hobbies, likes and dislikes and other things that help to assess an individual's character. These questions are usually aimed at seeing how sincere or sensitive an individual can be.

The interviewer will spend a lot of time trying to test the candidate's "quickness on his feet." The interviewer is not looking for how fast you can answer a question before you get on to the next one but rather how well you listen to the question and how successful you are at communicating your response. Content is important but not as important as quality and conciseness.

All interviewers have some kind of scoring system for assessing whether a candidate is a person they would want to bring into their organization. Keep this in mind as you prepare to sell yourself to this representative of the corporation.

# The Resume –
# A Description of the Property

A well-prepared resume is the most important thing you will ever prepare or have prepared to represent you. Keep this point in mind as we go through this discussion.

It amazes me how many people do not have a resume. If you are a student reading this book, you probably already have experienced a lot things that can be used to make up a good resume. I want to expel the myth that it will take a long time to prepare a good resume. The only thing that takes a long time to prepare on a resume is the experience you need.

Do not re-invent the wheel! Find professionals in the field or industry you are looking to enter, get a copy of their resumes, and use them as a blueprint to create your own. If you cannot find someone you know, go to your local placement center on campus. They usually have hundreds on file. College placement centers often run resume clinics and workshops and are more than happy to assist you in preparing your resume.

There are all kinds of formats to use for preparing your resume. Take time and choose one that will represent you in the style or image you want to project. (We will discuss image and style in a later chapter.) The format you choose should be one that will accommodate the amount of information you want to display. Remember, your resume is your first presentation of yourself to a corporation.

Selecting resume paper can be fun. You should select a medium bond paper with a nice smooth texture. If the texture is too coarse, it will not display the text very well. I like resumes with very soft colors. White displays black text very well. There are many other light colored papers that will allow you to express yourself, but save them for when you are an expert and the color of your resume will not matter. Try to have something about your resume that will be eye catching, but not something someone would find distasteful. After we choose the paper we are ready to prepare the resume.

Remember that computer we talked about earlier? Well, here is a good opportunity to use it. A computer and a word processor will allow you to prepare and experiment with formats for your resume. Only use a conventional typewriter if it is your last resort. The computer will also allow you to keep a copy on a storage device for future updates. (Have I sold you on acquiring a computer yet?) If you have a letter quality printer, you can prepare and print your resume at home. If you find preparing a resume a major task, there are services that will sit down with you and take you through the whole process for a nominal fee.

# You Are The Product

You are the product to sell — in an interview, have no doubt you must be fully capable of selling yourself. Everything is fair game: communications skills, presentation, sense of style, wit, charm, sense of humor, intelligence.

Be prepared mentally — Most people go into the interview process with many preconceived notions which set up a high anxiety situation. Your frame of mind will definitely affect the flow and outcome of an interview. I believe it takes more time to prepare yourself mentally than it does to prepare your physical appearance. The interviewer will test how well you think as well as your ability to perform the job. Your ability to hear and answer questions clearly is affected by your mental preparedness. Take time to rehearse in your mind what motivates you and what excites you. Be able to bring about a positive consciousness that permeates everything you do during the interview. If you are a person who is happy-go-lucky, who has a hard time taking things seriously, you may have just as much trouble becoming mentally prepared as a person who is very nervous about interviewing. Projecting the right aura is very important in an interview, and I believe it stems from your state of mind.

I once interviewed a college senior who interviewed in a hard-charging style. He came right at me. Before I could ask him a question, he was asking me questions and selling me on his approach to life. I was overwhelmed by him, and he did not get selected as someone I wanted to follow up. He struck me as arrogant, yet I do not believe he wanted to project that image at all. I believe he wanted me to come away from the interview thinking he was very aggressive. But I came away thinking the kid was pushy and hard to talk to.

Take the time to sit and think about an interview with the idea of being fully in control of yourself, and you will enjoy the interview. When I am the interviewee, I convince myself that the person on the other side of the desk is a person just like me. I work hard to bring them to a level that will allow me to communicate with them. When I am sitting in the reception area waiting for the interviewer, I bring my emotions into a certain harmony. I try not to anticipate what questions they might ask me. After all, the questions are about me. Who knows more about me than I? I tell myself that they will not try to trick me or mislead me. They really want to get to know me.

During the interview I take mental checks to see if I am still in control, and I take control of the interview when I feel it is appropriate. I want to interview the company as much as they want to interview me. I sit back in the chair to listen. I usually rock forward when it is my time to speak. If I want to show increased interest in what the interviewer is saying, I move to a position on the front of the chair. If the conversation moves to a lower level of excitement, I will settle back into my chair. These tactics work for me. But remember, the key to having a good interview is to find a level of comfort that will allow you a position of maximum two-way communication.

Dressing for success in an interview — We African American are very guilty of over-dressing. Face it, we like to look good. In an interview you must pay particular attention to how you look and what makes up your attire. The key is not to overwhelm the interviewer but to impress them.

If you walk into the corporate interview with anything other than a white shirt or blouse, you have just given up easy points for the interview. It is amazing how much the white shirt or blouse is accepted as a vital part of the appropriate attire. Even corporations that do not have a dress code, you will find receptive to the white shirt or blouse as part of the interview attire.

The dark suit takes on the same prestige as the white shirt. There are a lot of fancy dark suits in fashion today. Make sure you find one that is rather conservative. A new college graduate should first invest in a good suit to wear to interviews. This suit will be one of the best investments you will ever make. I still have my first blue suit I designated for interviewing. Blue is the color of choice. Black or charcoal gray will work, but dark blue is a safe investment.

The tie should be a color that has a red derivative. It does not have to be red, but keep in mind who is in the White House. I am not very fond of red ties, but I have three or four in my business wardrobe. I have been known to wear Republican Red on occasions. Keep the tie to a solid background with simple designs: stripes, dots and paisleys will generally be well received. Do not, I repeat, do not wear flowers. The women have a bit more freedom here, but make sure you have a closed neck type of a blouse and some kind of a tie. A string of white pearls will set a dark suit off nicely complemented by a tie of some sort.

Handkerchiefs in the suit coat pockets are a nice touch. I prefer white with unique folds. Matching ties and handkerchiefs work, but I find them too predictable and even a little corny. This is a matter of style, and I will discuss this in a later chapter.

As for shoes, I must confess, I just bought my first pair of wingtips during the writing of this book, and they are not of the conventional style. Wingtips are the accepted business shoe, and they come in three basic colors: maroon, black and brown. I think they are the worst-looking shoes on earth, especially if they have thick soles. My black culture prevails! Nevertheless, we shall endure and dress for interviewing success. You can wear loafers with tassels, and a lot of the older business executives are wearing them. I believe it is the Yale, Stanford and Harvard influence. Women should wear the basic blue or black pumps with mid-size heels. And please make sure those shoes are shined. I see a lot of my Black professional sisters with immaculate suits and dresses and badly worn heels on their fairly new pumps (those sewer covers will get you every time).

Flashy shoes send a bad signal to the corporate executive. They will immediately look at you as a "typical Black." Now is not the time to be typical if we are to choose our battles and win.

I would like to warn my Black professional sisters, you must take extra care to look your best and try not to be to ethnic. Dread locks will be the death of you; and even if you get through the interview, you will always be treated as one who swims against the tide. If you tie any kind of a rag around your head, I will personally come and shoot you.

Once you have done all you can to sell yourself to a corporation, then you should step back and let that well-prepared resume take over.

# Prepare For The Pitfalls

Many corporations use highly researched Aptitude Tests when considering a candidate for employment. These tests are very informative and do a fair job of predicting the success or failure of a prospective employee's performance.

These tests are almost always discriminatory. Most corporations run these tests through their legal departments to get clearance before they decide to use them. I found only one out of six Black candidates passed one test I administered. You cannot study for these exams because they are designed for psychological testing and reasoning, two areas where Blacks with limited access to the White culture do not test well. This does not say anything about our intelligence, yet it does say something about our cultural and developmental experiences. We Blacks do not tend to know a large number of analytical lawyers, doctors, accountants, and other professionals who help build these experiences. We usually do not have the opportunity to attend the best elementary and high schools which provide some of the preparation for this type of testing. Most of these experiences will occur on the job. We can pass these tests if we have done a good job preparing ourselves.

These tests are usually designed to weed out potentially low performers, and they are often successful. We must understand their purpose.

Some corporations will accept minority candidates who score in the average range of these tests, and the good news is that we are doing better and better at passing. I will not spend time giving you a lot of statistics to support this claim because that is not the intention of this book. But I have seen the progress. The fact of the matter is you should not let this be a deterrent to what you are trying to accomplish. I am confident that, if you are armed with the knowledge of what you will face during the interview process and prepare yourself appropriately, you will get hired. That is the intention of this book.

One last thing about these corporate tests: PLEASE READ AND FOLLOW THE INSTRUCTIONS CAREFULLY! Use the time given you to take the test wisely. These tests are not designed for completion, but for how well you answer the questions you complete.

A final pitfall note: There are going to be those interviewers who are a bit tricky, and you will spot them quickly. Keep your cool, chalk them up to experience and move on to your next project.

Preparation is the key!

# Taking The Advantage

The infamous GPA — One of the most important things corporate interviewers look at when selecting employees is the "GPA", better known in the corporate world as the Grade Performance Average - pun intended. The GPA is an indicator, as you know, of how well you performed while in academia. It is not an indication of how well you will perform in the business world. The GPA is used often by interviewers to decide who to interview. An interviewer will pick the best candidate s/he can to fill a position and use every indicator that will lead to that candidate.

Hopefully you still have time to influence your GPA after reading this book. I counsel young college grads to go back to school another year and retake courses that are bottoming out their GPA. It is not the easiest thing for a young college graduate to accept. We Blacks often come to understand the value of the GPA a little late while struggling to get through school. It is often too late to try to improve your GPA before interviewing in the corporate world. But this is something you should understand so you can control your strengths and weakness in order to better present yourself for being hired. Although it is a major decision criteria, it is only one of many in the hiring process.

Build a good vocabulary — You can build a very good professional vocabulary in a relatively short time. There are many ways to do this. If you put a word building program together for yourself, you can build a good vocabulary in six months. It will take hard work and discipline. A good vocabulary will be noticed in an interview. Some corporations have a section on the interviewing form for comments on the way you speak and present yourself.

Having a good vocabulary must be accompanied by the ability to articulate and enunciate your words and thoughts in a clear manner. Throwing out multi-syllabic words which add no value to a thought will be discovered and will weigh against you. If you were born and raised in a low income, urban environment, you probably use a lot of slang in your language. This is a problem I had to overcome, and I am still trying to improve the way I speak. It is a worthy quest. Practicing words in front of a mirror or into a tape recorder will work wonders for your enunciation. I am fairly well spoken at this point in my career, but I still struggle with grammar.

The interview can be compared to a child being born. The only way a person will ever come into the world is through the painful process of childbirth. The only way a Black professional can become a part of the business world is through the process of a good interview.

Get dressed! Be ready to impress! And your talents and skills should do the rest!

# Accepting The Offer

Accepting the offer is the most important part of the interview process, even though it can come days and even weeks later. Hopefully, you have made your intentions known about what salary you are willing to accept. Salary is the reason we go to work, so do not make it the last thing you think about when accepting a job. It should definitely not be an after-the-fact consideration.

Salary does not always mean just a paycheck. It can mean bonuses, stock options and other forms of compensation. You must do your homework if you are going to get a fair and equitable deal. Corporations are not looking to take advantage of you, but lack of knowledge puts you at a disadvantage. They want a happy and productive employee, and you want all you can get.

Benefit plans should be included in any offer from a company. Take a little time to read all the brochures they give you during the interview process. If they do not offer them to you, then you should ask for the information. Remember, you may be making a life-long decision.

# Chapter

# 8

# The Corporate Structure

*A* most interesting thing to study is the structure of the American corporation. There have been hundreds of books written on the subject, and you will find no particular one to be comprehensive. In this chapter I will point out some of things that are important to know about the way corporations are structured, information that will allow you as a professional to become a fully functioning part of a corporation.

Corporations can be centralized, decentralized, divisionalized or any permutation thereof.

A typical corporation will have a corporate headquarters. This is where all the major decisions are made. The chief executive officer (CEO), the president (the president and CEO may be one in the same in many corporations), the chief financial officer (CFO), and other major decisionmakers reside in the corporate headquarters. This is where they "count the beans" and allocate funding for the rest of the corporation.

A note of interest: most Fortune 500 companies have corporate headquarters in and around the New York Area. A lot of America's major corporations were founded in the New England States. The reason they are still there today can probably be attributed to the fact New York still has many of the nation's largest banks. New York is still the home of the nation's major stock exchange. It is close to Washington, D.C.

Typical corporations usually have a manufacturing division, a research and development division, and a marketing division with some sort of sales force. Depending on what industry the corporation represents, it can have other divisional entities. Trying to understand all of this can be challenging.

If you as an employee can understand the structure of the corporation, you can more easily align yourself and become a fully functioning member. If a corporation has been successful at communicating its structure to its employees, the corporation will probably function more smoothly and be more productive. If the employees understand what a division is capable of doing or why departments are structured a certain way, they will make better use of resources.

Some corporations are broken up by geographical area or by the amount of revenue that can be generated from a particular component. Some corporations structure themselves into territories or districts. One major part of the corporate structure is the organizational structure.

# Organizational Structure

The organizational structure defines the way the corporation uses its people-resources as opposed to the way it participates in its industry. The organizational structure also tells how decisions are made and who is responsible for carrying them out. The management of a corporation may spend more time reorganizing than doing any other major task in the corporation. They strive to find the perfect organizational structure that will allow the corporation to maximize its people, especially if it is trying to gain control of its expenses. Organizational structure, accompanied by the culture of an organization, is what allows a corporation to police itself and effectively conduct its business.

When we discuss the organizational structure of a corporation, we are interested in what makes up its parts: what departments are necessary to support the corporation in its mission to reach its goals and objectives.

An organization may use the "cookie cutter" approach where each divisions looks just like every other division. Each division might have a personnel department, administrative department, payroll department, etc. which form the organizational structure for the entities of a corporation. A corporation may use a "centralized" approach where payroll, personnel, and other departments may be at headquarters. A corporation may use an "autonomous" approach where each division structures its organization as it wishes. In the rest of this section, I will look more closely at some of the entities that make up the organizational structure of a large corporation.

The personnel department or human resources department is one of the most important parts of a corporation. This department is where it all starts for an individual entering the corporation. This is usually the department that houses the recruiters we discussed earlier. This is also the department that has the mission of keeping track of employees throughout their corporate tenure.

The personnel department is where you go to understand what benefits the company has to offer. Many Black professionals do not take advantage of the various benefits a corporation offers. I have had numerous conversations trying to convince my Black compatriots to invest as much as they can of the allowed percentage of their salaries in the various financial programs a corporation may offer.

This is also the department usually responsible for administering the employee stock option programs. The personnel department usually has a benefits coordinator who is responsible for insurance programs and medical/dental benefits which can be very complicated and may require assistance when you try to gain the maximum benefits. There are numerous other functions the personnel department may be responsible for providing to you, the employee.

The personnel department usually is empowered to act as your agent and counselor to assist you and the corporation. They can be very helpful through some of the most difficult times in your life. Do not hesitate to consult with a responsible member of the personnel department's staff. A note of caution — they are representatives of the corporation and will have the interest of the corporation in mind when dealing with you as an individual. They can work against you when you and the corporation are at odds or on different sides of a court room. If you use them in a consultative role, they should serve you well.

The payroll department is another department that can be of great service to you. Hopefully, you will be served by them without any efforts on your part. If you have problems with wrong information on a check or you need to make changes to information they have on file, do not hesitate to seek them out. If you are relocated by your company, the payroll department may become your best friend. They are usually responsible with helping you deal with expenses incurred to relocate.

If you find yourself owing a corporation money for any reason, make sure the payroll department is fully informed of the circumstances. I have seen many employees abuse corporate credit cards and find themselves in a lot of debt with no way to pay it. The cash funds which are usually a part of the payroll department can be a big help if you find yourself in a situation like this. Remember you can lose your job if you abuse corporate resources. Misusing corporate funds may sound like a hard thing to do, but many people find themselves short of cash and try to supplement it with the corporation's assets. Good planning can help you avoid needing this kind of help from the payroll department.

The administrative department of a corporation can be one of the most helpful departments in a corporation. This usually is where word processing and secretarial support report. A secretary can bail you out of the toughest situations. I work very hard to befriend every secretary I ever meet. Find the key secretary in your department, and you may have found the true seat of power. He or she may be your boss's secretary or the local executive's secretary. If you can win their trust and confidence, they can be a valuable source of information. If you have a department secretary, s/he can be your saving grace. There are many situations where my secretary has made me look sensational. They help you with letter writing, managing your time and in many other ways where a busy professional may need assistance. I tend to be a heads-down worker, and I can become so involved in a project I will forget my next appointment or obligation. My secretary has bailed me out of many uncomfortable situations.

Beware of incompetent secretaries; they can be the death of you. Make it a practice to follow up on any projects or items you turn over to a secretary, especially if they do not appear to manage well. This is more of a problem in a large corporation then it is in a more tightly controlled organization. Secretaries in large corporations are usually overworked and can be put in situations where they appear incompetent when they really are not.

# Levels of Management

Understanding how a corporation uses it management can be a challenge. In a day where corporations are spending a lot of time and effort to reduce their overhead by increasing the span of control a manager can have or by compressing the levels of management, it is becoming increasingly important to understand the chain of command in the corporate environment. To understand how decisions are made and accounted for, let's start out by discussing the field or line part of the organizational structure.

## *The Field or Line*

This is where day-to-day decisions are initiated. The line or field organization is the most important part of the corporation. It is where the work of the corporation actually gets done. (I will use line and field interchangeably in this section.) The field organization of the corporation is the first stop you will make in corporate America as a newly-hired professional. This is where you will train and gain the experience to successfully complete the first rung in your climb up the success ladder.

Most line organizations are the bread and butter of corporations. A line person usually has specific duties to perform and usually is not allowed to deviate from the tasks assigned. In the aircraft industry, line engineers of various disciplines work on the various parts of the aircraft. There is a great deal of interaction between various line departments in order to accomplish the task of building a multimillion dollar aircraft. The line organization must function properly if the corporation is to be successful at bringing their product to the market.

In the days of early car manufacturing, the assembly line was the place where most of the corporation's resources were used to make an automobile. They still use the assembly line to manufacture cars, although technology now allows a car to be assembled in hours rather than in days.

The sales force of an organization is referred to as the field organization. By now you probably have guessed, I spent the initial part of my career in the sales force of a major corporation.  The field is responsible for bringing the product to the customers' doors.  They are responsible for selling what a company researches, develops, and then manufactures.  Sometimes they are expected to sell it before it is finished being developed.

Most of us will spend anywhere from two to seven years working on the line or in the field organization of a corporation.  If you have been in the field or a part of the line organization of a corporation longer than five years, you ought to be worried.  You have probably become complacent and too comfortable at what you are doing.  You have set your measure of success too low!  Black professionals often spend too much time working in the field or in the line organization.  Once you have perfected the skills it takes to do a line or field job with some expertise, you should get very anxious about what is to happen next.

## Management Staff

This is where strategic decisions are accounted for and corporate objectives are turned into corporate strategies.  When you are in a management staff position, you are usually working with and supporting the line or field organizations.  Management staff positions can allow you to develop your skills.  There is usually minimal people-responsibility and more accounting for the use and effectiveness of corporate resources.

Most corporations use these positions as training grounds for all levels of management positions.  The staff management usually reflects the organizational structure of other departments in the corporation.  They can allow an individual to gain insight into the internal workings of a corporation.  They allow you to get a 10,000-foot-level view before you are allowed responsibility for the 1,000-foot-level functions.  This is where you learn what resources a corporation has available and how to gain access to those resources.  You either make a lot of friends while in staff assignments or you make a lot of enemies.  (Enemies are not so bad if you gain their respect but try not to make too many.)

Blacks can benefit a lot from staff assignments.  These assignments allow you to make a few mistakes and learn the ropes of a business environment. The games of the corporation are usually introduced here, and this is a good chance to learn the rules of playing the game. Do not spend too much time in a staff assignment. A year or two is plenty, and you should come away from these assignments much better prepared to function effectively in a company.

## First-line Management

This is where day-to-day decisions are made and accounted for and tactical decisions are implemented. The first-line management job is probably the toughest job in the corporate structure. The first-line managers are responsible for the day-to-day operations of the corporation. They are responsible for making sure the line and the field accomplish the tactical tasks to meet the corporation's overall objectives. These tasks can include anything from making sure a quota gets attained to making sure the wing of an aircraft is complete before the fuselage is ready to be attached.

The first-line manager is a person caught in the middle. They sit between the employees who are responsible for accomplishing the day-to-day tasks and the management responsible for tactical decision-making. The line manager usually has very little decision-making power but represents the corporation to the field or line as if they do. They are often responsible for hiring and firing, but not without consulting with second-line management.

I spent two years in this type of an assignment, and it was a very enlightening experience for me. I found this job to be very confusing. Your own creativity is limited to the parameters set for you by upper management. You are held accountable for all mistakes you make and the mistakes made by the people reporting to you. It is the first time in your career when you feel you are not in total control of your own destiny. You spend a lot of time reflecting on whether or not you handled a situation correctly. I have jumped from thoughts of firing a person to wondering should I be giving the individual a reward all in the same day.

This job is usually a reward to those who have proven themselves in a field or line assignment. By the time you receive this dubious honor, you have already gained significant recognition by your co-workers. You are now responsible for a number of the people you may have worked beside, maybe not from the same office or shop but of the same skill level. You are now a boss for the first time in your career.

The first-line management job is one you must experience before you can appreciate what it takes to motivate a person to get a job done. The rewards of this job are more likely to come from self-actualization than from personal accomplishment. You are now more the cause rather than the effect of getting something accomplished. The reward becomes the completion of a task . Very few kudos are bestowed upon the first-line manager.

Black professionals often make it to this position and do a very good job while in it. However, we often get stuck in this position and here's why. We set our expectation levels too low. Being the first-line manager gives you a sense of becoming part of the corporate power structure. The power associated with the average first-line manager's position is very minimal, but it is more power and control than most of us have ever experienced before. It feels good to have your own office or cubicle and a secretary though s/he is probably shared by several managers. You are responsible for evaluating other people's work, and you are also responsible for rewarding them. The average African American professional finds this very rewarding. We feel we have arrived. I did. We do not realize, and no one tells us that this is just the beginning of becoming a decisionmaker and a part of the power structure.

If Black professionals are going to truly share in the wealth and affluence of America, we have to learn to seek seats of power beyond the first-line management chair. Remember, the first-line manager is mainly a people manager and not a business manager. It is the managing of the business that allows you to be a full decisionmaker. The power to influence what a business's goals and objectives should be is at a much higher level.

One last note: A first-line manager must be respected rather than liked by his or her subordinates. If the people who work for you respect you, they will work for you. If they like you, they may or may not help you get the job done. If you can get them to like and respect you, you are probably on your way to becoming president of the corporation.

## *Second-line Management*

This is where most tactical decisions are made and accounted for, and strategic decisions are implemented. The second-line management position is still one of managing people and implementing strategies that come from above. It is still a line position, as explained earlier. You are responsible for planning the resources managed by the first-line managers reporting to you, and you hold the reward-power which, as I explained earlier, is usually minimal.

As a second-line manager, you will have your first opportunity as a manager to feel as if you are running the show. Second-line managers can have as many as eight to ten managers reporting to them. They can be indirectly responsible for as many as a hundred or more people. It is a position that allows a manager to make day-to-day decisions without having to consult with managers above them, unless it affects the structure of the organization. This level of management can have some budgetary responsibility and can start to participate in some of the bonus structure of an organization. Entry into second-line management is a start towards the power seats.

Black professionals are starting to arrive in these positions in most major corporations. These positions are the entrance to decision-making and can allow you to provide input into what affects the direction a corporation may take. We African American professionals need to strive to gain seats in these offices. Most corporations have very few Blacks who make it to these positions. I have noticed in the last few years we have become very interested in what lies beyond the first-line manager's responsibilities and that is a good sign. Once we feel we have access to such positions, we begin to ascribe to them.

Black professionals who are successful at this level of responsibility usually are capable of doing well in a corporation. Usually, if we have the skills to perform this job, we are highly marketable outside of the corporation. We are often sought after by other corporations. We may miss opportunities because we do not recognize how to play one corporation against another. This is a game we should learn to play. Most managers become very successful because they know how to take skills gained in one corporation and market them to another corporation within the industry. This is how you increase your salary and your position of authority. I have noticed if Blacks get to this level, we are usually motivated to return to school to get a higher academic degree.

The second-line manager's job is one to ascribe to within seven to nine years in a corporation. Patience is very important when waiting to be promoted to this level. Demonstrated leadership will make this promotion come sooner. This position can lead you to a career in higher management.

## *Functional Management*

This is where strategic decisions are initiated and tactical decisions are accounted for. Functional management can cover the power base of several levels of management. The key attributes for this job are demonstrated leadership and the ability to manage the business aspects of a corporation. It can include second-level management, especially in service-oriented departments and in some production organizations.

Functional management is where a corporation starts to pay you for thinking and strategizing rather than implementing and getting your hands dirty. You usually spend most of your time in meetings with other functional managers analyzing how things are being accomplished and what needs to be done to make it better. Analytical abilities and business management are now the focus rather than people. This is where the 1,000 foot view of the corporation is structured and accounted for.

Blacks are starting to arrive in these offices, but there are still far too few of us to say we have arrived as a people. It is a position in management where you may have the opportunity to manage a big piece of the corporation and where you are a major influence on what is being implemented.

Note: If you have the skills to be a functional manager, you are probably a candidate to run your own business.

## *Executive Management*

This is where corporate goals are initiated and

accounted for and executive decisions are made. These people run the corporation. These are the president, senior vice presidents, and other major decisionmakers of the corporation.

Corporate America is run by executive management and requires all the experience, strategies and tactics you can bring to the table. Skills must be honed to perfection, and corporate political awareness is imperative if you are to succeed. Is it for us? It can be if we want it bad enough!

It is fascinating to function as a part of a large management machine. Observing high level executives at work is like watching a movie production company at work. These executives are almost worshipped by the employees they lead. They often take on star status, and it is amazing to watch the work they create as they pass through a city. The CEO of one of the corporations that once employed me was out visiting another large corporate CEO. He and the other CEO had a short meeting during the visit. After our CEO left, several of us were dispatched to review a product the other company produced. We were treated royally by the management staff of the other corporation. We spent at least half a day in demonstrations and presentations. We loved the product. We reported this to our management, but we never heard much about the product or the visit thereafter. My colleagues and I scratched our heads wondering how did this all get started and what results did it produce. Much later we learned that during their visit the CEOs casually agreed that our CEO would use their product in our demo centers across the nation. It was amazing to witness the reaction such a casual conversation caused.

Blacks are rarely seen walking the halls of the executive suites. When we gain seats in these suites (and we will), we will no longer struggle for self-worth as a people. These are truly the power seats of corporate America. But even more — they are the power seats of the world.

This is where the economic policies of this country are written, and we must become an author like all of the other people who have come to America seeking financial success. Black Americans must become hungry and possessed with the notion of making it to the top. We must acquire a thirst that will only be quenched by running the show!

# The System

We often hear people talking about "The System." "You need to learn the system!" "You need to make the system work for you." "You can't beat the system." "You are a victim of the system." What is this "System"?

Everything we discussed earlier in this chapter all works together to form the all-encompassing "System." The system is something that intertwines itself throughout a given corporate structure. What is truly amazing is how well it works. (This does not mean it always works for the good of an individual or the corporation.) The system is also made up of several other elements that I have not yet discussed and are worth mentioning at this juncture. The system houses the corporate political mechanism. I will devote a whole chapter to this topic later. The system also has a component I call the corporate culture, and we will discuss this in a later chapter.

The system is an important entity to understand. You will become a part of the system when you sign a contract with a company. It is something that will work for you or against you (or without you). To set the record straight, you cannot beat the system. You may fake it out! You may manipulate it! You may get around it! You may have the opportunity to represent it! In order to be successful, you must make it work for you. Most of the time, this is not hard to do.

Learn what the policies and procedures are in your corporation. This knowledge can serve you well. Blacks too often try to beat the system because it never seems to work on our behalf. The unique thing about the corporate system is that it is not set up to work on behalf of any individual. It is set up to work for a "monolithic monster" called the corporation. This is why we always try to beat it, especially when it manifests itself in the form of authority. The most important piece of information to take away from this section and to learn is that the system is something you are a part of and you must understand how it works. Know when it is working for you and when it is working against you.

I will discuss this concept further in later chapters, but I hope I have at least tweaked your thinking for now.

# Chapter

# 9

# Corporate Dress Codes

*S*ometimes looking the part is the first step in becoming the part. In corporate America, the way you look and present yourself is half of getting the job done.

Corporate America has dress codes. For the most part, they are well understood and accepted. You will rarely find do's and don'ts in the policies and procedures manuals of most corporations. There is rarely a written document that tells professionals what they should or should not wear to work. Yet, there are some entrenched dress codes in almost all of the major corporations in America. Corporate dress codes are understood rather than strictly-enforced rules. The dress codes are usually communicated by the culture that runs through a particular organization. As we shall discuss later, when the culture of a corporation is involved in what can and cannot be done, it is hard to change what is in existence. You may find it interesting the way these dress codes are enforced and adhered to by the professionals that make up the culture of a corporation. You will surprise yourself the first time you start to conform to the cultural dress codes of the corporation.

You may see someone who chooses to dress outside of the codes. His or her co-worker might chide them by saying, "Did you forget to bleach that shirt?" The person wearing the shirt may answer, "No, why?" The chider says, "Then tell me why it's so blue" or they may say, "Where did those stripes come from?" This is usually done very discreetly and without malice. In fact, it is usually done in fun. But it is statements like these which help perpetuate the codes and imbed them in the corporate culture.

Do not misunderstand the importance of adhering to

these dress codes. Many professionals find their careers stifled because of the way they dress. Hopefully, you will learn, people who do what is expected of them and adhere to the norms are the ones who rise through corporations at a faster pace than those who do not. And, they are not always the ones most qualified for the positions they ascend to. You will hear statements like, "Well, he's just a good looking suit" or "She looks good, but...." I find that the professionals who are the objects of these statements are usually very smart and understand the corporate game of "Chutes and Ladders." They have learned to use what they have to be successful. The people who have learned to make the system pay off for them are brilliant if they play by the rules.

Remember, this is all about being successful in the business world. If you are going to be successful in the business world, you must dress for success.

# You Can Still Express Yourself

My fellow Black professionals and I find the corporate dress code one of the most difficult areas to deal with. In the Black culture, the way we dress is almost sacred. It is a form of cultural expression and communication. Corporate dress codes attack the essence of what we believe we do very well. Nothing offends us more than being told how to do something we know we already do very well. It infringes on what has been thought to be a true art form in the African American culture. Our clothing and the way we choose to wear it gives us identity.

What we have to come to grips with is that we can still express ourselves and adhere to the business dress codes. I see it as another opportunity to be creative and to rise above what so easily becomes a hindrance to us. Do not let it become another obstacle. Do not let it keep you from making it to those top level corporate offices.

On the other hand, the corporate world is fast becoming more liberal in what it dictates to its participants. More and more corporate executives are experimenting with different styles and fashions, not only fast-moving, young professionals, but also the older professionals who have been running corporate America for the last 40 years. In the next few years, I believe we will see more liberal trends in corporate dress. But for now, there are still enough of those old conservatives around to keep the older and more prevalent dress codes alive. One example of how much influence an executive can have on the way people dress is Ronald Reagan. During the Reagan Era, style was more conservative yet elegant. There are many who say Mrs. Reagan put elegance back in the White house. Some feel it was necessary.

There are those who will do what is expected of them until they gain the power seat where they are allowed to bend or break the rules. We once had an executive who was somewhat of a free spirit. She wore suits to the office most of the time and played the corporate game very well. She was told by her mentors, "If you're going to get anywhere in this company, you had better pull your hair out of your face." When she became the executive in our office, she kept the hair out of her face, but she often wore a yellow and black polka dot dress. The first time she wore it, every female in our office started wearing dresses instead of their usual business suits, at least for a few weeks.

It is the men of the business world who are mainly responsible for continuing the corporate dress code; they are more "stodgy" than women. They are usually the ones who do the critiquing. The ladies usually have more freedom to choose different styles of clothing. Women of the business world are more likely to critique whether you are up to date rather than critique the color of the shirt or blouse you are wearing. There are corporations that are so conservative the employees appear to coordinate buying their clothing from the same store.

In one of the corporations where I worked, we were required to attended a training program. The corporate dress code was totally embedded in the program from the executives who managed it to the instructors who taught it. It was comical to witness all of us trainees get up in the morning and dress for class in very similar business attire. On days we had major presentations or tests, we all wore blue suits. What made it even more comical was to see us all parade into the parking lot every morning and stand around looking each other over. We all got into rental cars which were all the same model, either blue, red or white. There were four of us to a car. If you stood in front of the apartments, you saw all these Escorts, each with four people wearing blue suits and white shirts, and more than likely complemented by some sort of a yellow tie. The place was a clone factory. We all started to talk, walk and think alike.

In the following pages, I will present several tactics and strategies that will assist you in becoming very successful in dressing for the corporate world.

# Elegance is Accepted

First and foremost, elegance is accepted by the business world. We know how to dress elegantly. We know how to take clothes from K-mart and make them look like they come from the most expensive clothiers of the day. We also enjoy shopping and buying expensive clothes if we can afford it. I must warn you early on, I have had a lot of friends who found themselves in deep debt from buying expensive wardrobes. They used the corporate dress code as their excuse to abuse their credit cards after convincing themselves this was necessary to be successful. Adherence, not over-indulgence, is the key to business dress codes.

As I explained in an earlier chapter, the white shirt is the foundation of business attire, especially if the corporation is conservative. I once was interviewed by a functional manager in a very conservative corporation. We were just about to conclude the interview when I got this overwhelming urge to ask a question that many of you might think I should not have asked. I looked this executive in the eyes and asked, "Is it true that you guys only wear white shirts?" He was caught off guard. He laughed and said, "I have twenty white shirts, and they make it very easy to get dressed in the morning. Does that answer your question?" I got the job, and I bought ten white shirts before I started work the next week.

The white shirt has been declared the centerpiece of the business attire. It usually has button down, performance collars (performance collars are a bit stiffer than normal shirt collars). The preferred shirt is usually a full cut as opposed to tapered and may or may not have a pleat in the back. This shirt should be at least 50% cotton blend. I prefer a 60% cotton and 40% polyester which has a smooth elegant look. A lot of professionals wear 100% cotton. If you are one who launders and irons your own shirts, you may not want a 100% cotton; they are hard to care for. Printed white material is accepted, but you are still flirting on the edge. If you walk into any store that carries professional clothing, you will find a wide selection of white shirts. Women will find blouses of the same description at your favorite fashion store. Again, women have a little more freedom; the business world does not dictate to women their business attire as much as to men.

Shoes for the corporate dress are equally as important. This is where you may struggle with the need to express your Blackness. We Blacks love to wear fancy shoes. You guys remember when your grandfather used to wear those Stacy Adams and wingtips to church. Well, he was spot on! That is the shoe worn by most executives in the business world.

I must admit I am rebellious in this area, but I haven't departed too far from what is accepted; and I do have a pair of Stacy Adams. I normally wear solid brown or black loafers with simple tassels, and I see a lot of higher level corporate executives wearing this type of shoe. This is not the preferred shoe, but it seems to be accepted. The shoe you wear is a part of the statement you are making, and people will judge you by it.

The upkeep of your shoes is also very important. Keeping your shoes shined is basic to elegance. Many women forget to keep their pumps shined and their heels in good condition. Make sure the soles of your shoes are kept neat as well. Stopping at the shoeshine stand makes for a nice break in your day, and it is relatively inexpensive.

Wear socks to match your shoes. Extremely colorful socks may make a statement, but they will detract from the elegance you are trying to create. Brown shoes should have brown socks and black shoes should have black socks. Argyles are chancy. Printed socks work if the prints are not too pronounced.

The blue suit is the selected uniform for the business world. It drives me nuts to walk into an important meeting and everyone in the room is wearing their blue suit. Both men and women! Nevertheless, the blue suit is the mainstay of the corporate attire. I have at least four different blue suits in my business wardrobe. Stripes are more impressive than just a plain blue suit. You will find your top executives always in stripes. Some corporations do not allow their junior colleagues to wear stripes. If you spend a little time observing the people around you, you will quickly learn what is allowed or not allowed. Double breasted suits are mainly reserved for the top executives in most corporations. If double breasted suits are allowed, do not spend all of your business wardrobe money on double breasted. The preferred style of suit in the business world is the single breasted, two button, with one slit in the back. Buy at least one.

Gray suits are being worn more and more. In fact, the charcoal gray suit with thin pin stripes is really starting to compete with the blue suit. I find charcoal gray to be more elegant than any of the other colors. Brown suits are worn, but not very often and tend to be worn more on the days when you need to roll up your sleeves. You might say the brown suit is viewed by the business world as a work suit. In one corporation, I observed the customer service engineers all wearing brown suits. I was told it was because brown is a color that hides dirt. But they still wore white shirts.

In the spring and summer months, you will see tans, taupes and khaki green attire. They are nice, but they tend to be less elegant.

The tie is a great place to show off your elegance, and you can probably get away with a little more flash. As I discussed in an earlier chapter, paisleys are usually in. Simple geometries are standard such as dots and squares. There are always some new designs coming onto the corporate scene. The main point here is pay attention to what is popular and stay to the conservative side of it.

Dresses are starting to come onto the corporate scene, and they are definitely elegant if properly chosen. You sisters can have a lot of fun dressing for success with the new tasteful fashions in dresses. Longer is better and more tasteful. Some women can wear shorter dresses but they become a distraction in the office environment. Secretaries seem to wear the shorter dresses; and you will have a hard enough time convincing people you are not on the lower paid administrative staff. The corporate professional woman usually wears clothes that complement the status they earn. If you walk into a room full of female corporate executives, it is easy to tell who are the movers and shakers. Suits will always win out over dresses. The higher the position the more conservatively women seem to dress.

Jewelry can be worn, but it must complement the attire. A female professional wearing a string of pearls over her butterfly neck ties is very elegant. A string of pearls can relieve women from wearing neck ties with some outfits. Earrings should not be too obvious and should complement the color scheme. Bracelets are cumbersome if they fall onto the hand and should be seen only when you are fairly close, such as during a handshake.

Brothers should stay away from all earrings unless you own the company and it is worth at least a million dollars. Earrings are cultural and should be saved for personal expression after work. Bracelets are acceptable if they follow the guidelines discussed in the paragraph above. Cuff links are nice, but they are out of style at this date. You may wear them to create an individual style as I discuss in the next section.

# Create A Style

Some of the most successful business executives and professionals are those who take the time to create a style or a "look." You can have a signature in your style. The manner in which you get things done can also be viewed as part of your style. A style is something that points back to you when heard, seen or experienced. This allows you to be easily identified by your peers and can make you stand out. Creating a style can be advantageous in improving your self-esteem. The most important thing about a style is to be consistent.

The way you arrange and decorate your work space or office can be a part of your style. Pictures on your wall can help you make a style statement. Keeping your work area clean not only perpetuates the work ethic but also will make people want to be in your environment. A few awards, especially those you may have acquired for overachieving, can accent your work space nicely. Displaying choice awards in your space can give people a sense of your accomplishments, even if they are awards you received in college.

Your pictures do not always have to say you are Black. Use your environment to show you are capable of having an expanded cultural experience. Remember, the business world already knows you are Black. If you point it out in everything you do, it will be read as a negative.

Established professionals have used the way they dress to express "a style" for years. They wear a certain brand of clothing or use a certain color scheme in their wardrobe. They are recognized by the style they have created. Michael Jackson is the epitome of creating and using a style to accent who he is. The sequined white glove became so popular, it was sold to his fans. Jackson's style provides good PR and profits for his corporation. Bill Cosby has created a soft style on his television program. He wears an assortment of sweaters and sweat shirts. If you have ever seen Earvin "Magic" Johnson off the court, he has a style that is sublime. Then there is Whoopi Goldberg who has catapulted herself into stardom with dreadlocks. Whoopi's style says, "If you don't like what you see, then it's your problem." If you took away her dreadlocks, it would not be Whoopi. There are other women who are in the process of creating a style, some of whom are sizzling, such as Jasmine Guy. Felicia Allen-Rashad is very elegant. Copying a style from someone who is already successful is not a bad way to create or implement your own style.

In the business world, you want to take care to adopt a style that will complement your business environment. Remember, we want to use style as a positive and motivational attribute. Once you have launched your career in the direction you want it to go, then you can add an exotic touch to your style. In any case, conservative is a safe bet until you are sure what works.

In creating your own style, one of the risks you run is that somebody can very easily copy you, and then you are no longer unique. It is the uniqueness of a style that allows you to attract the attention and curiosity of your colleagues and clients. It is very flattering when someone chooses to use you as a pattern for creating their own style.

Cufflinks, tie clips and collar tie-bars can help you create a style. I decided to wear a collar-tie bar to hold my collar down and prop my tie up instead of wearing collars that button down. Keep in mind, I have paid my dues in the business world, but I still feel I sacrifice something in order to take luxury in wearing the tie bar. Jesse Jackson and Lee Iacocca both wear a collar bar in a similar manner. I also wear a uniquely folded white handkerchief in my coat pocket of every suit. I try never to be seen without a Simms-folded handkerchief. I worked very hard to fold my handkerchiefs so that there are only three corners, folded in half and pointing uniformly in the same direction. It is uniquely me, and a lot of people are awed by it. I try to buy ties that always have some sort of white accents. I chose white because it looks nice with white shirts and those Simms-folded handkerchiefs. I get bored wearing white shirts, and I need something to give me a sense of uniqueness in the way I dress.

Your shoes are definitely a place to interject style in your business attire. Even my one pair of wing tips are unique. I may sound hypocritical, but I did not say I totally adhere to the corporate dress code and very few Blacks do. Providing you with enough information on what to expect provides you with the best shot at being successful in the business world. Now, if you adhere to all the "rules", you will soon be totally bored. Make sure you have some fun and do what you want, even if it means giving up a little of the success we are seeking.

As I stated earlier, the way you do things can be a part of your style. I interject a bit of style when I answer the telephone. I answer saying "Darrell Simms here." I have practiced using this phrase to answer the phone so it no longer sounds like I am "putting on airs", as my grandmother used to say.

Being helpful can also become a part of your style. I make it a point to be very helpful to secretaries and administrative people. For instance, I make myself available to the receptionist. When he or she cannot find the person responsible for a particular situation, I allow them to call me. Be careful. This can increase your workload. The secretaries and receptionists appreciate having someone they can rely on to help them respond to various situations that occur. A lot of the time, I simply take a message and pass it on to the person who is responsible. I find my co-workers also appreciate having their clients or situations handled in such a nice manner. If helpfulness becomes a part of your style, it will get around the office quickly, and your co-workers will like you even more.

If you can create a style that is your own and easily recognizable, you have created an ambiance that is uniquely you.

# Image

Projecting a positive image is essential in the corporate world. Image is mainly attitude.

Most people's first inclination about another person's "image" is focused on the way they look. How you look most certainly is important to the image you portray. Your outer attire is definitely the linchpin for "first impressions." You must take time to consider what image you wish to project as you create and implement your style.

Your grooming will affect your image. Black professionals must spend time on the way they wear their hair. The business world is discovering Black fashion and finally considering our styles as part of today's fashion. They are beginning to know when a Black person has recently had a haircut. I take every opportunity to educate Whites on Black style. We Blacks must be consistent in what we portray as good and bad styles. For instance, is a "flat top" business-like or is it street-like? Is a "shag" something a Black executive should be wearing? Is it conservative or liberal? You might be thinking at this time, "Has Simms gone off the deep end!" We take these haircuts for granted in the Black community as part of our culture. The business world must be taught to understand African American fashion, just as they understand the razor cut and keeping hair off the collar and slightly covering the top of the ears is a conservative White haircut—unless you are from the Eisenhower Era, where the less hair you had the more powerful you were. Most of the people in the Eisenhower administration wore crew cuts and most business executives also wore crew cuts.

The business world can be a little stupid at times. I had a very comical haircut experience. I had just gotten a fresh haircut, and one of the people I worked with passed me in the bullpen and said, "Something is different about you today. It seems you're darker or something." All I could do was laugh at her. She really was trying to be sociable, and I chalked it up to her ignorance of Blacks. I know she was not unique.

Women are scrutinized more for hairstyle and image. As I stated in the chapter entitled "Interviewing Tactics," you must wear your hair in a business fashion. Most of the Black professional women I have observed have well-groomed hair.

Black hairstyles for women are not that different from hairstyles for other cultures especially now that perms have been improved. When Black women start wearing ethnic hairstyles, it is picked up immediately. The key is, as always, to present a professional image. As we continue to take seats in the business bullpens, we are allowed to express ourselves more and more. Still, we must proceed with caution. The business world is experiencing a learning curve where Blacks are concerned.

By now, I hope you understand how important it is to communicate well in the business world. Communication is another place to build or destroy your image. Poor communication skills will create an instant image problem. Speaking, reading and writing are all a part of the image you will portray. This is another reason why you must work hard at building communication skills.

Cigarette smoking can hurt your image. If you smoke, you run a large risk of holding back your career. Today cigarette smoking is viewed as unhealthy. If the "powers that be" are smokers, than there is no problem with your being a smoker. But if they do not smoke, you want to keep your smoking a secret. The work place is now forcing smokers outside the building. You may be surprised to see certain individuals from your office standing outside of the building smoking.

Professionals in the business world are very conscious of fitness, especially weight control. I once had a client who wanted us to bring in a specialist to study a situation he was experiencing. When the specialist arrived, he was introduced to the client. The client became very stand- offish toward the specialist. One of the other employees in the client's office explained how the client felt about fat people. This specialist was bordering on obese. Without explanation, the client decided he did not want us to study the situation.

The car you drive will project your image. It is unbelievable how many people pay attention to the car you drive. The BMW, Mercedes, Honda and a bunch of newcomers are all cars of status. The amazing thing is, unless they are in sales, professionals spend very little time in their cars during work hours. Yet, everyone at the office will know what kind of car you drive, especially if it is an expensive car. Do not run out and put yourself in major debt trying to improve your image by buying an expensive car. Buy what you can afford.

The image you portray can be changed but not easily. Make sure you check the perception of your image on occasion. If you find you are not being viewed the way you want to be, make a change immediately. You do not have to put up a sign that you are making a change, but make the change in such a way that it is perceived in a positive manner. Be careful not to become reactionary at every piece of information or feedback that comes back to you. You could be put in a position of constant change which would be unsettling. It is not always easy to make a change, but if people know you are trying and you can be flexible, they will work with you.

As a Black professional, the corporate dress code will occasionally get in your way. Just remember, it has been around since the first business deal and will probably be around in some manner for the last one. Dress for success!

# Chapter

# 10

# Corporate Culture

*A* corporation that has a thriving culture will ultimately prosper! A corporation without a stable culture will struggle! A corporation that cannot develop or nurture a culture at all will die!

What comes to mind when you hear "culture"? I think of a culture as the accepted commonalties of a group of people, the way things are thought about within a group of people, the ability of a group to pass their practices from one generation to the next, the capacity for a group to make practices and beliefs difficult to change or unchangeable. Culture maintains or gives value to human existence.

I think culture has deep roots and is long lasting. It allows you to be proud based on historical experience. It allows you to belong. Culture can include me or exclude me. I think of heritage. I may or may not be able to relate to accepted societal norms.

The business world is not unlike other organized forms of society. It is made up of all kinds of people, places and events that somehow must be brought into harmonious interplay. What forces the business world to be different from most other types of institutions is that it is mainly centered around making a "profit." If people have common goals and objectives, a culture will be born.

The business world intertwines itself around every part of our lives whether we want it to or not. The culture spawned by the business world is focused on making sure it does not lose its philosophy, not what makes it profitable or successful, but what keeps it from deteriorating and dissipating, not unlike religion, race or society which are founded on the philosophy and culture they impart and nurture. Their success lies in their ability to convince people their way should be chosen as the best way. Businesses seek to have a philosophy that works. Once convinced of its philosophy, it builds a corporate culture to protect that philosophy.

There are numerous factors that force corporations to create and maintain their cultures. Competition pushes corporations into deep cultural fortresses. It is interesting to watch a corporation build and maintain defensive practices based on the effects of competition. There are many corporations that expect their people never to disparage the competition. Strong policing forces kick in if their policies are not adhered to. Only a strong culture can maintain these types of policing actions.

Corporate cultures vary widely depending upon the type of industry involved. For instance, the computer industry is geared to the highly analytical thinker which sets up a culture of planning and analysis. It also spawns management styles geared to measurement systems that are hard to tear down. It takes long hours to produce software that is useful and easy to use. Computer culture demands that people work long, intense hours in order to produce software products.

The finance industry is mainly made up of socialites. They are interested in doing business with people they know and like which fosters a lot of repeat business. The finance culture is one of conformity. Other industries that rely on bankers often find their business culture is a hybrid of the banking industry and their own. These businesses take on the culture of the bankers in order to participate in that arena, and they have their own idiosyncrasies spawned by their own industry.

Blending all the different industries into what I continue to call the "business" or "corporate" world makes for overall interesting cultural considerations. The business world provides a continuous influence that penetrates various industries, and many sub-cultures are formed. Sub-cultures exist in some form or other from the top to the bottom of organizations within an industry. A corporation's culture is varied by the participants and players and can be changed by those who are at the top of the organization.

In the Nineties, you are going to find businesses

being forced to change their cultures as never before. These changes will come because of the changing workforce. Attitudes once held in sacred esteem will come tumbling down after the last "old fogie" of a CEO is replaced. If he is not replaced, he will have been converted to a "Nineties person." (The business world is still currently run by White males, but that will change rapidly.) Corporate cultures are going to change from being organizations centered around an individual (me generation) to more collaborative and cooperative. The fall of the old, male- dominated business culture has begun. Businesses are now building day care centers for the children of those enthusiastic working professional women who are also mothers. The days of working sixty hours plus weekends are starting to vanish. You can stand in the lobby of most office buildings and watch the professional women leaving work at the published quitting time. What is interesting is they are accomplishing the same amount of work as the men they replaced, if not more.

Corporations are being forced to change their cultures to compete with the Japanese and other world market participants. This is an example of the effect competition can have on the business culture. Soon the United States will be competing with products from the Soviet Union and the Eastern Bloc countries. We Blacks had better be prepared to take advantage when these global business doors swing open. There will be a flood of countries representing a huge variety of different cultures running inside. I am sure there will be pushing and shoving to see which cultures can stand the test. I believe there will be a new, diverse business culture; and we can help shape it if we are in the proper position. It will be an exciting time if we can position ourselves to capitalize on the opportunities.

Keep in mind most of the cultures existing in the business world today were put in place at the inception of businesses developed by brilliant-thinking entrepreneurs.

# Diversifying Your Thinking

Business thinking is primarily collective thinking. It is brought about by circumstances and situations that are presented before boards, CEOs, management staffs, and other corporate leadership. The one thing all corporate management must be able to do is to change their thinking when necessary. They must not only be able to change what they are thinking about but also be able to re-prioritize what is being considered at a given time. Should they be focusing on increasing market share or increasing sales, expanding the work force or decreasing expenses? A final thing corporate management must be able and willing to do is change what their employees are thinking about, especially the acceptance of "imminent change." This I call "diverse thinking"!

Diverse thinking is not easy to accomplish. It is amazing how much we expect from one another in this work-a-day world we live in. What is even more amazing is how much we expect from ourselves in our quest to participate. We set out to forge our branch in the history of life and often end up with only a thinking process. If the thinking is right, we go on to accomplishments beyond our wildest dreams, creating enthusiasm in ourselves and, hopefully, in others along the way. If our thinking allows us to accomplish that much, we have been successful. I believe diverse thinking transcends process thinking.

Genuine enthusiasm is hard to conjure up for an individual who has had a limited chance to exercise true thinking until college. We Black professionals gain our first taste of business thinking during our college experience. A few of us have had the opportunity to gain knowledge through experiential development. By this I mean observing from a distance what was not locally available to us first hand, such as having a friend whose father is a doctor or lawyer or an engineer. This has motivated us to try to catch up to those privileged ones who have genuine business experiences all their lives. We must work at building a base of enthusiasm from every experience that presents itself to us. The moment we understand what is expected of us, we must start to deliver. This has to be projected in an overwhelmingly positive manner that will foster the developing of a business sense. We must develop this from whatever positive experiences that are available.

In the business world, there were times when I have felt as enthusiastic as humanly possible, and I was misread by my peers, subordinates, and management all in the same day.

My enthusiasm has been misread as too aggressive. These experiences make you very aware of thinking in the business world. It can make the Black Chip raise its dark side very quickly if you have not learned to adapt your thinking to different situations. One of the things the Black Chip will do is make you over-sensitive to what is often normal business interplay, such as jockeying for position at a business meeting. This is a normal occurrence. It is done by all. Once you have learned the game, you will do it.

All of the things mentioned above definitely lead to a different way of thinking, different than we have ever been faced with as Black people. Diverse thinking, as hard as it is to comprehend, has to become a part of our cognitive base. Therein lies the success we have recently learned to crave.

As we embark on our journey onto the corporate scene, we are going to have to think tactically and strategically, a type of thinking fostered by competition. This (business) culturally-based thinking is necessary for anyone wishing to survive and become a vital, participating player (or shall I say "owner"?) in the corporate world.

I cannot tell you how many times I have been sitting in a meeting with a great idea, but I was not able to put it in the framework or context of the individuals in the room. Today, if I get an idea, I will discuss the idea with all who will listen. Once I have convinced my close colleagues (friends) the idea is good, then I proceed to convince those who are capable of empowering me to act upon my idea. This is not an easy task. It really shakes me when I am treated as the "null" kid on the block. But if that is the way they want to think of me, then I should learn to take advantage of it.

The types of thinking a corporation may want you to do may not always seem logical to you, but remember the corporation does not revolve around you. (There are corporations who are starting to express thinking that appears to support societal needs rather than corporate needs.) Even when a corporation appears to consider the needs of the people who are employed by it, it is usually thinking of itself. Corporations are learning if they meet the needs of the individual employees, they are able to keep them as vital resources.

I have watched corporations make decisions that have

just baffled me. For instance, you are motivated to make a set of objectives. You attempt to make the objectives. Just as you are about to succeed, the corporation tells you not to make those objectives at this time because it is not in the best interests of the corporation. A case in point: A corporation decided it wanted product demonstration centers in various strategic locations around the country. They put everything in place to set up the centers in various locations and to make the centers successful. Once the centers were operational and running, the corporation decided it was not going to provide support to the centers any longer. Each center became dormant for many months. Each center cost approximately $500,000. The problem was that the centers were put in place before they were of use to the corporation. The products that were to be demonstrated were not available to sell, at least not in the fashion they were being demonstrated. I found this strange.

Diverse thinking is very important when you try to comprehend all of the different directions a corporation can go. Take incentive programs: I once found myself motivated to go against the strategic direction of a company. I was motivated to sell a product because it was necessary to achieve a bonus (cash). I attempted to sell the products in the way that I could satisfy the requirements for achieving the bonus. However, I started researching the possible repercussions and impacts that selling the products might have on the bottom line of the corporation. I found that, if I sold the products to meet the criteria for achieving the bonus, the corporation would gain revenue once and only once. But, if I sold the products the way the corporate strategy said you should sell the products, the corporation would gain a revenue stream that would last for years. If you compared the two ways of bringing revenue into the corporation, one way would actually double the amount of revenue the corporation would make. Yet, we were motivated to sell the other way.

In the chapter called "Twice as Good — Can be Good Enough," we described cognitive dissonance as a great mind protector. You will have many opportunities to use this to allow your mind to deal with what it must. Just think of some of the decisions people are forced to make in the business world. For example, in the car industry they have to decide whether or not to make a design change based on the number of people that are killed each year.  If the kill ratio is not high enough, it may be difficult for an engineer to financially justify making the change.  The airline industry will fly a plane knowing there is a minor problem with one of its parts.  A flight maintenance director has to decide if the risk of taking time to repair the part is greater than the risk of not meeting the schedule.  These decisions become everyday casual thinking.  I know we take risks every day when we drive our car on a wet street, especially if there is very little tread on the tires.  Making a decision that affects me is one thing, but thinking through a business decision that affects others takes a very different kind of thinking.  Cognitive dissonance, please stay close!

One final thought on this topic.  If you do not remember anything else from this chapter, please remember this:  Corporations need people who can think big, and I do mean BIG!  Thinking big is not as easy as it sounds, especially if you know you may have to sign up and deliver.  This is also a diverse form of thinking, but it is vital to American business.

# Corporate Idiosyncrasies

The business world has many peculiarities.  You are going to find yourself asking, "Who decided to do that?" or "Why are we doing this?" about accepted practices.  They may be things people have been trained to do or think about in a certain way or things that were just passed down through the culture.  Some of these things are going to make a lot of sense, and some are going to be just plain foolish.  When you consider them all together, they are the "idiosyncrasies" of a corporation.  And, they can be a vital part of the corporation's cultural makeup — right or wrong.

One such idiosyncrasy is called "technical."  (I admit I created this chapter mainly to discuss this thing called technical.)  What does it mean to be technical?  Before, I became as informed as I am claiming to be these days, I used to think technical included very few things, places or people.  Let's explore this a little.  Technical used to describe a little twirp of a person who wore thick glasses and carried around some type of number crunching machine.  It usually meant one who had a higher intelligence than the average person.  These are still accepted definitions. I have since learned technical is a powerful thing to be in the business world. If you can gain this status, you have done a good thing.

Everything in the business world is technical. I say this because it is very important to be known as someone who knows what should be known. Technical in the business world means to know something intimately, not only to know about it, but to know why it is, how it got that way, and what good it is to the person, place or thing that possesses it. Being technical about something is of no value unless there is a perceived business need for knowing it. I have learned that being technical is the best thing you can be in a business environment. Someone who has knowledge obtained from experience and/or training — does that sound powerful? I have often heard co-professionals say, "That is too technical for me." I have learned never to say something is too technical for my understanding unless I know I am an authority on the subject and I am just trying to be modest.

Another way of defining technical is having just a little more knowledge on a given subject than everyone else in a room. You are the one who will be looked upon as the specialist or maybe even the expert. Why is it important to understand this corporate idiosyncrasy? I thought you might have figured it out by now!

The person who is technical is allowed to spend more money and use more resources. If you are looked upon as the person most knowledgeable on the project or subject, you will eventually influence decisions. The person who is technical is allowed to make all the mistakes s/he wants if s/he is able to explain why the mistakes were made. One note of caution, if you are making mistakes and there are no beneficial results, you run the risk of losing your technical status.

As a technocrat you will enjoy a lot of wonderful benefits, as long as you can live up to the title. I once wanted a job that everyone thought required technical proficiency. I knew I was capable of doing the job. The position was a stepping stone to bigger and better things. It was a position with very short tenure. I watched several people hold the position, and I watched how they went about doing the job. Most of the people were minimally qualified to do the job. I finally got my chance at the job, and I went for it. At the time I was interviewing, the person who was in the job wanted everyone to know she was not technical. She thought this would allow her some latitude. She lost all credibility while in the position. I interviewed on the strength that I was technical. When I was selected for the job a short time later, I sent out a note introducing myself. At the end of the note I stated, "and I am very technical." That job became a major launch pad for the rest of my career. Ever since then, I always find a way to label myself technical.

Bankers, lawyers, business people and, in fact, every discipline allows you to be technical. It is not only the scientific aspects that allow you to be technical. In this world of computers, you have to be technical to get money out of your bank account or change the channel on your television set. Being technical means having a key knowledge base, even if that is just a little more than everybody else.

Another true corporate idiosyncrasy is the corporate handshake. I have never found a custom that is so highly regarded as the proverbial touching of the hands. It almost seems that members of the corporate world live for a solid handshake. Many deals have been launched and concluded with a handshake. Remember the manager who taught me how to say "ask"? He also taught me how to shake hands. He looked me sternly in the eyes and said, "Simms, you need to learn how to give a solid, firm handshake." I have learned to enjoy shaking hands. There is something about touching a person's hand that makes them feel a sincere thing is happening.

When you are in the business world, leave the ethnic handshakes home. I enjoy a good dap myself, but the corporate world does not understand why it is important or why it is a good thing to do. If your non-Black colleagues know how to execute the dap, they will let you know when they get to know you better. Even if a professional is Black, do not assume they want to use the Black handshakes or some other ethnic handshake. A lot of African American professionals reserve the dap for friends or for times and places they hold sacred and dear. This goes not only for handshakes but for any other Black ethnic or cultural thing we do.

Note: Do not assume every Black you encounter in the business world is your African brother or sister. You will set yourself up for a lot of embarrassment if you do. A lot of Blacks get high up in corporations by shelving the ethnic part of themselves. They are not necessarily an "oreo", but they have learned what is necessary to get in on the game.

The corporate dress code, as we discussed in the previous chapter, can be considered an idiosyncrasy. It is one of those things that is peculiar to the business world. You will find people clinging to dress codes as if they were sacred cows in a foreign land.

Another corporate idiosyncrasy is people's obsession with having an office. For one thing, having an office is an expensive proposition for a corporation. We all know the business world has established the office as a status symbol, yet they are major barriers to communications. However, I still prefer having my own office.

The car phone has become the new status symbol. It is well on its way to being considered an idiosyncrasy. It is amazing to listen to the radio on your way to work and hear all the people calling in on their cellular phones. I have one; it is just another telephone.

One of the biggest idiosyncrasies of the business world is eating. Whoever said, "The way to a person's heart is through the stomach" was right. Business people love to eat, and, as a professional, this is one thing you will have to learn to do properly. I have never closed a deal without at least one lunch date with a client or customer. The business world spends scads of money on food. If you attend a morning meeting, you will more than likely have donuts or pastries with coffee, tea, or orange juice before starting the meeting. What's even more amazing is that people expect to have these amenities.

The new ploy of the corporation is working lunches. Yes, gourmet pizza while you sit through the next slide show. Occasionally, I feel it is a cheap way to get another hour of work out of me. I have seen people sequestered from breakfast through dinner trying to complete a planning session.

The brown bag is now left at home. There are even subsidized cafeterias at most major corporate sites. And, guess what! The food is often very good. One corporation had the audacity to bring in a renowned chef for the corporate executives who spent most of their time trying to cut down and sell trees.  (Guess who?)

Planning session has become another name for meeting.  Sometimes they go by the name of strategy sessions. Everybody in America's corporations is planning for something. The strange thing about this idiosyncrasy is that the finished document is rarely used.  Here the process is really more important than the results.

# Two Different Worlds

The corporate world and the real world are very different; and, though the corporate world may be a unique subset of the real world, it operates independently of the rest of the world.  For African American professionals especially, these are two separate and distinct worlds.  Our challenge is to try to bring them together as one, to integrate the corporate world into our real world as most other cultures have successfully done.

I have heard many of my African American colleagues say they have a business dialect and a Black dialect. The business dialect is used for business conversations.  The Black dialect is used when they are home or among Black people.  Blacks are not unique in this situation.  Asians and other ethnic groups have a very similar problem.  They must speak English in the business world and speak their own language when they are home or among their own people.

The business world is a lot less forgiving and a lot more demanding than the rest of the world.  It thrives on concerted chaos and will run over anything that gets in its way. It will slowly consume anything it cannot run over.  We must learn to tap its strengths and take advantage of its weaknesses. For the last century, it has sapped our strength and taken advantage of our weakness as a people.

Business world players can be ruthless which is confusing to  many Blacks at first.  We can get a warped perception about ourselves and others if we are not careful. The game is for real and the winner takes all.  We must learn to be a part of this world that is so vital to our existence.  We can no longer be the lingering foe, or we may wind up like some of our friends in various third world countries.  Learn to play the game and learn it well.  Be demanding as you grow smarter, and become smarter about what you know. Learn not to take no for an answer. Say "yes" as often as you can when encountering new challenges and obstacles. Say "no" only when necessary.

A business is an entity that exists for itself. Within it we must find a place that will allow us to thrive. We must merge the world of business and the world of Black survival. Do not mistake what I am saying here as militant. I am talking about a world that will attempt to exclude any people who do not know how to participate. The good news is that the business world so far has accepted everyone who has taken the time to learn the rules and finish the game trials.

One of the things I have learned about business culture: you are allowed to make mistakes as long as you understand what the consequences are. I watched a major corporation which was founded on very strong basic beliefs be challenged by those same beliefs. It is struggling to change the essence of its culture, which was built on a lot of big, healthy, fat years. Now the industry it is a part of is trying to reshape itself in every way. This corporation is caught in a tailspin. The culture it spawned many years ago has become a millstone about its neck. The people of this corporation are still a devoted lot, but things that once worked well no longer work well enough.

This corporation is asking people to take risk and be empowered to make changes, but this has not been a part of the culture in the past. It will be interesting to see if this corporation can truly change the way it does business and the culture which has served it so well in the past.

As a Black professional I have learned in order to exist in the world of business as well as in the Black world, I must become very adaptable. I must learn to incorporate business in my way of thinking; but more than that, I must learn to incorporate business in my culture. This is not easy. Like the big corporation above, we Blacks must change the basis of our culture and the way we think. We must educate ourselves and keep changing until we find the right combination. We must force ourselves to integrate into corporate America, compromising only the things that will ultimately set us back.

What is more sacred than life is the ability to live it to its fullest. We must maximize our potential as Black professionals and never look back to the past anguish and lack of success. Integrating what makes us happy from the past with what makes us happy in the present will make us happy in the future. All that is necessary to keep these two worlds in harmony is success. Once we start to live and BREED success, we will push the two worlds into one; and that will allow us to be winners.

As we embark into the next century, we must create a place in the business culture of America that will nurture the Black professional. But we must not stop with America, or we will be left behind once again. We must proceed into the global market, along with Japan, Europe, the Eastern Bloc and the new kids on the block, the countries coming out of what was once the USSR.

# Chapter

# 11

# Managing In All Directions

*T*he most challenging thing to undertake in the business world is managing. Most people think managing is telling someone else what to do. If you do not manage all aspects of the job and the various situations that arise, you will constantly feel like you are a spinning top, spinning and gyrating in all directions.

In this chapter I would like to give you a sense of all the things there are to manage, things you probably have thought about but not necessarily from a managing perspective. Keeping track of time, or "time management", is the first thing you must learn to manage. Time management is a valuable skill, as we discussed earlier. Managing the resources available to you is a must. And, there are many other things we need to consider. Learning to manage can be easy in some aspects and almost impossible in others.

One of the most important things to manage is the people you work with and for, to manage the people who work for you and who help you accomplish company goals.

Getting people to allow you to do your job is not always easy. It is certainly not a gift you were born with, as is often believed. Acquiring this type of experience is what I call Managing 000. (You will not find this course in any college catalog because its contents only come from on-the-job experience.) This is not an easy course to pass because it is through trial and error and is self-graded on how well you accomplish your goals. If the mistakes outlast the trials, you have failed. You certainly ought to experience this course and understand what it allows you to do.

When you look at the total package that comes with

being educated and professional, you will find you need to manage everything. Most people shy away from managing because for years our society has taught young professionals that someone else will manage for you. By the time a person has graduated from college, they probably have had at least seven years of managing a lot of things. When you move from junior high school to senior high school, this is just about the time your parents start to let go of you. By the time you are in your junior year of high school, you probably manage mostly on your own, hopefully with a source of encouragement from your folks. Once you are in high school, you are not only managing yourself, you are also managing a schedule of day-to-day activities. As a Black student, you have probably worked a steady job and managed your life in order to complete college. This is all good experience. Notice, I am not yet talking about management but about managing.

## Managing The Middle – Yourself

If you cannot manage yourself, you will never be able to manage others or anything else!

Knowing and understanding what motivates you is of the utmost importance when it comes to getting what you want from the business world. Most people do not take the time to understand what motivates them. Most people do not realize how valuable it is to be able to make a decision that concerns themselves. Blacks on the whole are taught to survive rather than being taught to manage through the challenges that are presented to them. This is one of the reasons we have had a hard time assimilating into the American business world even after graduating from an Ivy League college with honors.

While I was in college, a radio station came by to interview all of the young Black students (including me) who were a part of a college equal opportunity program. They were awed by our success in the program. I always wondered why they were so awed by our success. Was not the mission of the program to take young Black kids and help them succeed? No! In their eyes, we were an experiment, and they were there to see if the experiment was working or failing. This type of thinking in our society forces you to learn what is good or bad for yourself. This takes a discipline anyone can admire, and we have it—survival.

In order to fully take part in the business world, we have to know what we want. We must take time to organize ourselves in such a way that we are fully understood, understood first by ourselves and then by anyone who is necessary to make the things happen we want to happen.

It takes a long time to learn to manage yourself properly. If you spend too much time thinking about what is necessary, you are still dreaming. If you spend a lot of time trying to convince yourself you know what is necessary, you are procrastinating. If you have an idea about what you want and are not quite sure, you are probably confused. If you know what you want but are not quite sure how to get it, you are not in control. If you know what you want and think someone else will get it for you, you are fooling yourself. If you know what you want and have some ideas about how to get it, you are ready to plan. If you know what you want and know exactly how to get it, you have a plan. Now execute the plan and begin to manage yourself to successful completion of the plan. If you get what you want through carefully considered plans, you can successfully manage yourself. Many people never put themselves through this type of reasoning. They usually go after what they want, and, if they succeed, they feel good about themselves. If they fail, they wonder what happened. If they fall somewhere along the way, they commit suicide. Learning to manage yourself is not an art form, and it is usually not hereditary. It is a skill you must learn and develop.

Developing this skill can take time, but most of us start developing this skill when we are very young. One of the first things we learn to manage about ourselves is our expectations. Do not mistake managing expectations as the status quo. Most people have a very hard time learning to manage their own expectations. In the business world, managing your expectations is most important. You will have many opportunities to expect things to go a certain way, and of course they will not.

One of the expectations I have learned to manage is my ability to read what effect something might have on me. The tactic necessary to counteract and manage this situation is to be able to assess how much I can affect the situation. Most of us hyperactive types have this problem because we want to do everything quickly.

I like to accomplish things and see completion. This is the perfect setup for having my expectations exploited by my own personality. I often build up my hopes and have them come tumbling down because of my own miscalculations of how soon something should happen. One of the methods I use to counteract this inability to manage my expectations is to be able to have a lot of different events going on at the same time. When one fizzles out another can take its place.

Building your expectations toward a goal before it can be completed can be very dangerous. I became bored with a job assignment I was on, and I decided to find myself another job. I was making an above-average salary for the geographical area where I was living. I found a job opportunity that I thought would be a shoo-in for me. I became very excited about this opportunity and obsessed with getting the job. I interviewed and all went well. I started to divorce myself from my current job. Bad mistake! My performance dropped, and I started attracting my current management's attention. I was really fired up about changing companies. The company where I was interviewing decided to fill the position from within. I lost my edge in my current job for about six months, and it took me almost a year to recover.

Again, learning to manage yourself is very important. You will protect yourself from numerous disappointments if you can manage and motivate yourself. It is very important to be able to derail yourself if it becomes necessary. If you are a person like me, derailing may have to become a way of life. I can get going on a project that will consume resources and time quicker than even I could have guessed. I have also learned to assess my progress. I can stop or start a project when necessary. This allows me to be more productive on average. If I need to derail myself from one project, I always seem to have another to fall back on.

Once you can manage YOU, then you are ready to manage other resources. There are those of us who should stick with managing ourselves until we reach a level of demonstrated proficiency. You will know this has been completed when you start to hear yourself say, "Yes I have completed that!" Then, and only then, can you think of managing other things.

# Situation Management

As you learned to manage yourself, you probably discovered you were developing the skill to manage what was going on around you. I believe some of the best managers are those who can manage situations.

You will have numerous opportunities to manage what is happening around you. Earlier, we discussed staff assignments and their importance. One of the key things about staff assignments is that they give you the opportunity to manage situations. To me, business is a series of events and situations that transpire around making money. This is the perfect environment to have things go right and to have things go wrong.

Situations can be managed directly or indirectly. This means doing the work necessary to get something done—assess the problem, understand the measurements for a given situation to be completed, put in place the steps necessary to accomplish the work, staff the problem and gather the resources to work on the problem. Resources can be you, a pencil, paper, and a telephone. Then do whatever is necessary to remedy the situation. Check the solution to make sure it will satisfy the requirements.

I find situation management to be fun and challenging. The results usually come from the gratifying accomplishment of simple tasks. You must have these minimal skills in order to be able to call yourself a professional.

# Managing To The Side – Your Peers

After mastering situation management, your next opportunity to manage will probably be that of managing the people who work with you and/or around you. This is where your skills must be accompanied by controlled emotions and patience.

Dealing with people is what life is all about! People were created to relate to one another. Managing is a form of relating to others. This is not management in the sense of standing in the center of the ring, cracking a whip and watching people jump through hoops. We will soon get to that form of management. This type of management is very similar to situation management.

Being able to manage your peers is having the ability to assess situations and then motivate those who work with you to complete the work. This is done without a lot of fanfare. Gratification comes when tasks are completed and the work is done by all who are responsible.

When you first arrive in a company, you will often ask yourself, "Why am I doing this?" Did someone tell me to do this or did I just figure out what to do after someone told me something needed to be done?

You can observe some interesting dynamics of peer management when you watch prisoners work together. First of all, they are not highly motivated to work for an authority figure. In fact, the more the authority is applied, the more resistance there is, especially those who have been incarcerated for some length of time. There is not a lot of classroom training or instruction on the tasks to be completed. Training may be available on an as-needed basis. Most of the training is done on the job (OJT—on the job training). Most of the training that is accomplished is done by the peer group, those who have learned what is necessary to get things done. There is usually a leader who is not always dominant. There is a major influence in the group to get things done out of necessity, not because of many positive incentives.

What I have just described for you is not just a prison shop but a normal, small company's office bullpen. To make the analogy of the prison fit a large corporate office, you must add in an extensive training program and an elaborate incentive program. The group dynamics are very similar to the prison. One unique difference in office environments is that creativity is encouraged and often rewarded, depending on the company's culture.

Peer management is a natural phenomenon in the business world. You will learn to manage your peers and they will manage you. We Blacks are quite capable of garnering peer management skills. Your challenge will be not to become frustrated if you do not succeed at first.

One of the things that allows peer management to work effectively is people's tendency to want to trust and confide in one another. As you think about the group dynamics of a work environment, you will find there are the usual obstacles we face, such as mistrust and non-acceptance. You will just have to work through these as always. Talent and skill will get you through these obstacles. Oh, and don't forget patience!

All of the success factors should apply, as they do in all aspects of the business world. Making the proper assessment of what to do and when to do it is still a valid concern. There will be jockeying for position, and there will be competition. I challenge you to keep it healthy and working for you, not against you. I encourage you to play along until it is your turn to take the controls. I often ask for the jobs others shy away from because they give me a chance to exercise my skills and demonstrate what I can do. Talent and skill will win out most of the time. Peers will follow the leader or will do their part if motivated properly. Peer management can be of all participants at once or it can be of any one participant at any given time.

In team situations, a leader always emerges, even if it is a quasi-leader. The work will get done, and if you do a little more than others without alienating yourself, you will be successful. Working with your peers is a lot of fun, and gaining their respect is very gratifying.

One of the things that is devastating to peer management is adverse personalities. Since I have joined the business world, I have seen more personality clashes than in any other organizational structure. You will learn to spot personalities that complement your own. You will learn to avoid those that offend you. Dealing with people you like is always easier than dealing with people you do not like. It is easy to work with someone you like unless you realize they are not capable of keeping up their end of the bargain. It is detrimental to work with people you do not like, and this situation should be fixed as soon as it is identified.

Peer management will survive most other types of management. It comes about more naturally than other forms of management. Do not be afraid to take your turn at the helm. Do not abuse the position when it presents itself to you.

# Managing Down – Subordinates and Staffs

Understand one thing, it is hard to manage something you do not understand. So take time to understand what you are getting into before you grab the reins. Many people think managing people is easy; you just tell them what to do and they do it. Managing people is not easy. It is not for everyone and can be detrimental to an already successful career. There are more books, magazines and training programs written on the subject of managing people than you would care to know. You could probably attend every class and read every book on the subject and still be unsuccessful managing people if it is not your forte. And, it is one of the most important job functions.

The business world must have structure or it will fail. It will only have structure if it has organization. It will only have organization if it has people leading and managing people. One of the things I failed to learn early in my career is that a manager is a person responsible for managing something; the key word is 'responsible', in this case, that something happens to be people. Each and every person is different, and that means they must be managed differently. In developing a style of managing, this should be one of your biggest considerations.

Managing people is the ultimate and most challenging responsibility. The main reason this type of management poses so great a challenge is because people have the ability to think for themselves. The minute you interject someone who will challenge the thinking of others, you have created a major challenge to your management.

"God created all people equal!" True! But the business world tried to improve on God's original dictum and created the "ORG Chart."

There are, indeed, many ways to manage people; and they all work, given the proper situation, or fail, given the wrong one. I have successfully managed a group of people, and I have also struggled to manage the same group of people. Both situations were major marks of learning for me. Sometimes, I find people don't need to be told what to do. There are other times when you must provide guidance and leadership for people in your charge.

In order to manage people well, you must have very good people skills which are some of the same skills required to function well in the business world. The ability to listen and understand what people say is a key skill for good people management. The ability to control your anger is a very good skill. A large amount of patience will serve you well. The ability to articulate your thoughts into clear and concise statements is very valuable. No matter how clearly you state yourself, people will often confuse what you say to them if you are the one who is in charge.

I once had a young lady reporting to me who decided I was out to get her and I was not to be trusted. She was used to manipulating her last manager and appeared to be very good at managing her peers. No matter how hard I tried to convince her she was a valuable player on the team, she continued to convince herself I did not like her or her work. She was right about only one thing: I did not like her. But I did like her work. One afternoon, I asked her to come to my office to discuss a project she was working on. I attempted to tell her how well she had done on completing the project. During the discussion, she started to cry, and I was flabbergasted. The next day I awarded her a bonus during a meeting. She was utterly surprised and embarrassed. She avoided me for several days after receiving the award. I finally cornered her and congratulated her on the bonus. She finally realized I was not criticizing her work but was actually quite pleased with her work. It was a very good learning experience for me. The lessons I learned from this situation were to smile a lot and speak very little when a person has a perceived mistrust.

Good leadership skills are very important. Leadership skills are those skills that make people want to follow your lead. Being a good leader makes it a lot easier to manage people. All leaders are not good people managers. If people see you as a good leader, they will look to you for guidance and consultation. Good leaders are always aware of what is important to the people they are leading. They are able to build confidence in the people they lead. They are able to give directions. If they are able to give directions without being dictatorial, they can be good people managers.

A people manager must be able to make good

decisions. Do not make the mistake of thinking a decision must always be made quickly. If an employee situation warrants a quick decision, then by all means, make a quick decision. For the most part, people do not want a quick decision as much as they want an accurate decision. If people understand the process used to make a decision, they are more likely to be patient until it is made.

One of the most important requirements for managing people is the ability to interpret what the strategies and objectives of a business are. People look to their manager as a source of information. You are the company. What you say is what the company says. Take time to understand company objectives and be able to articulate the business to the people who work for you. You will gain a lot of trust if people feel they are being informed and kept up to date. This is a valuable set of skills to have, and they should be garnered, cherished and continually improved.

# Managing Up – Your Manager

As a professional, one of the things you are going to find challenging is the ability to relate to your manager: the ability to manage your manager. The ability to convince the person who is responsible for signing your paycheck that you are worth that paycheck. The ability to convince this person you understand what is expected of you. The ability to convince this person you have the company's interest at heart. Learning to manage your manager's expectations and perceptions is the most important thing you will ever do. The higher up you go in the corporate business structure, the more important this becomes.

Your manager usually cannot make you succeed or fail, but s/he can influence which direction you take. Your manager is definitely the person everybody else in the corporation will look to if they want to know how well you are doing. Your manager should have your best interests at heart. S/he will usually prioritize that interest in the following manner: an interest in self first (and this should not be a surprise to you), next, an interest in company objectives, then, an interest in your success in the company(if your manager is a good manager) and finally, an interest in getting the company's objectives accomplished by managing you. This is the normal priority for managers, and, for the most part, it should work to your benefit. There are many reasons for learning to manage your manager but the most important one of all is that you usually do not have much of a choice.

Good managers want you to manage them. What do I mean by manage them? There are lots of things to accomplish in a given work day, and there are almost always too few resources to get these things done. When you are a professional, your manager is another resource available to help you accomplish your assigned tasks. S/he is not there to supervise you but to manage you. Your manager usually has some level of authority that you do not have. There will be times when you will try to push some piece of paper through the organization. You may or may not know all the steps it takes to get it done, and you will run up against some internal corporate obstacle. This will be the time to bring in your manager. S/he should be able to advise you as to what direction to go or method to use in order to accomplish your goal.

In one of my job assignments, I liked putting on grandiose demonstrations for my customers. I truly liked exploring what was out on the horizon, what was inevitably going to be viable in the not-so-distant future. I always needed resources that were outside of my boundaries of power. This is when I would press my manager into action, and I usually did not stop there. There was one time when I had three levels of management involved in pulling off one of my projects. Remember, your manager usually has performed your job in some form or another and is experienced in using the company's resources, or "working the system." Your manager can help you get things done if you take time to properly manage her or him.

Getting your manager involved can prove very helpful in gaining access to the resources you will need to make a project successful. Once I had a manager who was very easy to manage. I spent a lot of time keeping him informed, and he usually had to sign final documents. He once told me, "Simms, the only thing you ever need me for is my signature."

Taking the time to involve your manager in a project that you are working on can make your manager look good.

Making your manager look good in front of peers or upper management will do wonders for your career advancement. Good managers take pride in the accomplishments of their people. Remember, your manager has a manager. A note to your manager's manager at the appropriate time can do wonders for your manager's career as well as your own. Your manager will want to make your projects successful if they provide visibility for the department or group s/he is managing.

Part of managing your manager is keeping him or her informed of what you are working on and accomplishing. NEVER, NEVER ALLOW YOUR MANAGER TO BE SURPRISED! If your manager has nine to ten people working for him, he usually cannot keep track of all the details. You should take on the responsibility of keeping your manager up-to-date on what you are doing. I prefer to do this in writing. This allows me to go back and refer to a document if there is ever any discrepancy about what I accomplished.

Most managers will require you to prepare some type of report on your accomplishments in a given time period. If your manager does not require something in writing, you should prepare something anyway. A lot of professionals make the mistake of trusting their manager's memory. This is a mistake! Managers are human too, and they will forget and occasionally become confused about who accomplished what within their units.

Once the report is written, make an appointment to review the report with your manager. Reports by themselves do not always provide a clear picture of all the details of an accomplishment. Be sure to highlight significant accomplishments. Patting yourself on the back is allowed in the business world, if done tastefully.

Learn what your manager's "hot buttons" are and try to push them as often as possible. If you know your manager is a stickler for being on time to meetings, try to be in your seat when your manager arrives. Managers are very good at making mental notes of who of their people are working to please them. However, do not make it too obvious, or you may alienate yourself from the rest of your department. If your manager likes to co-sign letters even though his or her signature is not required, take time to allow this. This is another way of making your manager aware of projects you are currently working on.

Managers are not always the friendly, helpful type; and you should take care to observe if your manager likes the way you go about getting things done. If you find your manager is not very helpful or does not like you, do not panic! This is truly your opportunity to manage the situation. Take time to look for what might be turning the manager off where you are concerned. Try not to return animosity to the manager, or you will lose this battle. Continue to work hard, and, at every opportunity, allow the manager to see you in a positive setting. If you feel you have done all you can to satisfy your manager, and s/he appears to be working against you, schedule some time to talk to the manager about your concerns. Managers love to resolve problems before they get out of hand. If this still does not clear the air between the two of you, it is time to go over her head. This should be a last resort. (Many companies have processes and procedures in place to handle such matters.) Never ask for a transfer out of a group or department without first settling the controversy. If you leave the group, and the controversy has not been settled, it may follow you to your next group. Or, it may be waiting for you when you get there. Managers confide in one another, and they compare notes on subordinates. This is one reason why it is very important to manage the perception of yourself within an organization.

Corporations have various tools for assessing managers' abilities to effectively manage their people. There are things such as management assessment programs (MAP) and opinion surveys. These tools are administered to employees annually or semiannually. They allow employees to provide feedback on the style and methods their managers employ. They are also a good means of providing feedback to managers who may not be aware they are affecting their subordinates a certain way. Do not use these tools to settle personal vendettas. Be strong enough to discuss problems face to face with your manager; it is the mark of a good professional.

Black professionals must learn to build skills to handle these types of situations. Because of the cultural differences and stereotypes that exist in the business world, we must take extra care in these situations. The good news is that there are more and more women entering the ranks of management who seem to have a sensitivity that men lack. They often take a little more time to understand situations. My hope is that there will be more Black managers in place as this century turns. This will allow a better workplace for Blacks in general.

# Management Tools

Managers have many valuable tools to assist them in properly utilizing the company's people resources. These tools also work to assist the manager in managing a group of employees equitably. They can assist the manager in being fair when assessing the work an employee is putting out for the company. Every good company will have some such procedure. Different companies may have different names for these tools, but their methodology will be very similar. In this section, I will describe the tools I am experienced with and have had the opportunity to administer.

### *Development Process*

The development plan is one of the most important tools a manager can administer to increase your value — as an employee — to the corporation. This is a plan to help you attain the position you want in a company. This is a document signed by you, your manager, and possibly your second-line manager. (Most corporations use their second-line management to insure equity by having them review things such as development plans.) It is an agreement between you and your manager of what s/he is going to do and/or allow you to do over a period of time to enhance your skills or build new ones. I also believe it is the one thing companies have in place to increase your personal worth to the company.

The plan usually starts out with a statement or objective you wish to accomplish for your personal and professional benefit. These statements can range from "I would like to become a vice president of a division of the company" to "I would like to continue to build my skills as a bionic, technical, synthetics specialist."

The next section of the plan will have strategies

aimed at building specific skills or gaining knowledge in a given area of expertise. These strategies usually say something to the effect of, "build knowledge in a key skill area."

The final section is activities with completion dates. These activities can range from attending a night class at a local college to being allowed to work in some other area of the business for some period of time in order to gain the experience to help you achieve your objectives.

I once had a Black colleague who had been successful for seven years in an office working in the field. When I arrived in the office, I asked him what were his plans for moving forward in the business. He replied, " I'm not sure." (You must know what you want from a company before you can ask them to do something for you.) I asked him what his development plan had in it. He was not sure. We discussed his options, and I counseled him on what should be included in his development plan. He went to his manager and had those things added to his plan. During the next few months, he and his manager executed the plan flawlessly. He was promoted the next year to a staff assignment, which was part of the plan, and then promoted to a management assignment the next year. This story has a happy ending, but there are others that end differently for many of us Blacks.

There are many African American professionals sitting around various corporations going nowhere because they are not sure what to do next. The colleague I described above could have been promoted out of that office in four years instead of eight. The only thing he was lacking was a good development plan that articulated where he wanted to go and what steps were necessary to get there. One final note: most large corporations require minorities and women to have current development plans in place at all times. They are usually valid for one year.

## *Performance Process*

This is a contract between the employee and the company administered by the immediate manager. This process and its end product, the performance plan, explain the objectives the corporation will expect you, as their employee, to accomplish. This is probably the most important document you will need to understand as an employee of a company. They are usually valid for one year. Most companies hold managers responsible for having some sort of a performance plan in place, one month after an employee is on board or has entered their department.

The performance plan is constructed by your manager using the criteria and job description for your particular job and level. This is the only document in the company that tells you, in great detail, what your job task assignments entail. A lot of companies allow their managers to write the document and then solicit input from the employee. When your manager presents you with a performance plan, be sure to review it thoroughly. You may challenge any responsibility you feel is unfair or unwarranted. Most managers work very hard to include the things you and the company think should be in the plan. If you find a plan to be overwhelming, the time to speak up is when you are asked to review it or provide input. Too often, people accept these plans as the gospel and are afraid to challenge them. Managers are usually very happy to have employees provide input into the plans.

The performance plan is usually broken up into several sections. There are usually several sections on job tasks. There is usually a section on professionalism. These sections can be weighed by relative importance to one another. I always like to see a job assignment letter attached to the plan. For example, if a manager wants to hold you responsible for a certain duty in a given assignment, s/he can outline this in a job assignment letter. Joe is responsible for supporting sugar distribution to departments X, Y, and Z. Sally is responsible for sugar distribution to departments R, S, and T, and so on.

The employee is responsible for understanding the plan in all its detail. Again, challenge the plan before it is considered final. A plan is in final form when you receive a final copy. Your manager should make you aware it is the final copy. Once you have a copy of the plan in final form, you are responsible for executing the plan to the best of your abilities. Many professionals receive the plan, read it once and stick it in a drawer until it is time to have the formal appraisal review. (We will discuss the appraisal process in the next section.) You should read the plan thoroughly to make sure you are aware of all the things your manager is holding you responsible for. Then you should put it in a file very close to you. In the front of the nearest desk file drawer is a good place, not because you have to look at it often, but because it is that important a document.

I often look at my plan to remind me of what my manager and I have agreed my job is. I once had a manager who put very detailed activities in my performance plan. Later, she informed me she was going to appraise me, and I had not looked at my performance plan recently. Upon reading my plan, I found there was a control book she wanted me to put together, and I had not done it. I was very happy I took that one last peek and got the control book completed just a few days before she was supposed to appraise me. What made this more significant was that she ended up promoting me before she appraised me. The appraisal was a good one.

## Appraisal Process

This is the process that will measure you, the employee, against those objectives that were set forth in the performance process. This is where your manager tells you how well you performed over some agreed period of time against the set of objectives that were spelled out in the performance plan.

The appraisal process can be administered in many different ways. Good managers will provide you with feedback every week for your first 90 days and then will move to a quarterly schedule. If you are not getting feedback from your manager on a timely basis, ask for it. Sometimes managers get very busy and forget to take time to provide feedback. If a manager is often too busy to provide you with feedback on your performance, s/he is not a very good manager. I stated earlier, managers do not like surprises, and neither do we employees, especially when it pertains to our performance.

The final, written, formal appraisal is usually prepared by the manager at the end of the performance period of one year. If an employee is new to a company, some companies may have a manager appraise an employee after six months. Appraisals are written by your immediate manager and reviewed by your second-line manager. Your manager will make an appointment with you for about an hour.

Appraisal time is a time to pay close attention to what your manager has to say. They will usually give you very candid feedback, and you should learn something about yourself. Be prepared for constructive criticism. If you are the best professional in the world, there should still be room for improvement. When you walk away from an appraisal, you should feel really good about yourself, or you should have an understanding of what it takes to improve your performance. If you have not been performing well, then be prepared to receive feedback of that nature. Try not to fool yourself into thinking you have performed better than you have.

Black professionals must take extra care not to be over sensitive during appraisals and any other constructive criticism-type meetings. This is the time to take notes on your strengths and weakness from a manager's point of view. If you do not agree with everything that is said, that is to be expected. Be sure you continue to stay professional about matters. If you think you are being treated unfairly, do not sign the appraisal during the meeting. If you choose not to sign the appraisal, it will probably be reviewed by your second-line manager who may then want to discuss it with you. (In some companies this is a form of going above your manager's head. Be aware of the consequences.)

The performance plan and the appraisal are very important. People are selected to be promoted and given salary increases based on merit. These processes are part of the merit pay evaluation system. Do not take any of this process for granted, or you may find yourself very unhappy. If you perform well, expect to receive accolades and praises for your work.

## Salary Administration Process

Most companies pay you according to the years you are assigned to a particular level. The performance rating you receive during the appraisal process is used as a multiplier in a grid system in order to calculate your salary increases. Salary increases in most companies are given annually. There are corporations who administer pay raises semi-annually. The amount of the increase can be anywhere from 2% to 15%, on average. It depends on the job, the assignments and the other factors we discussed earlier.

Keep in mind, most companies use the merit system which allows managers to pay for performance. You should understand how this is being administered in your company. Salary increases are something we all work to get and yet are afraid to discuss. Large corporations make it taboo to discuss wages amongst peers. Here is a secret: most corporations have no written rules to stop you from discussing salaries. Salary information for different job assignments and levels is usually available from your manager and should not be unavailable for your viewing and understanding. Most of this information is published in some company document.

Black professionals are often afraid to discuss salary with anyone. Discussing salary information can both help you and hurt you. You should make sure you are as informed as possible about the salary program in the corporation you choose to work for; make sure you are being treated fairly. Understanding all of these processes helps to equip you to be as prosperous as possible in a company, especially when seeking a raise or promotion. The more you know, the happier you will be.

As we dare enter the world of business, we had better be prepared to manage any and all aspects of it. Do not miss any opportunity to grab a piece of the business and manipulate it for your success. Management is a way of life in the business world, and it leads to the ultimate success — running some part of the show or gaining access to making decisions. We should be up to it!

# Chapter

# 12

# Corporate Politics

"**P**olitics" in today's world can be defined as "convincing a person what you say, think, or believe is the way it is." Politics always exist throughout any organization of intelligent people.

From a professional point of view, politics can be defined as an awareness of what it takes to accomplish a particular task. There are many business people who would say it is your ability to be shrewd and/or clever or your ability to be tactful, especially when promoting your viewpoint, whether its a tactful, especially when promoting your viewpoint, whether it's a corporate agenda or a personal agenda. Politics often enters neither negative nor positive until they are first viewed in context. There are definite "do's and don'ts" in the world of business politics which often become company policies. The management aspects of a corporation will always include politics. When you are dealing with people, politics are inevitable.

Corporate politics are analogous to mighty ocean waves on which you and I are the surfers. The object of the sport is to ride the wave at a point where you can continue to stay afloat for as long as possible. You know you cannot control the wave; but you also know if you find the right spot, you can ride this wave until you reach a place of satisfaction. Surfers call this place of satisfaction "hanging ten." I call this place of satisfaction a point of "realized success." If you convince yourself it is not necessary to participate in the politics of a corporation, you have just relegated yourself to a "point of complacency."

"Politics" is one of the biggest motivational tools that

exist in the corporate structure. If a corporation does not have a healthy political structure, it will probably not experience much growth. If the management does not subscribe to a political structure, the corporation is not being driven to success. In spite of popular belief, politics allow corporations to continue to operate. How well the politics are played out decides how well the corporation will operate.

Most corporations come into existence through someone's dreams and well-conceived plans. If more than one person becomes a part of the corporation, a political structure is born. The size of a corporation will only make a difference in the complexity of the politics that must be played to get situations resolved. Every major corporation in the world has some form of a political structure that serves a purpose of checks and balances. Policies and procedures put forth by the governing body are usually the rules used by the political players of a company.

With all that said, why does everybody deny they are political? All anyone wants to do is to get the job done. If you think you have no time for politics, you have placed yourself at a serious disadvantage. People who claim not to be interested in politics are the people you must watch and worry about; they are the ones who make the rest of us think politics is a large negative force, always getting in the way of progress. They are what I call the "negative constituents" of a corporation. They are also the reason why you as a professional must understand politics in your business environment.

# Understanding Politics

The political structure of a corporation is different for each corporation. It can be compared to a person's fingerprints; we all have them, but each of us has a unique set. Understanding the political structure of a corporation is about as important as the payroll department knowing your name, rank, and serial number. Knowing the politics of a corporation is knowing how a corporation collectively thinks. It encompasses all of the internal workings of a corporation. If you can acquire this knowledge and understanding of a corporation, you can become a part of that thinking.

To exist in a corporation, you must become an active

part of the corporation. You must be able to evaluate what is good for the corporation and what is not. Even in your small sphere of involvement, the corporation depends on its pieces to survive and thrive. Most corporations that grow into mammoth monsters were once two- and three-person shops. Most of the major corporations of today started in somebody's garage or the trunk of their car. Great corporations have come from people's kitchens and closets. If you become a vital part of the corporation, it will mean succumbing to its political structure. If you want to become a part of it, then you surely must become a student of it.

Understanding the politics of a corporation means your survival as well. Most people become disenchanted with a company that does not seem to think about where they as individuals fit in. This is where we must change our thinking. We must realize we are only going to fit in if we choose to do so. We are now back to square one—understanding the politics.

Again, the political structure is the glue that keeps the corporation together and allows it to feed itself. Every time a new person, place or thing becomes a part of the corporation, the corporation has to account for this growth or addition. The political structure governs these activities.

The politics of a corporation is what lets you exist as you learn what does and does not work. A good political structure provides survival training for its members. I had a colleague who was top notch when it came to getting his work done. He was well respected by his peers. He had a manager who did not subscribe to office politics and who was therefore not very good at teaching him office politics. My colleague was annoyed by what was expected of him by upper management and just wanted to be left alone to do his job. And that was what he got; he was left alone to do his job. He then decided he wanted to be promoted. He was put up for promotion by his manager. His manager was told he was not ready to be promoted and should wait another year. (My colleague had been at the same level for many years already.) Everyone else who arrived in the business with him had already been promoted. He did not get promoted during that year.

My colleague's manager left the office and a new manager was put in place who was politically savvy. With delight, the new manager inherited the challenge of promoting my colleague. The first thing the new manager did was to help my friend understand the political climate in the office. She put a plan in place to get him more visibility with upper management. At every opportunity she encouraged him to get upper management involved in his projects. My colleague realized how important it was to understand the politics of his environment and became a student. Not only did he get the promotion he wanted, he was also the model used by upper management for someone who could get things done, which he had been doing all along. Understanding the politics of the organization obviously made a difference.

Take care not to abuse the political structure. Political structures often have fail-safe mechanisms built in that can destroy you. Once you understand a political structure, it can easily be abused and often is. Political structures in the business world are resilient and usually will expose those who abuse it. Examine the following story:

The Dog on the Log Syndrome — A dog was crossing a river with a thick, red, juicy steak in his mouth. He walked onto a log and immediately noticed another dog with a thick, red, juicy steak in its mouth walking on the log. The first dog opened his mouth to take the juicy steak away from the other dog and immediately dropped the steak it had in its mouth into the water. The steak sank to the bottom of the river. What the dog had witnessed was the reflection of himself with the steak in his mouth. Make sure you know what you have in your mouth before you open it.

This story can teach us a lot about corporate politics. Too often people are not satisfied with what they have accomplished in the business world. They seek more before they are ready to handle more or before they understand the full politics of the matter. They try to grab a bigger piece of the action and end up losing all they had. Politics can work for you, and it can work against you; and it almost always protects itself.

# Making Politics Work For You

Corporate politics is usually seen as a negative force by people who do not understand it and by those who do not know how to make it work for them. Politics is bringing the agenda to your side of the table, becoming a part of the existing agenda, or gaining the opportunity to present your agenda. I have had the opportunity to observe several people who have made company politics work on their behalf.

I once indirectly worked for a gentleman who understood very well the political system of the corporation that employed us. He knew the system so well he became a policy maker himself. He went as far as to put the company's initials on his license plate. In his case, he was very obvious in making the political structure work for him. In this particular corporation, it was customary to do a staff assignment before you received a first-line manager's position. This gentleman went straight into a first-line manager's position from a field assignment. In the corporate world, this is known as receiving a "battlefield" promotion. He finessed his way into a wonderful assignment where he knew there would be success. He worked hard at knowing all the key executives and always managed to get assigned to special projects that had high visibility.

When he heard from my immediate manager (who was his co-manager) that I was trying to get promoted, he said to me, "You are not the only one working on getting promoted out of here." He was promoted to a staff manager several months before I followed in a staff assignment. While on the staff assignment, I again had an opportunity to work with him on a very high visibility assignment. He politicked his way into being the manager responsible for chauffeuring the executives back and forth between the event and their hotel rooms. I heard one of the high level executive's wives call him by his first name.

When it was time for me to be promoted to my first-line manager's job, I called him. He knew all the details and helped me get the job. He was promoted to a second-line manager's job after only being in the staff manager's job for about a year. He was known as a great politician, and everybody seemed to accept it.

This gentleman was known as a "fast tracker." (As I explained earlier, a fast tracker is one who can get promoted very quickly from one job to the next.) These people are illusionists; they can make people see and believe what they want them to see and believe using the political structure of the corporation as their props. You always believe they are the next in line to get promoted because of who and what they know. They do not mind taking risks and will do things others are afraid to do. But, they have learned how politics can work for them.

In a meeting is where you can very easily observe the political dynamics of a company or a department. When you are in a meeting, pay attention to who controls the meeting. I am not necessarily talking about the person chairing the meeting. It is not always the loud and/or strong personality that controls a meeting. Sometimes it is the one most respected for his or her prowess. Sometimes it is the one who knows just the right time to raise their voice or lower their voice or keep silent. Meetings are a good place to learn business politics. These meetings are not necessarily formal meetings. They can be impromptu meetings that are held at lunch or near the water cooler.

Take time to learn the appropriate meeting etiquette for your work environment. Do not be loud and boisterous when everyone else is being soft spoken. You might start out by asking well-thought-out questions. When you decide to say something, keep it pertinent and meaningful. Do not be overbearing, even if you know you are right and everyone else is wrong. I struggled in this area when I first arrived on the corporate scene. I wanted so badly to be a participant. You will be anxious to participate, but take time to learn what works and what does not. There will be times when people will solicit your opinion in order to put you on the spot or to test your knowledge. Do not become the object of someone's political tactics. Do not be in a hurry to show what you know. When you feel comfortable with the political dynamics of your environment, then go for it.

If you arrive late to a meeting, be very apologetic. If you know you are going to be late for a meeting, inform someone who will also be attending the meeting. This will demonstrate your professionalism.

A good corporate politician tries to position him or herself to become visible. Office staff assignments are valuable for visibility. These assignments are usually above and beyond the call of duty. Be sure you have completed the work you are being held accountable for before taking on more work. Never take on an assignment you do not have time to complete unless that is understood up front.

There are staff assignments that are easy, fun and simple to perform. If the office is having a big meeting, take responsibility for organizing all or a part of it. If an executive is coming to town, ask to be the one to pick the exec up from the airport. It is a great opportunity to have a corporate executive all to yourself and have them learn to know you by name. Hopefully, they will be impressed with your professionalism. Professionals who want to be on the fast track make a point of taking on these types of assignments.

When you are the junior professional in your department, you will be expected to perform some of the more mundane tasks. Making copies for office executives can bring you in close contact with them. It also shows your willingness to contribute and be a team player.

Helping the office secretary is always a nice thing to do, and it is politically savvy. Secretaries are some of the most informed people in the office. They are truly the gate keepers to most executives and can get you in to see an executive when no one else is allowed. This is true not only for the secretaries in your office but also for the secretaries of your clients and customers. Trying to get in to see a busy exec who is a client or customer can prove to be almost impossible at times. If you have an "in" with the exec's secretary, it can be a walk in the park.

The executive interview, a meeting between a high level executive and a professional subordinate in the organization, is a powerful political tool. It is usually set up by your manager. If you become aware that an executive is going to be visiting the office and you did not volunteer to pick him or her up from the airport, this is another way to get time with the executive. These meetings can be invaluable and career-building. Be sure to prepare for these meetings. Be sure to learn what this exec's job functions are and his full title and name. It is embarrassing to have to go through a whole meeting trying to avoid calling an executive by his or her name because you do not know it or have forgotten it. I write the name on a piece of paper and stick it in my pocket. Asking for their business card can be flattering and allows you to keep their name in front of you during the interview. If you are politically aware, you will know their name long before they arrive.

Another form of the executive interview is the executive round table. This is where more than one person is allowed to sit and discuss issues with an executive. These meetings are good for allowing people to know who you are and can provide you with a chance to be exposed to the exec as well as your colleagues. If a very high-ranking executive pays a visit to your office, a round table allows several people to be exposed to the executive. If you are invited to participate in a round table or any other executive meetings, you have probably been identified as someone who does a good job in the department. Managers like to expose their good people to visiting executives. This is all part of corporate politics.

A political tool I have learned to use is to be a little controversial in some of the things I do. Being a little controversial can be good for the career, but you must understand how and when to use this tool. Not always going with the flow shows you are a creative thinker, a free thinker, and you can stand on your own. However, this must be tempered by good judgment, common sense, and sensitivity.

I have often chosen not to do things in the usual fashion. This is truly advanced politics. I have also had this type of politics backfire on me. I once earned the reputation of being "rough around the edges" which was not a good way to be thought of. It followed me for a couple of years. When I saw it was starting to work against me, I changed my style.

To continually be successful, you must continue to adapt to the business environment around you. This is where understanding how a corporation thinks is a major value. I discussed some of this when I discussed the corporate culture. The politics of a corporation is embedded in its cultural make-up and is a part of its survival mechanism. You, as a part of a corporation, must be equipped with similar survival skills. Too often we separate ourselves from the corporation. It becomes the corporation versus us, and we become alienated by the corporation's political make-up.

Black professionals must find ways to take advantage of the political structure of the corporation to the point that you become a vital part of the corporate structure. Most Blacks are turned off by all politics because it always seems to work against us. In this, we are our own worst enemy.

We must continue to find ways to move higher into the political structure of the corporation. That brings us back to becoming a decisionmaker, one who sets policy and direction for a business structure. We have no choice but to try and make it work on behalf of African-American professionals. We must become insiders in order to become powerful.

Work to gain a political sense of what makes a team player in your business environment. There are major requirements that must be fulfilled to become an insider. Loners in the business world do not often do very well. Most people want to like the people they do business with. A warm, friendly, politically astute and knowledgeable person is what is expected. Being able to interact in the expected manner is necessary.

Business protocol is easy to learn and is necessary for upward mobility. This is another area where we African-Americans must become students. We must ace this course. Because we are considered different, we must work to show we can fulfill the expectations. Protocol is not something you will be able to change. You will either subscribe or you will be an outsider.

If you study the government's political structure, protocol is obvious and can almost make you dizzy. One of the ways government officials must be proficient is to do what their constituents expect. This works in very much the same way between you and your management or you and your colleagues. I see protocol as your ability to meet the expectations of the policy-setting party. Of course, the ultimate thing to do is to become the one who establishes the protocol. If we are going to fully participate in the ceremony of business professionalism, we must learn and earn the authority to do this.

# The Rumor Mill – Corporate Hot Line

One of the best communication systems I have ever witnessed is the corporate "rumor mill." It is quite capable of handling as much information as can be levied onto it. It spreads throughout most corporations, and it provides information of all types. In my opinion, a healthy rumor mill can be very valuable to the professionals of a corporation.

I would guess more corporate information is communicated through the rumor mill than any other communications vehicle. I have learned of more organizational changes through the rumor mill than I have from an international corporate informational network. The telephone, coffee machine, water cooler, and lunch dates are some of the most widely used stations for information exchange. I have been on the East Coast of the United States and learned of something that happened in my office back on the West Coast.

The wonderful thing about the rumor mill—it is "user friendly." It can be a political tool extraordinaire.

When you are trying to get promoted, the corporate rumor mill can be very helpful in putting yourself on the market. You can leak information to your colleagues that you would like to be promoted. Your manager will pick this up from the mill and feel the urge to actually make it happen for you, especially if you are a good performer.

I have seen the corporate rumor mill actually police the corporation and help communicate corporate policy. For example, an individual was selling jewelry on company time. The individual was warned not to sell anything on company time. The individual stopped selling the jewelry openly and tried to sell the jewelry on lunch hours and breaks. The rumor mill carried the message of the selling activity. Management became aware of the activity and fired the individual.

The corporate rumor mill works best when you are a subscriber and an occasional supplier. If you put too much information on the mill, you just might become the owner of the mill and that is not good for your career. A politically savvy person uses good judgment and political awareness in how to benefit from using the rumor mill.

# The Power Tower

No two individuals are ever truly equal in a corporation! Even if two individuals hold the same job title, pay code, and/or job description, one will achieve a superior status over the other in what I call the "Power Tower."

The Power Tower is made up of several components. The Power Base is where you must first learn how to become one of the influential many. These people are not necessarily the decisionmakers, but they are the people who make up a big part of the politics of a corporation. They are not the policy setters, but they are often the ones who accept or reject what is being put in place.

I have been a part of this base in several corporations. You can become a part of this base by being politically aware of what the corporation is doing. You then subscribe to the parts of the policies that apply to you. These policies can be written or merely the political understandings that go on in a corporation.

People in the Power Base do not always know they are in the Power Base. People who are known for their peer leadership are usually ones who are a part of this base. They have a tendency to be in the right place at the right time because they do things in a fashion that places them there. First-line management may or may not be in the base. More than likely they were in the base at one time or another. You can move in and out of the Power Base and not necessarily at will. You can be forced out of the Power Base when people decide you are not one of the "difference makers" or you are a perceived stumbling block.

If you become a part of the base and you are fully aware of your position and the capabilities you have as a part of the base, you experience a good thing. You are probably very happy with your career selection and potential. This does not necessarily mean you are content with your current job assignment or the company you work for. You are probably influential among some set of your colleagues, which is a requirement to be a part of the base. If you are aware of your position, you are in a prime position to elevate yourself higher in the tower.

The Power Tower has "Power Trusses" which are people who are fully aware of their position in the tower. These people are influential, and they know who and/or what to influence in order to get things accomplished. I once worked with a young woman who understood her position in the corporation better than anyone I had ever had the opportunity to observe. She based her mode of operation on being politically aware of the things that were taking place around her. She was often sought out by upper management for her opinion. She was always being offered assignments that positioned her to be a part of the Power Tower. She used to say, "I am empowered by my customers." She often challenged upper management. She taught her people to do whatever it takes to keep the customer happy. I once heard her tell one of her employees if the company did not allow her to spend money on a customer, then she would pay for it herself. Once she made this known to management, she never had to do it. Another employee had a situation arise and he used the same line in a business memo. It worked for him as well. Most of the things she was able to accomplish were centered around manipulating the corporation to better support her customers.

She was truly a "truss" in the Power Tower. The only reason she did not move higher in the tower was because she made a personal commitment to her family. She took herself off the fast track and joined the "mommy track." (The mommy track is for women who have a career and have decided to have a family as well. They base career decisions around the needs of their family.)

The Power Tower has a "Power Tip" which is usually made up of people who are not only aware of their position in the tower but also politically able to influence the direction of the corporation. They do not necessarily have to be high up in the management chain or even a part of the management structure. If they are high up in the management chain, they are probably a de facto part of the tip. Those who are part of the Power Tip are the "movers and shakers" of a corporation. Large companies cannot survive without this part of the political power structure.

There are very few Black professionals in The Power Tip, although our numbers are increasing. Our biggest problem is gaining access to the requirements for those positions. The requirements allow one to politic their way into these positions. I do not believe they are blatantly hidden from us; however, I do believe they are not displayed so we may take advantage of them.

Whenever politics is involved, there will be gamesmanship with very high stakes. The biggest obstacle for Black professionals is to be allowed to make the mistakes that prepare you for access to the Power Tip. These experiences help you become familiar with the various strategies that are employed by the players of the Power Tip.

When we Blacks realize the amount of risk and energy required to play in these games, we often back away from the table. Those of us who try to embrace the rules usually have little support for our agendas. The Power Tip is a lofty place to be for all professionals involved, no matter what color you are or what walk in life you are taking. In order to get access, we are going to have to fully indoctrinate ourselves into what makes a business successful.

Another problem we face when we get to a point where we are ready to embark on these lofty positions is that we leave the company and start our own businesses. This is good on the one hand and bad on the other. Having our own business allows us to be owners of small businesses and make a few dollars, but we are usually resource-constrained. In the corporate environment, the resources are plentiful, and this allows us to accomplish big things. When we are out on our own, we can be successful, but we lack the bigness necessary to make big league power plays.

The Power Tower also has "Power Boundaries" which are necessary to stay balanced. Anytime you have a political structure, there is the necessity for "Power Balancing." If you allow too many players to gain too much influence, you will have too much contention. Corporations today are trying very hard to implement "participative management" which allows managed contention. Contention management is one form Power Boundaries can take.

Corporate cultures are having to change drastically in order for these types of measures to work. Corporate cultures are also having to change because of global competitive influences. Even the power of a CEO is bound. Today's CEO is far less powerful than the CEOs of the Seventies. They can be taken out of a job just as fast as they were put into it.

Some of these boundaries are clearly defined in the various instruments of the corporation. Some of the boundaries are understood and agreed upon through "gentlemen's agreements."

There are people in the Power Tower who do "Power Plays." There will be alignment of various factions within the Power Tower, a "pooling of power", if you will. Imbalances can force the tower to lean one way or another. Power struggles will often arise because of differences of opinions. Thus, you will find Power Boundaries become very important and need to be established on a continual basis.

A successful Power Tower will be one where the boundaries are clearly defined and enforced through cultural roots. However, the deeper something is embedded in the culture, the harder it is to change, when change becomes necessary.

The Power Tower can have "Irritants" who do not subscribe to the political structures within corporate structures. These people either attempt to overthrow the structure or eventually get pushed out of the structure. Oh yes, they are very much a part of the structure. They are the people who think politics is an unnecessary evil. They usually fight it at every turn of the crank. We Blacks have often been irritants in the government's political structures; and it has paid off for us.

We do not want to be irritants; we want to be players in the Power Tower. The irritants can be compared to fleas on a dog. They are indeed on the dog and may be seen as a part of the dog's environment. But, all the dog wants to do is get rid of them one by one, and it will constantly scratch the itch until it is gone. The dog will scratch hard enough to make itself bleed if that is what it takes. The Power Tower will do the same thing in order to survive, or it will die trying.

# Chapter

# 13

## Competing On The Corporate Front

*A* capitalist society breeds "competition" of all types. Competition allows the strong to survive and the weak to die. This may sound very dismal at its first hearing, but it promotes a strong society in the end. It allows society to utilize its resources in the most efficient way. Competition can often be beneficial to all participating parties. It becomes a negative factor when society allows any one competitor to dominate all others. Domination always lurks on the horizon of competitive situations, and it is this factor that drives humans to want to participate. We do not necessarily want to be dictators, but we want to be the chosen or accepted leader in whatever we are doing.

Here is where American business enters the picture with great thrust. Corporate America's first order of business is survival. In order to survive, a business must continue to build a competitive advantage. This advantage will insure viability and stability of a business. Most corporations spend a significant amount of their time and resources trying to remain healthy and competitive. Businesses start and fail every day based on their ability to compete in their respective markets and industries.

Here is where you, the professional, come into play. As I have stated over and over, a corporation is only going to be as good as the people who are a part of it. It is only going to be as competitive as its professionals. These professionals must strive to understand what is necessary to create a company that is competitive without sacrificing the strengths of its personnel. There must be people who can lead, analyze, effectively dispense resources, foster teamwork and promote healthy competition. These people must know how to reward success brought about through competition.

This all boils down to creating the right environment for people like you and me to compete effectively. Our first order of business is to find a place where we can learn the competitive nature of a business environment, a place that will allow us to utilize all of the factors we discussed above. This place must provide personal benefits for all of its professionals. If we can learn to compete on an individual basis, we will more than likely be able to learn to compete as a vital part of the corporation. Most people do not understand what is required to be a part of a competitive corporate structure. Often, professionals fail because they select an environment that is not conducive to their personal abilities. The business environment must allow the professional to build a competitive edge.

In a school environment, where most people have their first experience with competition, it is understood on an event by event basis. College kids understand what grading on a curve means to their personal GPA. They approach each test with the attitude that they must beat someone out if they are going to be competitive. They often bring this approach with them into the business world, and this type of competitive thinking does not work as well in the business environment.

Often in a corporation, you must help your colleagues become competitive as much as you must compete with them. Because of the delayed feedback system used by the corporate world, new professionals are often confused about how success is being measured. The paycheck is not seen as a measure of success or equal to the "B+" they used to receive in school. They must now learn to measure success as it applies to the corporation, as the corporation attempts to compete. This learning usually takes place during their first year in a corporation.

We Blacks are truly at a disadvantage here. We have not had the opportunity to gain the experience we need, and we are faced with learning how to compete. But, we have rapidly entered a decade where we will get the chance to participate and gain that experience. Our challenge is to challenge the status quo to allow us the time and resources to become competitive. This is one reason why I recommend starting out in a large corporation. The large corporation will be more tolerant of mistakes. It will provide the resources required to learn and gain a personal competitive edge. I utilized every training program, seminar, and class that was made available to me in my first few years in corporate America. These classes allowed me to build my personal skills as well as learn what the business was all about. Out of all of this, I gained a thirst to know more and started to compete, even before I knew I was competing.

Once you have found a place that allows you to compete, you will be able to contribute to a business. Your contribution will help a business get its share of its market place. It is now time to become the BEST! This is a quest that I will continue to preach to young Black professionals for as long as I have breath. If there is anything we should become obsessed with, this is it: becoming the BEST at whatever we attempt to do. This cannot be a passing attitude.

Once we were allowed to compete, we became the best athletes in the world! Sports figures such as Kareem Abdul Jabbar and Michael Jordan have shown us we can become a legend in our own time. Whitney Houston has shown us we can become the best musicians, if allowed. Bill Cosby has shown us we can become the best actor if allowed. And, Barry Rand has shown us we can become the best business professionals, if we are allowed to participate. Being a participant is the first step to competing. We have been a participant in the business world for the last twenty years. It is now time to compete.

# Trust and Confidence

One of the most phenomenal things that will be expected of you in the business world is that you be trustworthy and a confidant. People want to work with people they feel they can trust. People want to work with people they can share their ideas with and maybe even their secrets. The business world is the last place you would think would require such high moral standards. But if we go back to how most businesses got started, prior to large corporations, we quickly get a sense of why. One person had an idea, another had a few dollars saved, they put the idea with the dollars, and a business was born. Maybe it was a person bringing vegetables from their farm to a friend who would sell them at the local town market. Maybe it was a family who knew if they worked hard, trusted and supported one another, they could make an honest dollar. There were no instruments of incorporation or written partnerships. People came together and shared ideas. Business deals were set in motion by a good hearty smile, a twinkle of excitement in their eyes, and a solid handshake.

The carryover of the patriotic American value system is still prevalent in the business world today. Even the essence of Christian standards are a part of the business environment—waning, but a part. As hard as it is to conceive, we still choose our presidents based on their moral character. They can send us to war or spend all of our tax dollars, and, as long as they do not publicly cheat on their wives or get caught directly lying to us, we will tolerate them. This carries over to American business. You, as a business professional, will be held accountable for your actions.

Trust is a funny thing. We eat food in restaurants and never see whether the cook is a man, woman, Asian, or Ugandan. We simply trust they properly prepare the food we eat. In the business world, we may know a person for ten years and not allow them to ever see our confidential files. Why? The answer is simple—competition. We do not want them to know any more than they need to know within our business setting. We may ask a colleague to stand in for us or provide an excuse for why we are away from our post of duty. But, we will not give them access to our files. We drive down a busy freeway in a strange city. We trust that everyone will drive in their appropriate lane until they get to their destination. In the office we will not tell a colleague of 15 years how we discovered a new process for isolating errors in a computer program for fear they may want to share the credit.

Trust in the business world is fostered through mutual agreement. We decide what is to be entrusted into our colleagues hands. Professionals spend a lot of time trying to decide who they can trust and who is not to be trusted.

Confidence is even stranger. People must learn to have confidence in you and you in them. Confidence is not something you bestow on a colleague easily; it is something they must earn. I have learned to trust some people overnight because I need their assistance. Confidence, I find, comes more slowly and is harder to build. Confidence is often based on emotional experiences. People must have a lot more information about a person before they build confidence in them. It is easy to lose trust in someone, but I find it hard to lose confidence in someone. Once confidence is lost in someone, it is hard to build back to its original level.

Having trust and building confidence creates unique challenges for the business professional. It takes time and repeated experience. People grow to trust people, they see other people trust. They build confidence in individuals they have spent time with or have seen being reliable and trustworthy. You must find what it will take for others to build confidence in you. It takes hard work to make a management team believe they can trust you. It takes your being efficient and reliable.

Helping people as much as you can will allow people to trust you. If a person feels individually helped by you, they are surely going to trust you. As a Black, these attributes are of great importance. People in the business world today want to believe in people and to build their team. They want to work with those who are known to carry their share of the load. Teamwork is important. Look for assignments that will allow you to foster trust and confidence for yourself and others.

As you compete in the business world, you are going to want to trust people more than you need to. Take care where you lay your trust. Do not give it out without people proving they deserve it. There will be many opportunities to show trust. Make sure you do not become easy prey for your competitors. Some people will try to use you if they think you are the resource necessary to help them get what they want. Sometimes people's motives are hard to figure out. There will come times when you think you have a trust relationship in tact, and you will be disappointed. You should never get to the point where you trust anyone in the business world enough to surrender your "wits and guts."

# Don't Get Mad – Get Smart

Competing on the corporate front will pose many challenges, and none will be more career-threatening than wearing your emotions on your shoulder. African-Americans are expected to be militant and hard to manage. We have lived with this throughout our history in America. This is an image I have personally set out to change, starting with myself.

The forces of the Black Chip can be released in many ways, especially when provoked. This, again, is not to be thought of as right or wrong. We must make the Chip something we can use for the forward progression of Black professionals. However, we know it can manifest itself in very negative ways. Here is where we get to display our professionalism and wisdom.

There will be many opportunities to feel left out, neglected, overlooked, and segregated. This is the time to dig deep within yourself, grab all your "essence-of-success" resources and come out fighting. This time the fight is not won through physical aggression. The fight is won through skill and knowledge. Out-think your opponents.

Knowing your strengths and weaknesses will allow you to deal with all types of challenges. If you know when to use the appropriate body language to send the right signals, you are smart. If you know when to challenge a colleague (competitor) on an issue in a business-like manner, you are smart. If you understand the issues of a business transaction, you are smart. If you are the deal-maker and not the one being dealt with, you are smart. If you are the one in control of the situation and have it well in hand, you are smart. If your eyes start to roll around in their sockets, perspiration starts to bead up on your brow, your tongue gets a little heavy in the back of your throat, and you feel you have had enough, you are angry! You should find a reason to stop whatever is going on and leave the room until you can recompose. It has happened to me, and it will happen to you!

Dealing with adversity within the business world is inevitable for all of its participants. When money is the compelling reason to merit action, differences of opinions will occur. You must learn to manage adversity, just as you must learn to manage your day-to-day activities. The key is to not become emotional. If you find yourself losing control, you have lost your ability to manage the situation. If your colleagues realize that it is very easy to ruffle your feathers, they will use it every chance they get. It will be your weakness, and your weakness is their advantage.

Emotional control is a challenge for all people; it is that part of us that makes us a little higher than the gallant cockroach. It is part of our ability to reason. Being able to reason also means being able to be unreasonable. If we are to harness the power of the business universe for our success, it must be done with super-intelligence. We as Black professionals must learn to analyze the environment and then set the game plan of the hour. This is what getting smart is all about. If we lose emotional control, we have lost the game. This is true in any game you play. The team that wins is the team that remains in control and executes their plan.

If you find yourself being challenged in a way that is uncomfortable to you, take a step back from the game and re-think your strategy. I have often left a meeting wondering what I accomplished. I went away pondering the events and organizing my thoughts and realized I faired better than I thought. The times when I found myself angry were usually because of my own frustrations with myself, or when I found myself unprepared to handle the different nuances that were thrown my way. You will find that you are going to win more than you lose if you maintain control of yourself.

I used to spend a lot of time worrying about what people thought of me. I became obsessed with changing their thinking before I knew exactly what they were thinking. It was always me against them, and that was the way I approached my assignments. This is one of the worst frames of mind to allow yourself to fall into. It is very ineffective and always works against you.

If your competitors become aware of your insecurities, they are going to try their best to take advantage of you. I had a colleague who would offer his help in order to make himself look good. He provided practice for helping me learn to manage someone who I thought did not like me and was an opportunist. I learned to use his skills when I needed them. He helped me pull off a big meeting at one point in our career by presenting a key topic. He learned to respect me when I gave him an opportunity to look good.

Challenge yourself to be thought of by the actions you take. Do not spend a lot of time worrying whether people like you or not. It is nice to have people like you, but it is much more important to have them respect you for your actions and results.

# Get A Piece of the Action

In order to truly compete effectively, a new graduate from college should consider starting his or her career in a Fortune 500 corporation which tends to be large and have more structure to assist the new professional. I recommend you spend a minimum of two years, and as much as five years, in your first corporation. The large corporation can be a training ground and should help prepare you for the career you would like to pursue. It is an excellent place to acquire and build your skills. It will allow you to make mistakes and to recover from them. Your chances of building the type of network and support system it takes to succeed in the business world are increased. The larger the corporation, the greater the chance of having a larger number of Blacks employed.

Smaller corporations often cannot afford to allow you to make many mistakes. They rely heavily on the productivity of their professional employees. They can inhibit the growth of a new professional. I have known rookie professionals who joined small corporations which they soon found very unrewarding because of the lack of structure. You may think you want to be on your own, but don't try it before you are sure about what you are capable of doing.

Once you have settled into a company, you should find a "niche" that will allow maximum use of your skills and personal attributes. A niche is a position, assignment or job that allows you to work at your maximum potential or allows you to develop to that potential. It should allow you to continue to progress. A niche should be something an individual likes doing. If possible, try to find a niche that no one else is doing or, if others are doing it, that you are capable of doing better. Finding a niche is not always easy. Do not become discouraged if it takes longer than six months to find your niche. Some people take years to find their niche in a business organization. Some people have to create their niche, which is often better. If you create a niche, you will always be known for that niche. There is a niche for everyone that wants one. You may have to share it with a lot of other people, but it can still be your niche. You can also find niches you will like but which do not necessarily fit your skill set. This type of niche is all right providing you can assess your ability to learn the required skills.

There are times when you may have to do something no one else wants to do. Many companies will put new hires into the more mundane jobs as a first assignment. (Try to keep the Chip suppressed if this happens to you.) Jobs that are not the most fun can be the most important to a company and can allow you time to learn and grow.

Carving out your turf in a corporation is more than just finding a niche. Turf is defined as the area of the business for which you want to be held responsible. You must learn to set up boundaries that fence in what you will do for the corporation. This is something you will learn to do over time. You should start to consider what your turf is as soon as someone starts to explain your responsibility. When I was growing up, turf was something we took ownership of and great personal pride in, and we were willing to fight for it. This same type of thinking applies to the business arena. You should feel responsible for making your part of the business successful and not at the expense of the other parts of the business. The more ownership and responsibility you can show for a part of the business, the more you display your competitiveness.

Protecting your turf is important and simply means making sure you are doing all you can to maintain yourself as the candidate of choice for the assignment. If you start doing well in a job, there will be others vying for your assignment. This is an opportunity to show what you are capable of accomplishing. It is fine to bring others along, but make sure it is not at your expense. When I become the expert at a job, this is the time I start to reach out to help others. When you extend yourself to help, people identify you as belonging to the job assignment. When I heard someone say, "If you need help with that procedure, you should consult with Simms. He will be glad to help you." I knew I was becoming a corporate asset.

Making yourself a company asset should be a goal. To continue to compete effectively means you should become indispensable to a company or department. You should strive to build skills that are the best available. You should work toward making yourself the team member managers want, especially in a crunch. Spend time studying what it takes to become valuable to the corporation. Work at becoming the expert or the specialist.

Be careful not to pigeonhole yourself. There are times when you might want to move on in your career, and the corporation is afraid to move you because you have become so valuable in your current position. The backfill process has held up many promotions. It is a strange position to be in when you are told, "You are the best, and we cannot afford to let you out of your present assignment." It is desirable yet must be managed.

Black professionals must hunger for a piece of the action and must seek to secure firm positions in companies that will allow us to grow and become vital parts of the organization.

# Covering Your Butt

You will find that, when you truly start to compete, you will have the opportunity to make numerous mistakes. It is not bad to make large mistakes that can be easily fixed. It is bad to make small mistakes that can never be fixed. You will place an amazing pressure on yourself in order to be successful, pressure that will lead you to make important mistakes. Many people lose their drive and motivation because of little mistakes from which they cannot recover.

One of the most important skills you will need in the business world is your ability to cover your bases. Without this skill, you will have a lot of people on your back. If there is one area where I see Blacks fail, especially if they are new to the corporation, it is their inability to cover their butts. We Blacks often take the blame for mistakes we did not make because of our great pride. I am not discussing the ability to shirk responsibility or to not take ownership. No, just the opposite! I am talking about the ability to own the responsibility, and, if it is not good, we must be able to make it good.

If you know you are going to take vacation from the office for some period of time, take time to plan your absence. If you have projects that will come due during your vacation time, think about re-scheduling your vacation. A very stupid thing to do is have one of your colleagues baby-sit a key project while you are away. In the first place, you will probably worry about it the whole time you are away. This will lead to a wasted vacation. If the colleague botches up the project, guess who will receive the blame? You! Plan your vacation for a time when you know your business transactions will be at an all time low, when nothing needs immediate attention.

In my youth in a quota assignment, I asked an executive if it was okay for me to take my vacation during the last week of the year. The exec said to me, "You can take your vacation any time you want, that is up to you to decide." As the year ended, we found ourselves stretching to bring in every bit of business we could find in order to ensure our bonuses for the year. I was glad I did not take vacation that week. A year later, I found I had made all of my bonuses by the end of November. I confidently went on vacation the final week of the year and enjoyed every minute of it.

Covering your butt is a skill you will develop on the job. You will use it often. There are times when it will seem like wasted effort, but do not be fooled. The better you plan for not making mistakes, the fewer mistakes you will make. The time you put in to make sure you have done everything so that a task will progress smoothly is time well spent.

Keeping informed is another way to cover your butt. Here is a classic example of a sure way to fail in this area. I was trying to get a product installed at one of my customer's facilities. I assumed the people working on it were proficient for the task. I did not pay much attention to what was going on. I allowed myself to be blind-sided by the quality of the product, the skill base of the customer and the availability of needed resources. We spent a lot of time selling the customer on this particular product. This accentuated the problems because we felt obligated to make it work. We struggled with this installation for a month. When I finally understood the complexity of the problems of the install, I asked to fly in specialists. We did and it did not help. My boss was all over my butt.

I made another mistake with this installation by not keeping management totally informed. The customer called my office looking for help and ended up talking to my manager. My manager made a call on the customer, assessed the problem and blamed me. I owned up to the problem and took the blame, and my appraisal was lowered at my next performance evaluation. We not only lost the sale, we also had to pay the customer damages. I was not in this all alone, but I was the most responsible party.

I learned a lot about how to cover my butt from this incident. All I really needed to do was to make a call on this customer once a week and question the consultants as to how the project was progressing. I did all of that but after the fact. Yes, I finally cleaned up the situation but not without a bloodbath for all involved.

Some messy situations will arise in spite of your planning. You must stay alert and be aware of your responsibilities. A true professional stays on top of things. Covering your butt is the mark of a survivor.

Competing on the corporate front is an exciting and challenging endeavor. Black professionals are learning to compete on every avenue except that of a Fortune 500 chief executive officer. At this time, I do not see any in the making. I am not worried about it, because it will happen. I do want to keep this in front of us because it is another challenge that we must take on and win if we are to get a true "piece of the action."

Develop a competitive nature with a flair for business. Keeping your eyes open and your ears listening will definitely keep your brain thinking.

# Chapter

# 14

## Change Is Inevitable

*T*he one thing we can count on is "change"—everything will change. The world is changing. Global economies are changing. Unavoidable change is taking place in the way people are interacting with one another. Business is changing. The only thing that will not change is the color of our skin. Because we are Black, we must be willing to change everything that does not rob us of our pride, dignity, and self-worth.

The Black woman, the Black man, and the Black culture must continue to undergo significant change in the next decade, change that will allow us to successfully work and flourish in the American business world. These changes will make a profound difference in each of our lives and will allow us to fully participate in the American way of life.

I think of myself as one who wishes to make life better for others. I have been able to do this from time to time, but usually, not at my own expense. I often wonder how much I am willing to give up so that others might have more or are able to accomplish more. I try to foster this attitude in myself and in my children: start a legacy that has success for others as part of your basic foundation. If we can change our basic thought pattern into one of helping one another, I believe we will find success for the whole. I believe this is the essence for accomplishing as much as we dare to accomplish.

The ability to change one's thinking is the ability to become great—great in the form of controlling your own destiny, being sure of what you want to accomplish and how to accomplish what you want.

Look at the next two paragraphs and assess which

one applies to you. Be honest with yourself. This will help you start making some decisions about the way you think or how you might change the way you think.

The Optimistic Thinker: If you have good news and bad news to tell someone and you present the bad news first and the good news last, you are probably an optimist. You hope the recipient will go away thinking of the good news, since it was the last thing they heard from you. The optimist is very good at working things out for the better. Their approach to things is usually one of solving the problem.

The Pessimistic Thinker: If you always share the good news first and dwell on the bad news forever, you are probably a pessimist. The recipient usually goes away thinking only of the bad news which can be detrimental. The pessimist is very good at making matters worse. Their approach to things is usually complaining.

Now, does either one of the above paragraphs apply to your way of thinking? If neither one of them applies, you should probably put this book down and go read something else. If you find yourself a die hard pessimist, put a plan in place immediately to change your thinking. Pessimistic people are usually hard to deal with and can be very discouraging to all who must be around them. Pessimistic thinking is a destroyer of those who would be successful. There are more than enough pessimistic thinkers in the business world already. Pessimistic thinking is hard to change. This type of thinking allows people to be right more often than they are wrong. The only problem with being right as a pessimist is that it tends to work against being successful. A pessimist will often influence events toward a dark side; doom and gloom will always be on the horizon. Negative attitudes prevail over positive ones.

In order to change pessimistic thinking, you must stop negativity. You must help change what is currently influencing your reality. This does not mean building a bed of roses without the thorns attached. The thorns are reality, while the roses are success. The pessimist must learn to see the positive side of things and the ability to affect things positively. This can be a monumental task. But as Blacks we are used to climbing mountains no one else would ever dare attempt to scale. Pessimists must surround themselves with those who have learned that reality is something manufactured by the participants—those who are true optimists.

If you find you are the eternal optimist, stop kidding yourself. Take on reality, and start to analyze things for yourself. Stop accepting what everyone else is feeding you, and start to make decisions based on fact. Surprised by these statements? Eternal optimists are usually foolish thinkers. They usually do not get much done because they always keep things on the light side. They usually do not like to make waves. In the business world, they may succeed; but they are not the ones who make it to the top, which is what this book is all about.

The true optimist is one who is very much in touch with reality and has come to an understanding about what makes up reality for them in particular. The true optimist sees a glass of water and decides how full it is as opposed to how empty it is. This person never loses sight of the water in the glass and that it is there for a purpose. We must become true optimists and stop overshooting the mark for success. We know what we need to do, and it is now time we get around to doing it. Our culture must change. It must give up some things and add others.

Things that are a part of one's culture are the things that are hardest to change. We Blacks understand culture better than most people of the world because we have forged ours through so much struggle. Our challenge today is to be able to positively change ourselves and make these changes a part of our culture.

# Taking Responsibility

We too often get angry when we think other races are not taking the time to understand where we are or what we are trying to accomplish. It is our responsibility to educate them. We must work hard to change their thinking. This can only be done by becoming masters of change.

There are many who say we are a subculture. This disturbs us greatly. This type of thinking can only be changed by changing what others see and experience when in our presence. We are truly making strides in this area. We must continue to create and build examples that will not fail. When I see Blacks who become mayors of cities, who have convinced a

70 to 80 percent White constituency that they are the right person for the job, I am proud. When I see a Black woman who emerges from the deep south and becomes a top advisor on foreign policy to the White House, I am proud. These are the types of examples it is going to take to change other people's thinking.

We must take responsibility for supporting the efforts of people who are working hard to change the way America thinks about Blacks in the business world. We must learn to support each other's efforts and encourage one another to bring about positive changes. We must make sure our children see these examples and understand what is happening in America.

We must take responsibility for funding our own educational growth in America. When we hear of people like Camille and Bill Cosby using their fortunes to support Blacks in higher education, it should spur us on. We must learn to pool our resources and share our wealth to improve the whole. Education is the key to it all. We do not stand a chance if we do not come up with ways to continue to educate ourselves. Our children are going to face the same obstacles we face, and education is the miraculous salve to be applied to our gaping wounds inflicted by history.

We have tried the systematic approach which appears to work for a while before it fails miserably. The System will give one day and take it all back the next. We are our own responsibility and we must act responsibly.

# Role of the Black Woman

The Black professional woman in the business world is becoming a bright shining star. She is learning to capitalize not only on what civil rights has done for her but also on what the feminist movement has been able to accomplish. With some assistance from her White sisters, she is stepping onto corporate carpets with preparation and self-assurance. She can be furiously competitive. The Black woman is starting to flourish in business. She is often not seen as a threat to others who must compete against her. By the time they discover she is a threat, she has successfully accomplished what she set out to do. She has done well over the last 20 years and is well on her way to making a difference.

Now is the time for you Black women to continue learning all that you can. Prepare yourselves to meet the challenges that are going to be put in front of you. You have not yet arrived because the only way you will arrive is when we as a people have arrived. You are truly making strides in the right direction. You must continue to not let your pride get in your way. You must continue to encourage each other. I believe that it will be you who will receive the magic key to the corporate kingdom.

The business world can be a lonely world for the Black woman, especially as she climbs to the top. I have had the opportunity to work with many of my Black sisters. They are a force to reckon with in this male-dominated business world. The one thing that encourages me is their ability to maintain their desire and quest for success, in spite of this loneliness. I see her working late into the night and not having anyone to go home too. I have spent time discussing this plight of career versus social life with many successful Black women. They are often faced with no male companionship and not by choice. They would love to find someone to share their success but not at the cost of compromising what they have already accomplished.

There are not many Black men who can accept a successful Black woman without feeling threatened by her success. (I will address the other side of this in the next section.) Black men have always felt a need to dominate their households. I understand how this thinking came about.

I ask you, my sister, to press on and get your due reward. I also ask you to be patient with us Black men. We would like to think we are one step ahead of you when we are really one step behind you. We need your encouragement and your support. We are changing just as you are, and we hope to meet you at the finish line.

# Role of the Black Man

The Black professional man is starting to emerge as a business man. He is starting to gain access to the corner offices, but this is a slow process. He has indeed come a long way. He is still seen as a threat by most of his colleagues and has to compete on all fronts. The feminist movement has helped in some ways, but the jobs that were once slotted for him are being filled by ready and able women. The business world is not going out of its way to include him. It allows him to come in and expects him to be prepared and ready to perform. He knows he has to work for everything that he gets. He is becoming clever and is starting to learn not only survival skills but also how to compete.

You young Black men, please keep your eyes open and your hearing sharp. Do not settle for second best. Look behind you at every chance to make sure that those who are following you do not get lost. Focus on today and tomorrow, but do not forget what happened yesterday. Do your homework; be thorough, complete, and accurate. Make your mistakes count toward valuable experience. Hard work should be a given, and it should come easily without much forethought. Once you feel you have what you want, go after more.

Be sure to encourage one another and try to assist each other in every way. Allow change to carry you into the future and continue to assess where you need it most. You are going to find there is still a lot of change necessary if we are going to have our fair share of the pie. Learn everything that will allow you to help yourself and someone else.

Take time to be responsible to your family and your female partner. She is a valuable asset, and she is worth all the time you spend making things good for her. It is time to act responsibly and time to stop wasting her time and energy. There are a lot of Black professional women who are looking to partner-up and be successful. You are still a man even if you do not make the largest salary. Money should not be an issue if you have enough to do the things you want to do. Having an educated and successful woman in your life will only accentuate what you are. If she is more powerful than you, you now have a local measuring stick. Continue to encourage her in every way you can. I know this is not easy, but, if you start changing now, you may be there at the finish line.

Take time to help those in the community around you. You will benefit as much as the people you help. We will all benefit if we can stop this world from teaching us we are second class citizens. You are still the one we look to as a leader. We Black men must continue to enhance what we are all about.

The business world is now accepting applications for all Black men who desire to be successful and who are willing to prepare themselves. It is soon going to need you as much as you need it. There will come a time when you will have accomplished all you set out to do. This is the time when you should be proud. Then revise your plans, because you set the bar too low.

# Time To Wake Up

Wake up Black Americans! We are now in a position to bring about great change. Why? What has changed?

We have changed! We have come from the cotton sacks to the Cadillacs, and we are starting to acquire BMWs. We have moved from the back of the bus to the front of the bus, and we are now becoming owners of the bus. We have learned to fight with the pencil, and we must now learn to put it in ink! We have been castrated, degraded, segregated, integrated, and now we must become affiliated. I really do not mean to play on your intelligence, but everything above is true. We have endured much change. It is time to capitalize on what we have accomplished.

We must continue to change, but we must become the authors of these next chapters of our history. We must continue to ask the questions: Am I prepared? Have I done everything that I was supposed to do? What else do I want to accomplish? How can I help you? Can you help me? Then we must answer all of these questions: I know I am prepared! I did everything I was supposed to do! I want to accomplish everything within my powers! I can help you! You can help me!

These are all questions and answers that bring about change! Use them at every opportunity, especially, in your corporate meeting rooms.

Sitting around a corporate table is the only way to truly change things for ourselves in the world of business. Continue to seek ways you can gain access to those tables and chairs. Every time you get a chance to participate, do it!

As we embark on this journey to the top of corporate

America, let us remember we must be willing to change everything that does not rob us of our pride, dignity, and self-worth.

Change it or let it change you!

# Chapter

# 15

# Networking –
# A Support Structure

**B**lacks discovered the wonder of "Networking" in the Eighties. It will become even more valuable for Black Professionals in the Nineties. Unfortunately, for many Black professionals, networking has become a buzzword that basically means getting together. Too often, this getting together is only for social pleasure. Time spent with friends or colleagues socially is time well spent, but spending time socially should not be the sole basis of our networking.

Excellent networking arises out of informational seminars held in large cities with large concentrations of Blacks. The seminars center around well-known Black speakers and can be very enlightening and informative. We should continue to find creative and productive methods to spend time with other professionals. In the Nineties, networking must take on a much more enriching role in our lives, as we attempt to develop careers in the business world.

In the business world, very few people make it alone. If you are Black, it is almost impossible to make it alone. Networking is going to have to become much more than attending a seminar to hear a good speaker or swapping business cards over drinks. Networking is going to have to take on some of the same characteristics as Harriet Tubman's "Underground Railroad." The railroad worked so well because people were committed to helping one another. The underground railroad had "conductors" (Harriet Tubman was one) who risked their lives by leading slaves out of the treacherous South. There were also people called "station masters" who used their homes to shelter and hide slaves as they were conducted along the underground railroad. The conductors and station masters of the underground railroad were willing to risk all they had to see people become free. Networking must now embody similar principles. It must become a mechanism that will accentuate our success and survival in the business world.

Our tasks today are similar to Tubman's objectives but with far less severe consequences, although some would probably argue that point with me. We must build support structures within the business world that will allow us to aid and assist one another. These networks must be built around the problems and obstacles we face in the business world today. These networks can be informal weekly meetings of Blacks who have common goals and aspirations inside large and small corporations. In large corporations there are very few support groups for professional Blacks. I have been a part of several major corporations; I have never found any such network or support structure. I was always happy just to see another Black face in the company cafeteria or at a recognition event.

When I think back to the support structures I had in college, it was the college support groups, such as the National Society for Black Engineers, American Black Business Society, or the Black Student Union, with a networking emphasis that helped me make my way through. These support groups met frequently and regularly. They were more than social clubs. They taught and gave me the opportunity to conduct a meeting. The members were people I studied with or who helped me find answers to complex problems. In the business world, there are similar requirements that can be provided by well-planned networking.

We must not be afraid to set up networking structures within corporations. These networks will allow us to support one another and help us to be better employees for the corporations. Understand, the unions of yesteryear have instilled fear in a lot of corporations, and any kind of group meetings can be viewed as threatening to corporate management. We must help corporations understand that we are trying to become better employees. This will allow us to be better contributors as their employed professionals.

Black professional networks can be a key to sustenance of Blacks in the business world. You who understand how to provide leadership and organization should head up these networks. Once in place, these networks should solicit members who can contribute to the success of the network. Their agendas should be based around solving immediate as well as long-range problems Blacks face daily. Agendas should include clinics, workshops and seminars that can be conducted by its members and/or other successful Black professionals in the area. Membership dues should be small or nothing because of the fiscal responsibility they spawn. Projects should be funded on an as-needed basis. Emphasis should be placed on utilizing members of the group to run seminars and workshops. Community facilities should be utilized if corporate facilities are not available.

Black professional networks, if set up properly, can transcend corporation boundaries. There are professional industry groups who are setting up networks to share industry knowledge. There needs to be more such networks put in place to function as backbone support for local networks.

We must continue to build networks that will allow us to share ideas, information and strategies with each other. Once we are sharing ideas, then we must support one another in our business ventures by buying goods and services from one another. This will only work to strengthen our networks and allow us to become self-sustaining. We too often shy away from one another, seeking to distinguish ourselves from one another. We must stop competing on a Black basis and start competing on a business basis. We must learn to trust and depend on one another. We must become supporters of ourselves. If we do not put these things in place, who is going to do it for us?

# Take Care

As we attempt to build our networks within the corporate arena, we must continue to learn who is friend and who is foe, who can contribute to making our networks stronger or who will seek to tear them down. I hate to think that there are Black professionals who will sell out for their own benefit or who choose to go it alone. They will soon fall by the wayside. But, we must face the facts that there are Blacks of this nature. Leave them alone!

I have found Blacks who choose not to help one another. Unfortunately, this is not a rare occurrence. There are many Blacks who have decided they do not like to make waves and they do not want to be near those who choose to. They feel they have managed to get theirs and you ought to be able to get yours. Once you identify who these people are, avoid them at all costs.

In the corporate environment, everybody who smiles at you or laughs with you should not be given carte blanche to your network. There are people who would just as likely use you as they would try to help you. These people can be Black or non-Black. The same things that promote the free enterprise system are the same things that make people take advantage of each other.

We Blacks like to physically touch people we become acquainted with, especially if we think they are our friends. We are very creative when it comes to greeting one another. We have wonderful ways of saying hello and shaking hands, such as high fives and daps. Touching in the corporate environment can be a very sensitive area. Be careful who you choose to touch and the manner in which you touch them. A man touching a woman who does not sanction his touch can very easily be in trouble. A benign touch can easily be mistaken as sexual harassment. This could cost you your job. I often place my hand on a person's shoulder when I am talking. I have had people pull away from me when I touched them in this manner. People can act very strange to a touch, especially if they feel you have not earned the privilege of touching them.

I was once teamed with a very nice young lady. We had been working together for a few months and had developed what I thought was a pretty good working relationship. I put my arm on her shoulder as we were discussing a chart. She pulled away from me abruptly and did not say a word. I quickly realized she did not like to be touched. I cannot tell exactly when we became great friends, but today, whenever she sees me, she almost always greets me with a hug.

Women are not exempt from this discussion. There are a lot of men who, for whatever reasons, do not like to be touched and will not hesitate to let you know. There have been women charged with sexual harassment in the business world. You also run the risk that a guy will think you are flirting. Take care to not be put in a position of trying to explain that you were not flirting, just trying to be friendly.

Becoming a true professional takes being aware of what you are doing. It is very easy to be misread or have your actions mistaken. Do not be over-sensitive or too careful as you present yourself, but stay alert and sharp. It will carry you far.

# Mentoring

This is a most valuable tool for building a strong network. Every good support structure should have a mentoring component. This is how the "good ole boy" network was able to continue for the past 100 years. Our White counterparts have nurtured and cultivated one another since American business was invented. Mentoring allows us to grow and nurture Black professionalism.

A mentor is more than someone you can look up to. A mentor is also someone who cares about another person. They are willing to take time to help others benefit from their experiences and become successful. You do not have to be vice president of a company before you start mentoring those who are less experienced than you. I was in a company training program that taught and fostered its trainees to begin mentoring one another after three to six months in the program. I have seen new college graduates come into companies and immediately look for opportunities to help others. A mentor can make life a lot easier for new or less experienced colleagues.

Most of my mentors in the business world have been White. They were very helpful during the early stages of my career. White mentors very seldom understand the struggles we Blacks face as we become a part of the business world. As I became seasoned in my profession, I needed different types of mentors. My White mentors were mainly consulting mentors. If I needed to talk to someone about a business issue, they made themselves available to help me. A true mentor can help you avoid many of the pitfalls in the business world by sharing their own experiences. But remember, we are the first generation of American Black business professionals. I longed for a mentor who would watch me, take me aside from time to time, and counsel me on the tactics to use in given situations. Someone who would say, "You talked too much and did not spend enough time listening during the staff meeting." I believe you will need some type of mentor throughout your career. I still long for a Black mentor, someone who understands the business issues as well as the cultural issues.

Once I became knowledgeable, I made myself available to mentor other Blacks who were coming up behind me. Sometimes, it was the blind leading the blind, but just knowing someone is there for you is encouraging. I must admit, I have often become a mother hen by not giving my less experienced colleagues room to grow.

As we attempt to build more networks and support structures, we must keep in mind the young Black children who will make up the next generation of Black professionals. One thing that keeps Blacks at a disadvantage in the business world is a lack of early business experience, the experience young White kids bring to college with them, the experience that comes from being exposed to professionals when your are still at an impressionable age. These experiences allow kids to choose directions and set goals for themselves while they are still in high school. When they arrive on the college campus, they have a good idea of the things that might interest them. White kids often come to college with a good strong vision of what they want to accomplish. We Black professionals have got to take more time with our Black youth. They need us. We must take the responsibility to assist them in becoming productive people.

We can continue to give back to the community through strong networks that have mentoring programs. These programs allow professionals the chance to give young Black teens the opportunity to talk to engineers, doctors, lawyers, and other professionals. The sports community has always done a fairly good job at this. These types of mentoring programs allow professionals to take pride in their accomplishments. One of my proudest moments was when a young kid in his first year of college approached me and reminded me of a visit I paid to his high school. I had recently graduated from college and had been asked to speak to a group of high school juniors. He said, "After I heard you speak, I was inspired to go to college and become an engineer." He also let me know college presented him with many struggles, but he was determined to make it.

As we look to each other for encouragement and help to succeed, networking can and must play a major part in the exchange of ideas, the sharing of information, and the caring for each other. The more we do it, the better we are going to be able to do it. Pooling our wealth to fund our growth is the only way we can expect to gain viable seats in the corporate board rooms.

# Chapter

# 16

## Risk

---

*T*here is an amazing thing that happens to a woman or man who has decided success is something they must experience. Their thinking becomes "what if", and their "emphatic no" becomes a "confident yes." Fears are replaced with self-assurance. They start to realize they can do things that appeared to be beyond their capabilities. They progress with relentless authority through tasks that will make up their success. They are always aware that things are changing because they have learned to experience the change. There is a driving force that will not let them regress until they have either succeeded or failed at the task they wish to accomplish. Success will halt the process, but failure will spur them on. This is a person who takes "risk."

There is nothing in this world today that does not have some form of risk associated with it. Remember earlier I discussed eating in a restaurant and never seeing the cook, hoping and trusting the meal will be good: Risk. Being a passenger on a jumbo jetliner and flying across an ocean to a foreign country where no one knows you: Risk. Going to work for a corporation that has been in existence for two years: Risk. Success is no exception and is often born out of risk.

There are varying degrees of risk which is why we can accept it, allow it, take it, reject it, and ultimately live with it. Degrees of risk are often in the eye of the beholder. What is of minimal risk to me may be of great risk to you. What may be of minimal risk to you is something I will not chance. For me, eating in a restaurant is a low risk proposition. Flying in an airplane is medium risk. Taking drugs is a very high risk situation. These varying degrees of risk allow us to decide whether or not we want to participate in a particular activity or take on a certain task.

In business, risk is a process that we hope to avoid yet we often end up seeking it. Professionals work very hard to minimize it, yet they risk whenever possible. Capitalistic business thrives on risk and all that goes with it. It took me a long time to understand why risk is so important to business success.

First of all, most opportunities are immersed in risk. If you ask someone to put up capital on a venture that you have convinced yourself is going to make millions, you are asking them to take some risk. You may not make a penny. In fact, you may end up losing their money and your own. This type of risk-taking happens every day, a hundred times a day. Yet, without risk, most businesses would have nothing. Risk often decides the value.

Earlier I discussed risk-taking as one of our elements of success. Those who accomplish a lot usually have learned to take some risk. They have learned not to expect failure; and, when it comes, they have learned not to accept it as the final result. If the risk becomes too great, they have learned to manage it until it can be minimized.

Blacks in business America must become greater risk-takers. If we are going to attempt to climb the tall corporate ladders that are facing us today, we must realize there will be risk at each rung. The higher we climb, the greater the risk will become. We must learn to accept risk as a part of doing business. We must learn to expect risk each time we feel there is more to be accomplished.

Black professionals are just starting to understand what it means to go after the high and lofty positions of American business. Politics has allowed us to test how great risk can be. In politics, the stakes often start off low and eventually become very high. We have learned to approach the campaign trail with a lot of preparation, and we are learning to win. Politics is a high-stakes game that allows us to get in with minimal initial risk. If we lose, we still have opportunities to start all over again.

In the corporate environment, we do not have the luxury of losing a few times before we win. The path to the corporate board room is long, narrow and arduous. You may have one or two chances to get side-tracked, but you had better hope no one remembers.

Blacks must take on as much risk as they can, assess the risk and minimize it. I know this is not as easy as it sounds, but with great skill it can be done. If we do not learn to do this, we will continue to meander through corporate hallways never going any further than first-line management.

Accepting risk is our biggest challenge. We learned a long time ago, if we accept risk we lose everything. We have been taught by history not to accept risk. History, of course, is never wrong; but it has often made the future appear to be a liar. If we are afraid to override what history has taught us, the future becomes a repeat of the past. We usually meet the challenges if no one tells us how much risk is involved in meeting those challenges. The ability to accept and assess the risk now lets us make the future into what we want it to be. Accepting the risk is a major part of accepting the challenges.

# Accepting Challenge

The world has repeatedly challenged us! We know what it means to accept challenge, especially if the challenge is basic to our survival. If it becomes a matter of survival, we Blacks will accept whatever challenges that are placed in front of us.

Business is now a matter of survival. In business, these challenges are different than most of the challenges we have had to face. They are different in that they are not being forced upon us. We are knocking on the door of business, asking to be presented with these challenges; and they are hesitantly being pushed our way.

Accepting challenges that you have asked for is an easy thing to do. What complicates this acceptance is the risk that is associated with these challenges. The risk is increased because of increased levels of expectations.

What do I mean by this? We are asking to be given a chance to show we indeed can run large operations in major corporations. Corporate executives are responding very reluctantly, "Well, I'm not sure you can handle that much responsibility. That is a very important part of this business, and we cannot afford to put it in the hands of someone who could possibly fail." With this reluctance comes increased pressure that Black executives will fail. This increases the risk of failure for all of us. Once we obtain a noteworthy position, we are afraid to bring on other Blacks because they might increase our risk of failing.

What are we to do? Accept the challenge, and then perform like we have never performed before. And at every opportunity, help another Black professional into a corporate chair. Our White counterparts have been doing this for centuries. Our Asian counterparts are learning to do it as fast as they can; and they are starting to own major portions of American business.

If we can learn to accept the challenge and then minimize the risk, we are in for some profitable times in the Black community. The key is to be prepared. There is a scripture in the Bible that says, "Do not be anxious about anything." The scripture goes on to tell us how to minimize the anxiety of dealing with this world. If we can learn to be prepared for the challenges, we can accept more risk. If we are going to accept more risk, then we must learn to measure risk and calculate it.

Calculating risk is what a successful risk-taker has learned to do. Risk is automatically minimized if we know how much we can take on and still win. Learning when to buy into a project is a key factor. Weighing the factors that make up risk will allow us to assess risk. Once we learn to calculate the risk associated with a task, we are ready to move ahead in accepting the challenges that have risk associated with them.

After we accept and meet these challenges, we must then become the creators of the challenges. There are many Blacks accepting the challenges of the business world but very few who have earned the right to create them.

# Taking It

The biggest risk we must learn to take is on ourselves as a people. We must learn to support one another. We must learn to seek out Blacks who have learned their part of a business and push them forward, whenever possible. We must take the risk of becoming alienated in a corporation if it means advancing ourselves as Black professionals.

If there is an opportunity to hire a young Black professional, then we ought to do it. This is when risk becomes a difficult assessment. When we are given the opportunity to help each other as well as ourselves, it should be worth the risk.

I once found a job in a different department I knew I would be successful doing. The first opportunity to take risk was when I asked the manager of that department if there were any opportunities. He was surprised because in this company you always worked through your own manager to find new opportunities. Next, I brought my manager on board by telling him I wanted the job. I did this very carefully. My manager and I agreed it would be a great job for me. My manager and the manager of the other department discussed the opportunity and agreed they would attempt to make it happen. There was one hurdle to clear before the deal could be consummated. There was an employee holding the position I wanted who the other manager needed to place. Just when we thought we were ready to move forward with all sides of the deal, the company announced a reorganization and froze everybody in place. Several months went by and the vice president of our area came to visit for an awards meeting. I knew him fairly well. I took my biggest risk at this time. I told him of the situation and asked if he could help me. I expected him to tell me to work with my management team. Instead he asked, "Do you really want that job?" I answered, trying to speak over the pounding of my heart, "Yes sir." He said, "I will see what I can do." The risk paid off.

After weighing the cost, take the risk!

# Assuming The Responsibility

One of the most important parts of taking risk is understanding what is at risk and then assuming the responsibility for that risk. Too often, people take risk but do not want to accept the responsibility for it.

If you take risk and hope that luck is in your favor, you are a dangerous risk-taker. Luck is a highly undependable force. It will fail you every time you depend on it. I personally do not believe in luck. I believe in preparation and hard work. With risk comes responsibility. A lot of people will take risk readily if they feel they do not have to take on the responsibility that goes with it. These people are also dangerous risk-takers, and they should be avoided. If you decide to take risk, do take time to assess the responsibility that goes with it. If you are not willing to take on the responsibility, do not take on the risk.

Blacks often fail when it comes to taking risk with responsibility. Many times I have encouraged my Black colleagues to move higher in America's corporations. They often resist this encouragement. Many will say, "I do not want to manage because I do not want the responsibility." I applaud their assessment of the risk. When they find out there is responsibility involved with a promotion or a better opportunity, they say no. I perceive their "No" as not only fear of the responsibility but also fear of failure.

In the previous section I discussed accepting the challenges. One of the biggest challenges for Black professionals is overcoming this fear of failure. We must learn to manage this fear so that we can overcome it. Otherwise, we will never be a vital part of the business world. And we will never be true risk-takers but will continue to be "at risk!"

# Chapter

# 17

# Negotiating

*N*egotiating is a process that you will use throughout your career in the business world, and it is not to be taken for granted at any time. Negotiating in the business world may test the power you hold. Negotiations are often based on the information that is available. Time may or may not be a factor in negotiating.

Some people think negotiating is an art. Some people think it is a science. I believe negotiating is both an art and a science. Whether you believe it to be an art or a science, it is highly dependent on the skills of the one doing the negotiating. A good negotiator should have good verbal communication skills. Sometimes negotiating may draw on one's writing skills. Negotiators must also be able to think quickly and accurately. A good negotiator must sometimes be clever and other times appear coy or even ambivalent.

From the time you sit in your first job interview until the time you become the CEO of the corporation, there will be negotiations. Businesses thrive on negotiations. Leaders of a business must know how to negotiate if their business is going to survive and grow.

Negotiating allows businesses to assess value, and everything that has value will be negotiated at some point in time. One of the first things you will probably negotiate is how much should you be compensated. In most businesses, salary is negotiable. There are guidelines for how much a newly hired employee should make, but it is often negotiable. Each time you change jobs, salary should come back to the negotiating table. If a company is located in more than one location, the location where you will work may be negotiable. These are just a few examples of negotiations that take place in the business world.

Understanding when to negotiate and when not to negotiate is part of the art form. The ability to bring about the desired outcome will be attributed to the skills you possess. The business world will present you with numerous opportunities to negotiate. There will be times when you will have to negotiate without much notice. There will be simple negotiations, such as trying to compete for time on a colleague's calendar. There will be complicated negotiations which will require time and preparation. You will have to learn to assess when you are in a dog fight or when you are simply jockeying for positions. This will lead to different styles of negotiations which I will discuss in the next section.

Negotiations are often necessary because they allow parties to maximize the use of a company's resources. Companies who teach their people how to negotiate usually have a healthy, vital environment. There will always be individuals in a corporation who will try to take advantage of the system. These people have not learned that their success is based on the success of the corporation. They are normally very selfish, and they only think of helping themselves. Large corporations often have problems getting their people to negotiate for the good of the corporation. This is because large corporations are divided into departments that function as mini-corporations.

Some corporations use the process of negotiation very well. They encourage departments to negotiate amongst themselves. A corporation may have a print shop in-house that sells its services to the other departments in the corporation. A department who needs printing may go outside of the company and find the same services for less cost. The department needing the service may come back to its sister department and negotiate some agreement that is workable. If a department competes against outside sources and cannot match or beat outside cost for services, the company may opt to close the department and buy on the outside.

There are many ways negotiating will manifest itself in the world of business. We Blacks must become highly skilled in negotiating. Being Black in the business world can often be a point of negotiation. When assignments are being given out, management often has to take into consideration what the makeup of their workforce should be. As we move more and more into what we are calling a diverse workforce, this is going to become a bigger issue, not necessarily from the standpoint of quotas or tokenism, but because of the fact that the workforce is going to demand it. For example, if a department has 50 Whites, 20 Blacks, 15 Hispanics, 10 Asians, and 5 American Indians and 50 percent of this department is women, there will be many interesting points of negotiation. If the department managers are now considering who is going to be promoted, they are going to have to take into consideration this diverse workforce. If this group of people works up to the expectations of the company and are meeting the company's objectives, promotions will have to be negotiated. Questions like, "How many Blacks have we promoted this year?" are going to have to become relevant and necessary. We as Blacks must understand the advantages of being in a diverse workforce.

If we Blacks are now becoming a part of America's business management team, we are going to have to be good negotiators for the sake of other Black professionals. In business meetings, the question "How many women have we considered for the job?" is now a normal topic; and it always comes to the table. Women managers are very good at making sure they are represented in all matters of the business. "How many Blacks have we considered?" is an occasional question though it mainly comes up around EQUAL OPPORTUNITY Awareness Week. If a department has ten managers, five of whom are women and two who are Black while all the others are White, we are still at a disadvantage. If the Black managers have good negotiating skills, this may help even the score until we can get more representation in the corporate conference room.

# Whatever Works For You

Though negotiation is not a pure science, like any other process requiring skills, you will have to practice and become experienced. You are going to find that there are several styles of negotiating in the business world. One day you may be trying to increase the budget for your project. Another day you may be trying to win a bid on a proposal.

The style of negotiation that most people are familiar with is when one side wins and the other loses, I call this "competitive negotiations." This is a style of negotiation that has competition as its main theme. You are competing with another party for the same resource, and only one side can win. This may be a situation where you are trying to convince your senior management to give your department the last of the budget dollars which may mean shutting down a sister division.

The style of negotiation that allows no winners or losers is "give-and-take negotiations." The parties involved split the resources. The only real debate is the issue of how to share the resources. This may be used when two groups may have to share a computer system. They negotiate who will use the system at what times.

There is a style of negotiation where you let the other party win. This is the "accommodating negotiation." This may be done because you come to the conclusion they need the resource more than you do. Or, you may want to lose this round to position yourself to win the next one. You let your co-professional take the first project in hopes that the second one may be just as good or better.

Most negotiations within a department or group are usually "collaborative." Everybody is trying to work for the same end result. You will simply look at the immediate problem and try to solve it. This is a style that will allow both parties to win in some fashion. Maybe you are trying to get your boss to give you more resources in order to complete the work you have been asked to do.

Listen - Think - Assess - Give - Take is a style of negotiation I have learned to use. It is aimed at assessing a situation and trying to put a plan in place that will allow the parties involved to get what they want or need. It is different than the others in that it lends itself to setting up the use of the other styles. It can stand on its own if the corporation is continually shuffling resources around in order to assure progress is being made in all areas. This style allows many parties to negotiate at once. There are many winners. This is often used by corporate executives in their planning sessions.

Information-gathering is key to all of negotiating. The source of the information may be more important than the information itself. No matter what type of negotiating you may need to do, make sure your information is good and you understand it well enough to use it.

In the day-to-day business world, negotiating lets you acquire what you need. Your ability to negotiate will depend on how much value is placed on the desired results. Find what works for you and become proficient at it. As for getting what you want out of the business world, do what it takes and play fair.

# Selling and Buying

The ability to take what is in your possession and convince someone they want it I call Selling. Selling is a form of negotiating. It is the classic case of putting a price on something you have, then convincing someone to pay that price.

One item you are always going to be selling is yourself—your talents, your time, your skills and maybe someday your products and services. Whatever you have to sell, especially if it is yourself, know its strengths and weaknesses. Many of us try to put ourselves in markets where we are not prepared to participate. Selling something that is very good to the wrong market can be compared to selling a bad product in a market that has a high demand. Both situations lead to flops.

Learn this form of negotiation as soon as possible and try to learn all you can. You will get better over time as you gain experience. You know you have become proficient when it is working for you and no one knows you are actively negotiating. We Blacks must become better at selling ourselves out of the corners we so often get painted into.

Negotiating what someone else has in their possession and you want I call Buying. In the business world, you have many opportunities to buy. Remember, whenever someone is trying to buy something, it must be bought from someone who is willing to sell it. In the business world, you may have to buy as often as you have to sell. Many times if you are dealing with a customer (and this customer may be your manager or colleague), you will be the buyer. In many situations, you will find yourself being sold to.

Trying to launch a career in an industry that is most conducive to your ideals and skills puts you in a buying mode.

Shopping for a company where you may spend the next five to twenty years of your life is a big buying decision. Use the elements of negotiation that allow you to get what you want. If you need to compromise, be willing to do it. If you need to accommodate someone, do that as well. Most of all, do your homework. You would never try to buy a car without spending time seeing what various dealers are offering. If you are buying a house, you investigate who is offering the best interest rates on a home mortgage. Do the same type of homework when you are the buyer in the business world, especially if you are looking for a job.

There will be times when you are the one who needs to be sold on an idea from a colleague or a manager. Make sure you make them do their homework. Then do whatever is necessary to allow you to make good decisions. You are the one who has to live with whatever you buy into, and sometimes that may be a long portion of your life. Buying can be fun or can be traumatic. Buying, for the most part, puts you in control, so try not to lose control.

Negotiating through buying and selling will be a major part of your business life. Prepare for both and make them work for you. There is an important message from Wall Street that I think is appropriate throughout the business world. "Buy low and Sell high!"

# The Bottom Line

One of the most important things to know when negotiating is, "What do you want?" Know what you want and know what you are willing to give to get it. A lot of people find themselves around the negotiation table without this piece of work done. If you go to a negotiating table without this analysis, you have set yourself up for failure. You must know your bottom line, and you must be ready to walk away from the table if things go beyond it.

The second most important thing to know is, "What does the other side want?" Many times you will not be provided with this information until you are at the table. This is another good reason to know what you are willing to give up and what you are willing to accept. If you have the luxury of knowing what the other side's bottom line is, you are in a good position to negotiate and get what you want.

I once had a large corporate client who was very smart. The whole management staff appeared to be highly trained in negotiating. No matter who my colleagues and I approached during the sale, they all knew what their company wanted and was trying to accomplish. They all knew the bottom line, and they stuck to it throughout the negotiations. They played fair for the most part. They found a point of weakness in our strategy, and they took advantage of it. They knew when to use the competitive information they had gathered, and they accomplished it with skill. They were familiar with all the players on our side, and they made sure all their players were in place at the appropriate times. They set deadlines to have various transactions completed, and they allowed us to push them past their deadlines only when it benefitted them. The final deal was very complicated and we made the sale, but it was at the value the client had placed on it.

There was true professionalism throughout the negotiations, and everyone involved learned something. What I learned from this event was: know your opponent and stick to your bottom line.

# Chapter
# 18

# Do What You Can
# With What You 'Got'

*I* would like to share a thought that came to mind one night when I was writing checks to my creditors. As I was writing the checks, I realized there was no more money left in my checking account. Yet, there were still more bills to be paid. I ask you take off your grammatical hat for a paragraph or two to fully appreciate this thought:

FOR ALL WHO MUST DO!
Do what you can with what you got!
Until you can get what you can get!
Or, until you can get what you need!
Or, until you can get what you WANT!

I now live by these words, and they help me control the desperation that sets in when I become overwhelmed by my lack of ability to control certain situations and/or circumstances. You too will often have situations that are within your power to control, but you have not yet learned to control them. Now if you can reach down and pull up the Black Chip, which you have been learning to suppress for the last few chapters, and any other protection mechanisms you keep way down deep in your guts, you may find an answer to the problem. Just remember one thing, "Do What You Can With What You 'Got'"!

One of the things people fail to realize once they have gained a portion of success is they have also gained some rather interesting challenges—challenges such as the way you used your time and resources, accessing the skills you already possess, or the way you look at life itself. Your approach to solving problems will always present you with challenges. Once others deem you a success, the way they view you will also create interesting circumstances for you. You feel the same, but your world appears to have changed all around you. Everybody continuously reminds you that you have joined the prestigious and the elite. Welcome, my friend, to the world of being a professional.

You must now take control of what happens from here on. Brace yourself for all the things that are going to start happening to you. And, guess what? You can continue to enjoy all of the things you used to do as well. But, keep sharp and alert and keep your wits about you because there are some weird events waiting to creep up on you. Working late! Working weekends! Not getting enough rest. Continuing to ask questions like, "Where are my friends?" "Have I spent time with them lately?" "How many new toys have I bought?" and "I had better keep track of how much all these new toys are costing me!"

Along with your new challenges, there are also a lot of new activities that have been added to your life. You need to assess them and make them fit the new game plan. Take note of all that fattening food they serve at those customer/client lunches. Watch out for the sugar in those chocolate covered donuts that are always waiting for you at those early morning staff meetings. Do not forget to come in early enough on Saturday nights, so you will be able to stay awake during Sunday Service. Somebody might just ask you what the sermon was about.

In the rest of this chapter, I will discuss tactics for keeping a well-balanced life now that you are a part of the corporate business world.

# Do Not Forget To Enjoy Your Life

Think about this: In the business world, you are expected to work at least 40 hours a week. Most professionals work more. Some will often work a 50 hour work-week. If you add a half day on Saturday in order to catch up on paperwork, you are now at 56 hours per week. If you add what I call "shine time" (the time spent making sure your work is exceptional), you will work another 10 hours. If you perform the simple math calculation on this, you will find this adds up to about 66 hours a week. I have just described an illness called "Workaholism." It is very common in the business world for those who have misunderstood what it takes to hold onto their success.

The business world can rob you of a social life. We professionals too often lose this battle with little sign of struggle. I have seen a new hire fresh off the college campus come into a company, bright-eyed and bushy-tailed, only to become what I call a "social deprivate." This is one who has become impervious to all social attraction and activities. It is a tragedy. These are the same kids who, six months ago, were enjoying the good life. What happens is no mystery, and that is why it is tragic.

These kids come into a large corporation. They are introduced around and welcomed. They are congratulated and told how fortunate they are to have been selected to be a part of such a prestigious company. They are immediately told to work hard and success will follow. We show them their desks, telephones and order their business cards. They are so proud to see their names embossed on the same cards as the company logo. Then, we do it to them! We dump the largest stack of manuals you have ever seen onto their desks, and we tell them they have four to six weeks to learn it all. I still hear myself saying those very words. From this day forward, we have begun the destruction of their social life.

As I stated earlier, professionals so easily give up all that is good in life to accomplish their objectives. There is always a deadline to meet or a meeting to prepare for. There are more widows to the "corporate sunset" than you would dare to think about. (The corporate sunset is the time professionals start doing their paperwork. It usually starts around the published quitting time.) Women professionals are often worse than their male counterparts. As I mentioned earlier, they decide not to get involved romantically for fear of commitment. Instead, they marry "Corporate Harry", the copier machine. They find themselves on more dates with the janitor as they walk to their cars, one of the last ones in the parking garage. You know this is not what they thought being successful meant. Have I scared you enough?

This is a good time to go back and re-read the

sections on what it takes to be organized under "Perpetuating The Work Ethic" and understanding the value of your time. Taking time out for yourself should be more important than the time you put in for the corporation. I ask myself often, "What good is all the money if you do not take time to enjoy it?" When you sit through your first corporate time management class, make sure you extrapolate it to your social life.

The business world too often becomes your Family, your Friends and your Loved ones. Professional life will take all you are willing to give it and more. Plan time for your social life, just the way you learn to plan time for your professional life. Work hard, and after work, play hard, even if this means curling up with a good book in a cozy apartment after a nourishing meal. You are no longer tied to nighttime study assignments. If you are, quit now and find another job. If you are training, do it during business hours and leave it at work when 5:00 or 6:00 o'clock rolls around. Take yourself on a date at least once a week. If you are already married, schedule time for your spouse no less than weekly. (Do not spend all your money on partying. I will discuss more of this later.) There are more divorces because professionals do not take time with their spouses than most other causes of divorce. Do not become one of these statistics. Take time out for your friends and have routine time set aside to have fun. Be involved in your community. Learn to live a balanced life.

Corporations like to see their employees live balanced lives. Being involved in community activities shows you are well-rounded. Being involved in the community can also be good for career development, especially if you are involved with some type of organization that allows you to network. This is a good way to make contacts and broaden your horizons. If you have not done it already, it could help you meet the man or woman of your dreams. Being involved in the community will allow you to give something back to the community.

Be careful of over-committing yourself or becoming too involved with too many projects. I have observed those who find themselves more involved in the community than they are at work. Shoot for a balance. I spend a lot of time working with youth groups. They keep me young and vital. They also help me keep up with the latest fads and fashions as well as allowing me to develop young people for the future.

Spending time with your friends, family and acquaintances is very important for your whole person. People who work all the time become very poor souls after a few years. They actually lose their zest for life. Make time for the good things in life. Part of your definition for success should include living well and enjoying all that you build for yourself. Time spent on you is better than time spent on anything else. Enjoy your life, all of it!

# Spiritual Health

The biggest investment you will ever make is in becoming knowledgeable and developing your mental capacities to their fullest potential. It is amazing how much time and money we spend gaining knowledge. Once we have it, we take it for granted; and we usually do not do a lot to protect it. Oh sure, we try to keep up on the latest news. We may read a good book occasionally as we set out to enjoy life. But, how will you maintain a good attitude? What is going to help you through those times of crisis which will happen. What is going to keep you from driving your car over your boss when he or she takes you for granted, or he or she does not notice how much time and effort it took to accomplish your last project. This can all be handled by a stable mind.

Make no mistake, mental stability comes from the "spiritual aspects" of your life. Your spiritual health must be nurtured and cared for just as your physical body must be nurtured and cared for.

At the risk of ruining what you thought was a good book up until now, I will offer you some of my most personal thoughts. This does not fall under the guise of business tactics, strategies, or experiences, but it is important for taking care of the total person, which should definitely be a part of your life-strategy. I ask you to accept it as another example of the things you must consider if you are going to have true success and keep it. You must have a plan for spiritual growth just as you must have a plan for financial growth.

My theory is that we humans are made up of three things: One is a physical being; another is a financial being; and finally we are a spiritual being (some people call it a soul).

As a spiritual being, we must do things to enhance and grow this spiritual part of ourselves. I believe this is a part of us that should be taken care of first, and the others parts will fall in their proper places. Some of you are fully aware of what it takes to keep this being alive and well, and to you I say, go on to the next section. For those of you who need a little guidance, hear me out. If you are reading this line, thank you.

Your spiritual being must be fed spiritual food. Of course, it will continue to function whether you pay attention to it or not, just as your arm will continue to move your hand whether you exercise it or not. The question is how well and how long will anything function if you do not take good care of it?

What can you do for this spiritual being? I believe this is where having a personal relationship with your creator is of the utmost important; for me, it is God. (Most top executives attend church which says something about their moral character.) Because I am Black and was once very disadvantaged, I needed something that would never let me down, no matter what the circumstances were. God lived up to my expectations. Now, I try to live up to God's expectations. I have been able to count on God ever since I learned God's capabilities. I have found that there is nothing I cannot endure, if I put my faith in God. I try not to limit God to fit what my simple, yet complex, mind can conjure up. I believe God is all-knowing, all-present, and almighty. Not bad, huh! I have also learned not to try to force God into the business world except where it concerns me. People are going to believe what they want. I believe in God.

Exercising your spiritual being is more important than exercising your body muscles. There are going to be times in the business world when life will not seem fair. There will be times when everything you try will not work, and you will be at your wit's end. When you find yourself in this situation, and you will, you had better have a strong spiritual makeup—one that will endure the world and all of its challenges. I have been unsuccessful many times which was very hard to face. I have had people tell me I was not doing a good job when I thought I was doing my best. I have been devastated by what people thought of me at given times. Each of these times I turned to my God and prayed, and it always worked out well on my behalf. I know I have been blessed more than I can ever comprehend!

It is your spiritual being that helps you keep things in perspective. Cognitive dissonance is helpful, but it cannot get you through what I am trying to describe here. The spiritual being is a survival mechanism of the deepest kind. The more you develop it, the better it will serve you. Some people may call this your "guts". I think it is more. I think it is the seat of your consciousness. It is where you make those hard decisions where the facts seem to stack up one way, but something inside of you tells you that you can do it. A strong spiritual being will push you past those obstacles that pop-up out of nowhere and try to hold you back. Humans will prepare for every physical catastrophe they can foresee. But they have trouble when it comes to spiritual preparation. Hmmmm!

In fact, during the week I was writing this chapter, America waged war on Iraq. The one thing I heard everybody talking about, but not understanding, is how could this man be willing to submit his little country to such devastation. The answer is simple! Saddam Hussein had spent years preparing his understanding and his commitment to what he believed in. I am not saying he was right or wrong, but he was prepared to die for what he believed was right. Imagine the strength and power that comes from this type of mental preparation. We Americans have a hard time imagining this type of commitment. The President of the United States, at the time, called the most well-known evangelist to the White House to pray for the government. The war may have never come had the government been praying all along.

As African-Americans, we have had to turn to higher spiritual powers. It is a major part of our culture. We need to look back and see what brought our ancestors through their hard times. I think you will find it was their spiritual beliefs; they did not own anything else. Even if there were no God, the very belief in God generates a tremendous mental power base; and we need everything that will help us be strong. Most of your battles, as a Black professional, will be mental ones. These are the battles that are very hard to prepare for  Dr. King said, "You cannot kill an idea." I will add, "An idea will never go forward unless you are willing to stand behind it."

I say again, most of the challenges you will face in the

business world are mental challenges. If you have prepared your seat of consciousness that harbors your mental abilities (this I call the soul), then you are prepared to think clearly and precisely. May my God be with you.

# Physical Health

People today are very health conscious. The business world is probably a major contributor. No matter where you are, it is very important you learn to think clearly, look good and feel good. Physical endurance and overall physical stamina are very important in the business world, where your day may start as early as 5:00 a.m. and continue non-stop until 6:00 p.m. or later. If you are going to be able to think clearly and precisely throughout the day, you have to learn to take care of your total person. If you are truly mentally stable, you will want good physical health.

It is now fashionable to look healthy, and people go to great lengths to do so; but looking good is not the place to stop. You must also feel good. This is not a temporary situation. Part of being confident and self-assured is because you take very good care of yourself. One of the first things I noticed when I arrived on the corporate scene was that everyone looked great. They were well dressed. There were not many people who were extremely overweight, although you will see those who are a bit portly. When you are out at lunch, everyone talks about having to lose weight. I found that to be just another thing people talk about as part of lunchtime conversation. Dieting and eating properly leads to good health. The business world believes good health is a major part of being successful.

You will find your business colleagues, for the most part, are very careful about what they eat. Restaurants sell more salads at lunch than all other entrees. All of the fast food chains now have some type of salad on their menu. We have become a world that eats "lite". Light appears to be a marketing tool, but it also keeps everybody thinking about what they eat.

Eating properly is just plain good sense. If you watch what you eat, you will feel better in the long run. Eating properly will help control your weight, providing you do not have some other health problem. I must admit, we Blacks love to eat things that taste good, which are usually the things that are not the healthiest. I love eating a good pork chop with deep fried potatoes, a piece of french bread and a large coke (with sugar). If there is a piece of "one step pound cake" for dessert, I am in seventh heaven. But I learned to watch my diet when I joined the business world.

I had the honor to be teamed with a health conscious Black brother on my first assignment. He was from Kansas City. We were always running from one client to the next, and lunch was on the road. We frequently stopped in the various fast food restaurants. I always ordered the biggest hamburger. He would look at me and say, "Simms, that stuff will kill ya"! I would look up from my plate and give him a sheepish smile. He continuously told me how much better he felt since he stopped eating red meat. After about a year, I started paying attention to my diet; I decreased my consumption of red meat and started to eat more fish and chicken. Increasing my chicken consumption was not a hard thing to do. I still prefer it fried over all the other ways it can be prepared; but we all know that is the unhealthiest way to prepare it.

Good dietary habits are very important because they lead to better health. Diseases such as hypertension (high blood pressure) kill us. It should be easy to decrease your salt consumption. Here again, you must have a dietary program. Planning your meals is essential. One of the side benefits I receive by watching what I eat is the discipline it adds to my life.

Eating properly must also be accompanied by getting enough rest and relaxation. The relaxation is equally as important as the rest. If you are a hyper person like I am, you probably have a need to slowly shut the body down after a busy day at work. There are many ways to do this. One of the things I have learned to do is read. I was not taught the value of reading as a kid, but being in the corporate world has shown me how important it is to read. I try to read things that are informative; but if I am relaxing, I try to read things that I enjoy and that do not tax my mind. You can think of any number of things that relax you. I encourage you to take good care of yourself.

If you listen to the various talk shows, you have probably heard how deprived the world is of sleep. I can tell you from first hand experience, it is true. The business world is part of the problem. Business professionals work long and late hours which lead to sleep deprivation. Sleep deprivation leads to ineffectiveness at work. You must get enough sleep in order to have good health. You also increase your effectiveness if you are fully rested when you come to work each morning. Save your late nights for the weekends. Arsenio may have a party every night, but remember he is at work and getting paid for it. It is very unprofessional to sit in a meeting and nod off to sleep. You may have missed a major opportunity to get your piece of the action. You will be embarrassed each time someone has to nudge you in order to wake you up. Yes, I speak from experience.

If, for some reason, you are unable to get enough sleep before attending a meeting or class, you should quietly and politely stand in the back of the room. Standing will help you keep from falling asleep. It is not unusual to see professionals standing during long meetings or classes. Sleep is sometimes a by-product of boredom. Find a different way to handle the boredom. However, be sure you understand the politics involved in the company before putting yourself in a precarious situation. If your management team does not like people standing in the back of the room, you may bring unwanted attention to yourself.

The last of the programmatic things I want to discuss is exercising! Women please take heed. Fat hips are out in corporate America. I have yet to see an overweight woman in a highly-paid executive position, let alone a Black, overweight woman. Good eating habits will not lead to total good health without exercise. It is "in" and it is necessary. You will find professionals using their lunch hours to exercise. Some people have learned to exercise in the morning using cable TV. My wife justified cable TV in our house by convincing both of us it was a good use of our money and provided a major benefit to her and me. She religiously exercises every morning in front of the television. I myself exercise most mornings in the bathroom before my shower. It is very easy to put a personal program together. It takes discipline to keep it going, but so does everything that is worthwhile doing.

If you are one who needs encouragement to exercise, find a buddy who shares your interest in exercising. If the budget allows, join a health club. There are numerous aerobic classes offered which are very reasonable in price. Many large corporations are adding facilities and programs to encourage good health. Corporations often will assist you in paying for accredited exercise programs. Take advantage of these programs. They are a part of your benefits package.

Here are a few thoughts on things that work against good health. They also work against a good business image. Drinking can be detrimental in the business world. The stress that you can come under is a powerful force. Drinking is often a "crutch". Alcohol is often misused and abused in the business world. It may be called social drinking, but it often becomes a part of the business culture. On business trips, the thing to do after class or a busy day is to head for the bar in the lobby and have a drink. Unfortunately, it is never just one drink. A lot of professionals use alcohol to unwind. They become dependent on it for this reason. Drinking is widely accepted in the business world and can be expected in some settings. Do not fall into the trap of having to drink to accomplish your business.

As a non-drinker, I have learned to go out with clients and colleagues and drink non-alcoholic drinks. If I am discussing business, I stay sharp and focused on my objectives. If it is strictly social, I enjoy the interaction of my colleagues more, and I am in a better position to assist them if they become inebriated. My main objective is to stay away from alcohol.

Science has proven cigarettes are unhealthy. The business world is currently shunning the smoker. Cigarette smoking is now unacceptable in the work place and there are fewer and fewer people smoking every day. Most work places do not allow smoking in the main work area. In most companies smoking is only allowed outside of the building.

Cigarettes take away from the clean cut image we discussed earlier. If you smoke, you will smell like smoke at the most inopportune times. More and more people are irritated by the smell of cigarette smoke and will be turned off if you smell of cigarette smoke. Cigarette smoke yellows and dulls your teeth. Smoking takes away from clear thinking. I once had a boss who was a fairly nice guy. If you were discussing a problem with him, and he needed a smoke, you could tell. He would have less patience with you during this time. He was short with his answers if he needed a cigarette. In meetings, people who smoke are often disruptive because they need more breaks in order to smoke. They often try to shorten a meeting because of their addiction to cigarettes.

Cigarette smokers are a dying breed, pun intended. This habit causes major risk to everyone's health. It has been studied and proven: cigarette smoking is hazardous even to people who do not smoke—those who are exposed to the cigarette smoke.

Drugs are a total cop-out. Unfortunately, there are business professionals who think drugs solve some of their problems. I do not need to spend a lot of time on this topic. We all know that drugs are bad for our health, and they kill. There are so many other hazards in life, why take on those we do not have to? Most corporations have programs in place to test you for drugs. You will ruin a prosperous career if you are caught taking drugs. They may not always get you fired, but they most certainly will make you an outcast or considered untrustworthy.

Underneath all of the possible health abusers above is the need to "Manage Stress." You can simply avoid the cause and alleviate the problem by overeating, drinking, smoking or doing drugs. Job deadlines, trying to get promoted, trying to prove excellence are all factors that create or contribute to the stress you experience. Stress is unavoidable in the business world. I experience some type of stress every single day. Sometimes I am aware of it, and other times I am not. It can be very detrimental to your health and must be dealt with in some fashion. There are no real preventive measures. Situations arise and your body will react to those situations.

There are many healthy ways to manage stress. I love to play golf. For some reason, to go out on a sunny day and walk on well-manicured, plush, green grass, and hit a little white ball around makes me relax and forget about my troubles. Often I play with my colleagues and discuss work related matters, yet I do not feel stressed. Playing the drums allows me to relieve stress. There is a release when you do something physical. Driving on an unimpeded highway relieves my stress. One of my favorite stress-relieving activities is riding a bicycle.

Institutional Racism is a big contributor to stress. If I think someone is treating me a certain way because of my color, I experience stress. This is a stress factor that you ought to be aware of. If you are feeling out of sorts some days, and you cannot seem to place the cause; this may be it. This is not one to dwell on or it will continue to negatively affect you. Just be aware that it is another factor to manage; and whatever you find to relieve stress, you may have to employ it during these times. Networking can help you with this problem. Being able to discuss issues with someone who understands and cares will help release some of the tension you build up over these matters.

Most corporations are putting programs in place to assist you with almost all of the problems discussed above. They are a part of your benefits package. Take advantage of them if you find you need them. Please do not let your personal pride destroy your ability to be successful. Enough said?

# Financial Health

The one main reason I was prompted to write "For all who must do" was for the time in my career where I was spending more money than I was earning. It was not that I had not learned to live on my income. I learned to do that a long time ago when I was a pre-college graduate making $6,000 a year. In those days, I had money to burn. But, something happens to you when you graduate from college, and a large corporation starts to pay attention to "little ole you." You get this feeling of invincibility when you receive a check for more than $1,000. You now know, you have the capability of making a lot of money. You learn to spend money as fast as you can make it. Then there is an amazing discovery: you learn that you can qualify for every credit card in the nation. Now you learn that you not only can spend all the money you make, you can also spend all the money you are going to make in the next five years. The next thing you know, you are in debt up to your armpits.

In America, money and knowledge are power. They are both things you have to work very hard to acquire. This is the reason we must learn to make them both work for us. The knowledge we have acquired while attending college is now being employed by American business. In return they give us money. We now have the ability to buy. Buying power in America speaks loudly, but, if you buy before you can afford to, you lose your power. You will soon not be able to buy anymore. I have known several professional people who made a lot of money. They spent all of that money and more and went bankrupt. The only reason this happened was because they forgot one thing: do not spend more money than you have. In fact spend less than you have, and save the rest for a rainy day.

There are seven wonders of the world. I believe one of them is interest. At least it should be, because it has allowed millions of people to realize great fortunes. We Blacks must let interest work for us. Corporations have learned a happy employee is one who is not worried about where the next dollar is coming from. They have implemented numerous programs that help employees take hard earned money and make more money. Part of your personal business plan should be to take advantage of every program the company offers.

Most corporations have some type of profit-sharing program. Some companies have stock-purchasing programs, usually at a discount to their employees. They have savings programs that allow you to have the payroll department send funds to a savings account, usually with above-normal interest rates. Some companies will match your savings if it is tax-deferred for long-term investing. If you are not taking advantage of the maximum limits, you are missing out on part of your benefits package. Some might call it free money. It is advantageous for you to attend every financial seminar the company brings to town. You cannot lose! I am often very upset with my Black colleagues when I attend these seminars, and I am the only Black in attendance. Being the pushy person I am, I challenge them. Some of my Black colleagues have actually said they were not interested. I believe they did not understand the importance of the seminars and were either too embarrassed or too proud to admit it.

Again, these plans and programs are part of your benefits package. They usually cost nothing more than a little of your time to understand how they work. There is usually little to no risk. Before you invest money anywhere else, you should find a benefits coordinator to explain corporate programs to you. They are worth all the time you put into understanding them.

Personal Budgeting is a key to financial planning. By now you know I believe you should a have a road map for everything you do, even if it is a once-a-year exercise. It is especially important to plan your finances. Sit down and map out where you need to spend your money, and where you want to spend your money. You will be further ahead if you do. A personal budget should be flexible but adhered to as often as possible. This is another area of your life where you can build and "capitalize" on discipline.

Uncle Sam will see your checks before you see them. He will take as much of your hard-earned money as he can. You can not beat him at his game, but you can minimize his taking. Buy a house as soon as you can qualify for it. I know you have these lofty ideas of the big house on the hill with the ten feet by ten feet windows overlooking the lake. It will happen but not as soon as you think. I am still trying to get that house. (If you buy enough copies of this book I will get it.) Start small and work your way up. You are not successful until you own a piece of property. It is a proud moment when you receive your first set of keys to your own house. Guess what? Uncle Sam will allow you to deduct from you annual income all of the interest on your mortgage.

Earlier I mentioned tax-deferred savings programs. These programs allow you to save money while giving you a tax break. If these programs are no longer in place, there will be others. Understand these programs and learn to use them to your benefit. Beat Uncle SAM!

When all is said and done, Do what you can with what you "got", until you get what you want!

# Chapter

# 19

# The Asian Success – What Can We Learn?

*I*f you are just completing college or have been working for a short while at your career, the chances are you have an Asian colleague or friend. Have you spent any time observing them and watching how they go about getting things accomplished? They are indeed an amazing people. The Asian people have been on American shores for a very long time. Their history in America often parallels the Black plight in many ways, except they have managed to capitalize on their misfortunes in America.

The Japanese bombed Pearl Harbor and then suffered deeply after the Hiroshima bombing. They were placed in concentration camps during World War II. They started receiving restitution for being put in those camps a few years ago. They overcame a devastating tragedy and then used their own enemy to rebuild their land. They accepted and learned all the U.S. offered and taught while the U.S tried to apologize. The knowledge gained by the Japanese from America is now being used to achieve technological superiority over the whole world. The Japanese have exceeded, or are on the verge of exceeding, the U.S. in most of the highly technical industries they have chosen to enter. They have become a formidable competitor in World Trade.

The Koreans fought against the U.S. then turned around and fought beside the U.S. They now are participating heavily in the U.S. economy. The Vietnamese fought with us and against us and are now migrating and assimilating. They started out from their shores on ragged boats and are now cruising luxurious Cadillacs and Mercedes Benzs on Rodeo Drive.

The Chinese are deeply rooted in the U.S. and have managed to keep their culture solidly in tact. They are now in the throes of seeking democracy as it has never been sought before in China. I think their youth will eventually prevail even though they are fighting one of the strongest cultures that has ever existed.

If young educated Blacks could learn from the Asian cultures, we could truly take our place in the American business world. The adversity we have overcome has indeed made us stronger. It is now time for African-Americans to use the lessons we have learned as these Asian Cultures are doing.

A great characteristic of the Asians is their ability to assimilate into other countries, while continuing to foster their cultural beliefs and principles. My Asian friends and colleagues are very adaptable to their environment. They have mastered the process of assimilation without giving up what is important to them as a people. Asian people are willing to start from the bottom and work their way up.

When I was in college working a part time job at a local hospital, I remember meeting a gentleman who was a janitor in the hospital. He was a doctor from the Philippines continuing his education in order to meet the requirements for the medical board examinations here in the United States. He needed two years of course work to take this exam. He had come to work in the hospital to pay for the schooling he needed. He also continued to take care of his family which was still residing in the Philippines. His family also realized he was trying to create a better life for them here in the U.S. He was willing to put down his credentials and his pride to improve his lot in life. His desire to succeed was overwhelming.

An Asian willingly works in a hamburger joint for a minimum wage, asking himself only one question, will this help "me and mine" get ahead? They have learned to find "honor in whatever they do and they do it honorably." They have high integrity and high moral standards. This combination can take you far. This country has lost many of its moral standards, but I don't believe we have forgotten them. We still honor high moral standards.

The Asians appear to enjoy the process; they appear to enjoy the preparation for accomplishing a given task as much as finishing the task. Take martial arts. They enjoy the pain-staking preparation and the hours of practice. They have learned to finish whatever task they start. They calculate risk very well in order to minimize failure.

# The Art of Discipline

The main ingredient of the Asians' success is the deeply rooted "discipline" that has been handed down over thousands of years. This discipline manifests itself in all aspects of their life, especially in their work life. It is more than just a characteristic; it is the fiber that has been interwoven throughout their culture. They have developed discipline into what appears to be an art form.

It starts when they are babies in their cribs. They are taught to respect their elders. Discipline runs throughout all that they accomplish. The Asian child knows he must do well in school. It is not the reward/punishment system that drives this child to excel. The Asian children excel based on good sound logic and respect for the family which says, "If life is to be good for you, you must be good for it." The Asian child has been taught good grades in school will honor the family.

From my experience, the Black child is usually reinforced with negative pressures or stimuli, such as, "Child, if you don't go to school, you're just going to wind-up on the streets as a drug addict." Asian children have been taught that being average is unacceptable; over-achievement has become the norm.

When you attended college, who was setting the bell in the grade curve? In my classes, it was the Nguyens, the Okas, the Chins and Chows, or the Shigiharas of the world. The Ottems, the LaVerns and the Bigelows were riding the "means" of the curve. The Pattersons, the Stubblefields, the Beards, the Marshalls, the Turners, the Escribanos and the Simms were trying to cling to the "standard deviations." The Asians seemed to accomplish those good grades effortlessly, while we gave it all we had and still seemed to come up short. But don't be fooled. They worked very hard!

When you have learned to master everything that is presented to you, you no doubt will be ahead of anybody who attempts to measure up to your standards. The Asians are now starting to set the standards. The Japanese have become masters of quality. They assume zero defects in the products they produce. It is ingrained in the essence of what they are made of. It is hard to beat.

If you find you have superior study habits and the ability to walk away from distractions before they can ever take hold of your attention, you truly have something going for you. I worked hard to enter into the Asian social circle. Once they allowed me in, I was able to become friends with many of my Asian colleagues. I learned to study with them and enjoy their company. It took a while for them to accept me, but after they did, it was a very wholesome and trusting friendship.

I have become intrigued by their methods, habits and application of discipline. In the workplace, they are sought after for their discipline. Everyone seems to expect the best from them. This only perpetuates what is already a part of who they are. This discipline allows them to spend a lot more time thinking and listening rather than complaining and questioning. From my observations, they appear to enjoy their work more than most other cultures represented in the workplace. If they are not enjoying their work, they have mastered the art of hiding it.

The American-born Asian seems to have the advantage if their discipline has been kept in tact. They not only understand the American culture, they also have an inbred discipline which comes from their Asian culture.

Our Asian friends have brought a great gift to America, and we ought to capitalize on it. We are learning their martial arts and the ability to train the mind and the body to work in harmony. We must continue to imbed discipline in our thinking and abilities. If we can make discipline a part of our professional makeup, and it becomes a part of our everyday lives, we will indeed be better professionals.

# Patience Is A Virtue

I believe patience and discipline go hand in hand. If you are a disciplined person, you most certainly have learned not to rush things.

The Asian appears to be very patient in most everything. They seem to have the ability to wait a long time for things to get better or turn in their favor.

Patience is a valuable asset. It is very helpful while you are waiting to be promoted. I do preach patience much better than I practice it. I find I tell myself constantly to be patient! To become very good at anything, you must have patience, first, with yourself and then with other people or projects.

People who have little patience expect others to have a lot of patience. The business world is intolerable of people with little patience. Patience is the best manager of anger and provides a platform for stability in your life. There will be numerous opportunities to develop patience, and there may be times when you are forced to develop it whether you want to or not. And, I guarantee your patience will be tried, time and time again! I have been in numerous situations where patience was the only skill I could use. It is the one thing that will help overcome frustration. There will be times when you know you are ready to move on in your career, but the needs of a business will not allow you to do that. You will need your patience! There will be times when you need a resource from someone, and you must be patient until you can acquire that resource.

The application of patience is an area where we should learn from our Asian colleagues. When I think of the Japanese professionals who try to supply basic necessities for their family, I am in awe. In Japan, it could take a highly educated and highly skilled individual years to buy things Americans can afford at the drop of a hat. To own a car in Japan is more than a luxury. It is not the car that is at a premium, it is the place to park it. They must save money for years before they can start to buy a house that will never be paid for in one lifetime. Their children are obligated as early as birth to continue paying for this house. It requires patience to simply live in a country like Japan.

The Japanese patience is paying off for them in the United States. Now they are buying San Francisco, Hawaii, and other major real estate in the U.S. They are making investments that will continue to grow for the next decades. Their patience is allowing them to acquire all that their hearts desire and their growing pocketbooks can afford. I am sure, if you have completed any major task in your life, you have found patience to be a virtue.

# Combine And Conquer

The family is the key to Asian success. The family provides the support structure to succeed. You know the old adage, "Behind every successful man is a good woman." As antiquated as it has become, the principles that surrounded it are still valid. My Asian friends almost always have stable homes and family life. They have very supportive mothers, fathers, brothers, and sisters. Their extended families are equally supportive. In the Asian family you will find an uncle or aunt to be just as much of an authority figure as a father or mother. The uncle or aunt may spend a significant amount of time leading their nephews and nieces to a successful position in society. This is all done to bring honor to the family name.

If there is a big spread in age between the siblings, the parents require their older children to help with the discipline necessary for a successful family structure. It is no wonder they are up to the challenges that are put in front of them. If you know you are loved, and you have a family that cares and will do all it can to help you succeed, what can come against you?

Asians appear to have the utmost respect for one another. This is clearly expressed in their family structure. You will find a younger sister giving due respect to her elder sister. When you explore their language, you will find it is permeated by respect. For instance, in the Filipino language, the younger sister will call her older sister "Ate" which means older sister and shows respect for the older sister. When the Filipino says good morning, they say, "kumusta kayo po." The "po" is an understood "Sir" or "M'am".

Asians help one another. They work to support family members in their home countries while they continue to progress in the United States. The Vietnamese have acquired more wealth by working together. They make it their business, if at all possible, to buy one another's goods and services. They have learned to grow from within their own communities.

The Korean businessmen in America have monthly social gatherings where they come together to share ideas. They pool money from their profits and set it aside for whichever one of them has the biggest need. The money is then given to the individual. What a way to perpetuate the growth and prosperity of a community and a people. Everybody wins!

You will find if a neighborhood has one Asian family, it will soon have two and then three and so forth. These people have an overwhelming desire to be near each other. Their cultural ties are so powerful that they are drawn together from thousands of miles apart. The White community has learned the Asian family will enhance a neighborhood once they become a part it. White communities readily accept the Asian families into their neighborhoods without appearing to think twice about it.

You may find two or three Asian families living together. They buy a house just big enough to accommodate their needs. They all find jobs, often in the same company. They will buy their first car and share it for as long as necessary. You can see why they try to work together. Working together accommodates their sharing of limited transportation. If they have to wake up at 3:00 a.m. to get everybody to work on time — No Problem!

Next they buy another car. They keep pooling their resources until they all have exactly what they want. I once lived next door to an Asian family who appeared to have jobs that started at all hours around the clock. There were several very nice, economical cars parked in the driveway as well as in front of the house.

Once everybody is working and everybody has a car, they help one another buy a house. They have a tremendous ability to save money in order to fund their transactions. They often hurt themselves by buying with cash and never developing credit. They might be better off if they purchased commodities on credit and invested their cash. On the other hand, maybe they are smart to buy with cash. They don't get in debt like millions of Americans who are prisoners to interest rates that often outpace their return on investments.

I once listed a house through an American realtor. A Vietnamese realtor came by to show the house to his clients who tried to buy the house but could not. The Vietnamese realtor liked the house and became determined to sell the house. He did not hesitate to tell me and my wife just that! He did not stop until he had put a sound deal together we could not refuse, and he remained pleasant through the whole transaction. The buyers he found were Vietnamese. They had only been in the country a short time, yet they had saved enough money to assume a pretty healthy mortgage. Needless to say, I was very pleased with the outcome of his service, and I admired his business sense. He was persistent!

I do not wish to misinform you or leave you with the impression that all is well with the Asians who have become a part of these United States. There is growing violence in their communities which is threatening what they have accomplished. Drugs are starting to take a real toll on their children, eroding their discipline. In American cities, Asian gangs are becoming more violent than other inner-city gangs. "Evil and crime" know no color or other boundaries.

# Other Diverse Cultures

I want to discuss another ethnic culture which is starting to take a piece of Americana: the Mexican Invasion. We can learn from this minority group as well. They are quickly increasing their numbers in the workforce and in this country and will soon surpass the Black professional in business attainment.

These people come into the country, for the most part, on work visas. They are invited to do this because they will work for minimum wage and will do labor we U.S. folks are too proud to do. They will often sacrifice much of their personal wealth to gain more; in America we call that investing. You will find them all over the West Coast in the berry fields and other agricultural industries. They have learned the secret of success in America; if you work very hard, you can earn a little money. They know that, if you save your money, you will soon be able to buy your way into the U.S., permanently. On occasion, I still see them living in trailers on berry farms and working in orchards. Once they have the money, they seek citizenship and enroll their children in school. Soon they are making wonderful homes for their families and becoming contributing citizens to their U.S. communities.

I remember when there were those who used to say, "Look at those poor Mexicans." Now, those poor Hispanics own large portions of the southern United States. The Hispanics have learned, like the Asians, that if you get a good education, you can enter into the good life of the United States. You now see them stepping into the political arenas. They are formidable foes in the business world. Some statistics show them becoming the largest minority group in America by the year 2000.

There are other cultures that we as professional young Black Americans can learn from: the Indians from India are entering science and engineering programs in American Universities and surpassing even the Asians. They too have a discipline and commitment to family which carries them into the middle echelons of the business world. They have not yet learned to be as aggressive as our Asian counterparts, but what they lack in marketing "savvy", they make up with a tremendous "technical prowess." Here we can learn what it means to be persistent.

The Laotians, the Burmese, Taiwanese, and a host of other Far and Middle Eastern cultures all seem to have the ability to rise above the oppression the "American way" places in front them. They seem to have the ability to find solace from within their culture, allowing them to endure the American economic and social structure. We Black Americans must learn to use the system and make it work to our advantage. It is time to become a part of the big picture, in a positive way. We most certainly have endured the struggle!

The Asians are the successful "people of color" to date. Their success has come from within. Education has been a cornerstone for their success, and it is valued only second to love and respect for one another. They value the family and the honor associated with being a part of the family. We Black Americans need to continue to reach back and pull each other forward. We can do this in this decade. It just might be the chance we have all been patiently awaiting. We must learn from our Asian brothers and sisters to seize the moment and the opportunity.

# Chapter

# 20

## What's Next?

W hat's next? Even as I pose this question to you, the reader, I am continuously challenged by this question. No matter how successful you or I become, this two-word question must be answered again and again. It is a question I hope I can continue to answer for as long as I live. It is what continues to provide me with the vitality for my life. It is what I hope will allow me to get that house up on a hill, the sports car in the garage, and money in the bank, all while keeping food on the table. It is the question that will allow me to help someone else. And, once I have all of that; it will allow me peace of mind.

For you, the Black professional, this question should open up a plethora of thoughts and ideas. It should stimulate you to explore what is possible and what is not. One of the things I am still learning to do is to keep my thinking pertinent to my abilities. I try not to limit myself only to what I can do today, but I try to look at what is possible for me tomorrow. What am I capable of accomplishing? This type of thinking leads me to prepare for what I want to accomplish next.

Many people have a tendency to shoot for things they can never reach. This will only frustrate you. You can waste a lot of time and energy. There are others who plunge head first into whatever is before them, but they soon find they do not get very far. They may be ready to work hard, but if the opportunity has not yet presented itself, it could be just a genuine waste of time. If you are one of these, Stop — Step Back — Analyze, Analyze — Plan — Then Proceed!

We all have a crystal ball we can use to help us choose what direction we want to take in life, and we should learn to use it. It is not a magical thing; it is made available through the knowledge we have obtained. The more knowledge and experience we gain in this life, the more accurately we learn to use our crystal ball. You will be amazed at how much insight you can gain in a year. I have seen people go from bumbling around in the dark to knowing exactly what to do next.

Throughout this book,, I have talked about what it takes to be successful in the corporate world. By now you have probably gathered that it will take thorough planning to accomplish whatever you set out to do. Many people finish college and set out to make a career for themselves. They find there are a lot of different ways to accomplish things, and some take longer than others. They find numerous stumbling blocks along the way. If you have not yet sat down and given some thought to what you want to accomplish in the next few years, especially where your career is concerned, now is a good time to do it.

# Career Planning

Whether you are just leaving the college campus or thinking about a new career after working twenty years in the old one, you should plan your next steps. People who know where they want to go in their career usually get there.

I once had a Black colleague who was a relatively sharp individual. He and I worked together for several years. He had several very successful years and won a large division-level award that put him in the limelight of the company. He attracted the attention of upper management. He was invited to an executive interview with a fairly high level manager. He was asked during this interview, "How far would you like to go in this company? What are your career plans?" His answer was, "I don't know!" Never, never let these three words come from your mouth when someone asks you what you would like to do, especially if they are empowered to help you.

It takes a very short time to look around a corporation and pick out several jobs that could possibly capture your interest. I am often intrigued by the titles of some jobs, although I may not know the details of the job description. The day you walk into a corporation, you should start looking for the last job you would like to hold in the corporation before you retire. This should be a job you believe one day you will have. If it is the CEO position, I hope one day to work for you. The steps it takes to go from your current position to that final position from which you will retire is what makes up your ultimate career plan.

The ultimate career plan is not something most of us complete during our first year in the profession. Some of you may never complete it because it will continue to change. That is okay. The key is to have a plan and follow it as often as life will allow it. If it gets modified once a month, it is probably not a good plan. If it gets modified once a year, you probably have something you can work with. Do whatever works for you.

There are many things you can consider in your career plan. The more things you consider, the more thought you will give to your life; and you can never spend too much time thinking about your life. The events in your plan should allow you to be progressive. They should allow you to contribute to your profession which, in turn, will allow you to be a good contributor to society and someone we all can be proud of. The next few paragraphs should help you get started or reassess what you want to do.

In an earlier chapter, we discussed some of the "Essences of Success" which really translated to characteristics, traits and skills a professional might possess. It is rare to find someone who possesses all of them at once, especially if it is early in a career. One of the first things we need to do as a part of our career plan is a Self Assessment. Ask and answer the following questions: Who am I? What are my qualifications? What do I care about in life? What gives value to my life? How far do I want to go? How far do I really think I can go?

These are just some of the questions that will start you to thinking about your career and your life. You may be surprised at what you learn about yourself as you attempt to build a career plan.

Next, put together a Skills Inventory. This may be hard to do if you are an inexperienced professional. You will be amazed at how long this list will grow in the first three to six months in your profession. I was once training several new professionals who were very eager to learn everything that was put in front of them. I told them, "You will be assisting and teaching me inside of a year." They went on to promising careers in the company. One of them was able to explain several things to me within the first six months he was in the profession.

Your skills give you value. They are the commodities and treasures you will market as you move through your career. Your skills will often dictate what you become and how fast you become what you want to be. There are skills you will always need throughout your career: writing, listening, and communicating. There are skills you have to continue to hone: teaching, leading, managing, and counseling. These make you invaluable. There are the skills that will make you a part of your profession: the skills of a surgeon or the skills of a design engineer. Inventory your skills early in your career. Learn what skills need to be improved and what skills you need to add to your tool kit for success.

Strengths and Weakness are things you will tend to overlook, especially the weaknesses. If you are aware of your abilities, you should be aware of what makes you excel. If you are aware of your inabilities, you should be aware of what holds you back. Learn where you can excel quickly and build on the things that move you forward. Avoid environments where you cannot thrive. Try to improve those areas you find to be weak.

Many professionals deny having weaknesses. This denial never allows them to overcome their weaknesses. It can be compared to people who have a drinking problem who say, "I can stop whenever I want to." Yet, they will not admit when they have had enough. Know your weaknesses and have a plan either to overcome them or to get around them.

Strengths are not easy to assess for everyone. There are many professionals who do not get maximum use of their strengths because they do not realize what they are. I have known professionals who demonstrated great leadership, yet they shy away from leadership roles in their professions.

The ultimate goal is to be a creator of the profession, not just a doer of the profession. Maximum satisfaction in a profession comes when you are performing at your maximum potential. Operating with your strengths at their peak levels of power will always allow you to compete. Survey your strengths and weakness, and be sure to make this a part of your career plan.

Your Definition of Success is probably going to be

one of the most important things you ever define. We Blacks often set our success expectations, too low. If there is one time we fit the stereotype of being lazy, it is when we define success. I know this because there are still too few of us in the sacred halls of corporate America. That is what this book is all about. We must stop letting American Business define success for Black Americans. We must take on this very important challenge and be the business people we know we can be. We must continue to strive for success on all terms, especially our own terms.

Your career plan should lay out your success, and there should be levels of success. As I stated in an earlier chapter: goals must be clearly defined and measurable. American Business has learned to measure everything that can be measured. Each level of success you obtain should be a cause for celebration. Celebrating each level of success will encourage you to complete the next parts of your plan.

Career-Planning may be one of the best things you ever do for yourself. Take it seriously and enjoy each step. Your pride and ego will love it. The corporate world plans everything. So should you. Your only enemy here is yourself. When teamed with hard-core procrastination, you are easy to conquer.

Many human resource departments have booklets that will assist you in putting together a career plan. Most bookstores carry career-planning guides, but they should be used as guides only. If you try to make your career-life plans fit the guidelines of some book, you probably have not done a good job planning. You are the one who must build and tailor your career plan to fit your life and profession.

# The First 90 Days

This section is to be used not only for your first job assignment but also whenever you are starting a new assignment. No matter how well you performed in your last assignment, you should approach each new assignment with the same vigor and enthusiasm you showed when you received your first assignment. I offer this section as tactics and strategies that may be used in the first 90 days of a new job assignment.

One of the most important times in your career is

when you are the "rookie". Rookie status can be fun, challenging and frustrating. You are usually learning what to do. You are probably dependent on someone helping you to do your job. You are usually non-productive for a period of time. Your learning curve seems endlessly steep. In most jobs, you want to maintain being the rookie for as long as a corporation will allow. An enthusiastic rookie is enjoyed by most veterans. A rookie can renew the vigor of a company.

Professionals too often want to be the "pro" before they are ready, which often leads to frustration. I remember being a rookie in a corporate training program. I thought about how non-productive I was those first months on the job. I wanted training to be over as quickly as possible. I remember somebody saying to me, "Don't rush your training, you will get your chance to produce." I used to say to myself, "I can't believe they're paying me all this money to train." Two years later, when I played a major role helping to sell and install my first $10 million worth of products, I realized I had paid the company in full for my training, and I started to think, "I'm underpaid." The company had realized its return on its investment in me. I was now ready to get my return on me.

Being a rookie has its advantages. You are not expected to be at maximum performance. You are allowed to make mistakes and correct them. People feel a need to help you, and yes, sometimes this may frustrate you because of your desire to excel. There will be times when you will be asked to perform the more menial tasks; just remember, somebody has to do them, and everyone has to pay their dues in one form or another.

When you are a rookie, try to learn as much as you can. Being a fast learner is not as important as learning the things you need to know thoroughly. Again, stay a rookie for as long as you can. Once you are not, your colleagues' expectations of you may rise ten fold.

During your rookie days is when you build your image. This is normally when you will set up the way you want to be perceived. People will remember your enthusiasm for a long time, and this perception will follow you for a long time. On the other hand, you have the opportunity to damage your career if you project something less than what is expected. Build a good image, and let people know you are committed to being a part of the "A-Team".

Put in a good working day. Try to work a little more than what is expected. If eight hours is the norm, I work eight and a half to nine hours. When projects require overtime, I work the necessary hours to complete the project. I try not to overwork myself. Many professionals start out working too many hours. If you work long hours when it is not necessary, you will set a level of expectation you may not be able to continue. A company will take as much time as you are willing to give it. You are a professional, and you will probably not have to punch a time clock. Professionals are measured by the way they perform, usually not by how much they perform.

Take time out to know the people in your office, shop, lab, or department. This world is all about people; and, if you learn to enjoy the people, you will more than likely enjoy the job. Allow people to get to know you and be a fun person to be around. The first 90 days is when people are trying to size you up and see how well you fit in. Read the chemistry of your environment and try to blend into it. One way of learning who is who is by inviting people to lunch. People love to eat and talk. This is also a good opportunity to find who can be a resource to you or who you may be able to help.

While I am on the subject, lunch time is one of the most important times of the day. Take time to have lunch and refresh yourself. Many professionals eat at their desks trying to get one more thing done. Nobody pays you enough money to make you work five to eight hours without a break. Your lunch hour is for taking a break and refueling. Use your lunch hour to do something leisurely. If you want to work, bring along a colleague and discuss it over lunch. You will both be better for it. People who do not eat lunch are often less patient in the afternoons.

In those first days in a new assignment, take time and learn the business and what it is all about. There are many professionals who work very hard at what they do who never take time to truly learn the ins and outs of the business. Professionals who become very successful in a profession usually understand their business climate very well. During these early days of your assignment is an opportune time to do this, before you are under the major pressures of the job assignment.

In your first 90 days in a new assignment, you will have many opportunities to do things that could make your next few years count for a lot. Take advantage of the opportunity and enjoy the interaction. Set the standard for success.

# Chapter

# 21

# The End or The Beginning?

*W*hat I hope has happened during the time you have been reading this book is that I have stimulated you to think about what success means for you in the business world. The information presented here is invaluable, and it is difficult to get without experiencing it for yourself. The more insight you have going into a new venture, event or problem, the more chance you have at being successful with it.

I hope I have stimulated you to think about what you really need to enjoy your life as a business professional. Blacks are not only out to gain "Affluence", but we are more interested in gaining the "Influence" where it counts the most.

Throughout the chapters of this book, I have tried to be an inspiration to all of you who would dare to be professional. Now that you have read this book, I would encourage you to find your own source of inspiration. I hope it comes from within you.

I would like to leave you with one final question: Is this the end of this book or the beginning of something big for your life?

Corporate and Business America will not do much for you. All that will get done on your behalf will be done by you, so

Do Your BEST!

# Additional Resources

Earl G. Graves. Black Enterprise Magazine. New York: Earl G. Graves Publishing, 1991.

Wilmer C. Ames Jr. Emerge Magazine. New York: Emerge Communications, Inc., 1991

Roger Fisher and William Ury. Getting To Yes. New York: Penguin Books.

Thomas J. Watson Jr. A Business and its Beliefs. New York: McGraw-Hill, 1963.

ODLC

**Black Experience, Strategies and Tactics**